The Tornado Years

For my grandchildren
Oscar, Douglas,
William, Stewart,
Beatrix and Montague

To the Memory of
Flight Lieutenant John P O'Shea
1957–1988

Tornado Navigator, Qualified Weapons Instructor
and, most-importantly,
father of my two step-daughters,
Helen and Hannah

By The Same Author

The Buccaneer Songbook
Adventures of a Cold War Fast-Jet Navigator: The Buccaneer Years

Short stories contributed by the same author in:

The Buccaneer Boys
Out Of The Blue
Out Of The Blue Too

The Tornado Years

More Adventures of a Cold War Fast-Jet Navigator

Wing Commander
David Herriot

Foreword by
Air Marshal
Sir 'Timo' Anderson KCB, DSO, DSc (h.c.), MA FRAeS

AIR WORLD

First published in Great Britain in 2019 by
Air World
An imprint of
Pen & Sword Books Ltd
Yorkshire – Philadelphia

Copyright © David Herriot, 2019

ISBN 978 1 52675 8 941

A CIP catalogue record for this book is available from the British
Library

Typeset in Ehrhardt by
Mac Style
Printed and bound in Great Britain by TJ International Ltd.

Pen & Sword Books Limited incorporates the imprints of Atlas,
Archaeology, Aviation, Discovery, Family History, Fiction, History,
Maritime, Military, Military Classics, Politics, Select, Transport, True
Crime, Air World, Frontline Publishing, Leo Cooper, Remember When,
Seaforth Publishing, The Praetorian Press, Wharncliffe Local History,
Wharncliffe Transport, Wharncliffe True Crime and White Owl.

PEN & SWORD BOOKS LTD
47 Church Street, Barnsley, South Yorkshire, S70 2AS, England
E-mail: enquiries@pen-and-sword.co.uk
Website: www.pen-and-sword.co.uk

or

PEN AND SWORD BOOKS
1950 Lawrence Rd, Havertown, PA 19083, USA
E-mail: uspen-and-sword@casematepublishers.com
Website: www.penandswordbooks.com

The Tornado Years

More Adventures Of
A Cold War Fast-Jet Navigator

who was often

'Temporarily Unsure of My Position'

Tools of the Trade (J.F. Herriot)

*A professional navigator is never ever lost, although he may sometimes be
temporarily unsure of his position!*

Contents

Acknowledgements

Writing the two volumes of my life and career in the Royal Air Force has been a great trip down memory lane, but the greatest delight has been the recalling and describing of the incredibly enjoyable years that I spent, as a fast-jet navigator, flying in two of the best two-seat, fast-jet, strike/attack aircraft ever built. My keyboard can now take a rest after the pounding it has taken these last five years it has taken me to commit to manuscript, and publish, the story of my life in *Adventures of a Cold War Fast-Jet Navigator: The Buccaneer Years* and now this, *The Tornado Years: More Adventures of a Cold War Fast-Jet Navigator*. But it would be unfair of me to proclaim that this has been a solo effort. It could not have happened without the willing support of others to whom I will remain forever grateful.

Certainly, I am sure, that no book has ever been published, in such fine hard copy, without the help and assistance of others at the coalface. From my first contact with Pen & Sword Books Ltd in May 2016 I have had nothing but the most professional support, assistance and guidance. Laura Hirst, History Production Manager/Coordinator, has been outstanding in her backing of both manuscripts and was responsible for getting the ball rolling. I am truly indebted to her for her professionalism and understanding throughout. Martin Mace, Publisher at Air World Books (an imprint of Pen & Sword Books Ltd), had the grim task of reading Volume One before he had to make the decision as to whether to go with this volume or not. Thankfully, he enjoyed both! He too has been a stalwart with his support and encouragement for which I am most grateful. Throughout the publishing process, Amy Jordan, my production coordinator, has had to respond to my requests for more time and my 'Oops, I missed that in the contract' moments. She has done so with great patience and tact and never once discouraged me from the direction I wanted to take. I owe her the biggest thank you of all.

Once again, I am eternally grateful to Ken Patterson, my editor, who, after having to cope with my grammatical idiosyncrasies in Volume One, was brave enough to accept the challenge of working with me a second time. He has patiently ploughed his way through the required edits and has provided me with very helpful suggestions where necessary to enhance my text. As an ex-Royal Air Force man himself, he has easily understood the subtleties of my tale, which has helped him understand much of the goings-on thereby, I hope, easing his task hugely. Ken's relaxed attitude has helped immensely with ensuring that this book is still my work, in my style for which I now have to take full responsibility.

The names of friends, colleagues and characters are peppered throughout this story. Far too many to name them all individually here, but all of whom have featured in my life and are listed in the index. Most I have lost contact with, some are acquaintances whom I occasionally meet on social media or at reunions and a number have become firm friends. Some may be surprised to discover that our association was worthy of mention and others might even be amazed that I did not defame them in the process of telling my tale. Others, I hope, will just be pleased to know that the events that unfold in this tale are lodged firmly, with happy recall, in my memory banks. I am grateful however, to a number of individuals who have been kind enough to give me permission to write about our adventures, good, bad or embarrassing, in this memoir. They are, as mates, listed without rank or hierarchy in alphabetical order: Gordon Buckley; Chris Lay; and Dick Middleton. I am grateful to all my colleagues, whether mentioned in this work or not, for their support and friendship throughout my RAF career and elsewhere.

No aviation memoir would satisfy its audience if it did not contain a number of photographic plates that help to illustrate the words on the pages. Whilst I hold a significant stock, some of which are included, this book would be nothing if I had not managed to secure the assistance of others to gain some high quality shots of Tornado, and in one case Typhoon, taken through the lens of a professional photographer. Cliff Waldwyn, an ex-colleague from my days defining air-to-surface weapons requirements in MOD, but now with MBDA, was instrumental in obtaining the release of the two excellent photographs of the Storm Shadow-equipped Tornado (one of which adorns the back cover) and the Brimstone-armed Typhoon. MBDA featured strongly in the latter half of my RAF career, both when I was writing the Conventional Weapons Employment Manual and, subsequently, when I was in MOD in the mid-90s. I am most grateful to the company for allowing me to use their excellent product, to Barry Guess of the MBDA Archives for releasing them and to Cliff for once again being my 'go to' man. I am also extremely grateful to Iain McNicoll, whom I flew with a number of times when we were on 17 Squadron together, for providing me with a host of very good photographs of our time on detachment in Decimomannu, Goose Bay and Las Vegas. Unwittingly, by supplying them, Iain also helped jog my memory back to some of the more hilarious events that took place in those three locations. Most of the excellent photographs of the Tornado are rightly accredited to the Crown, but, in this case, the man behind the lens deserves credit for his excellent camera work too. Rick Brewell, erstwhile Warrant Officer RAF Photographer who, amongst many other postings throughout his long career, served for nine years as the RAF's Public Relations Photographer working out of MOD in Whitehall. As far as I am aware, Rick was the only groundcrew member of the RAF to be issued with his own stock of personal flying clothing. Not only that, he did so much flying in the back seat of two-seat fast-jets and in the cabins of helicopters and on the flight deck of 'heavies' that his Boss in DPR(RAF) ensured that he received flying pay! It certainly paid off and I will be forever grateful to Rick for sending me the high quality images from his personal archive and, in particular, for the top quality photograph of the Tornado office that adorns the front cover.

All photographs in this volume are copyright and, where appropriate, that copyright is acknowledged with each photograph presented.

Sir 'Timo' Anderson was but a young and enthusiastic second tourist Tornado pilot when I was foisted upon him as his back-seater in 1986. Like my first squadron pilot on the Buccaneer, Tim and I flew together for much of my short time on 17 Squadron at RAF Brüggen in Germany. Whilst, as he states in his foreword to this book, it was occasionally inharmonious in the cockpit when our Celtic temperaments clashed, it was, in truth, a 'marriage made in heaven'. His exceptional ability as a pilot, coupled with his unmatched knowledge of the Tornado systems, complemented perfectly the tactical experience and weapons knowledge that I brought with my 2,500 hours on the Buccaneer. Together, we very quickly gelled and became leaders on the squadron and were, more often than not, at the forefront of operational training missions. Tim and his wife Ursula have remained good friends throughout these past thirty-three years. During a very low period in my life, they were there to support me and provided me with breathing space, sustenance and advice when I needed it most. Our career paths have criss-crossed often and culminated in Lincolnshire when Tim was Commandant of the Air Warfare Centre at Waddington and I was commanding his training wing at Cranwell on my last tour. I am grateful to Tim for many things in my career, but particularly, in the context of this book, his honest foreword.

Finally, there is one person who deserves my greatest appreciation for her unstinting support and encouragement from my very first scribblings. My wife Jo, who has had to put up with much since we married on Christmas Eve 1993, has been behind me all the way. When I first sat down to jot a few notes that would form, for my children and grandchildren, my 'never-to-be-published' biography, she thought it a good idea. As the first volume progressed, and Jo read every chapter as my first editor, she too became engrossed in the project. It was Jo who, having completed her task, encouraged me to seek publication. Without her 'push' this memoir might never have seen the light of day. Jo has been my main source of motivation and encouragement throughout our married life. I am so grateful to her for so many things.

Foreword

Air Marshal Sir 'Timo' Anderson KCB, DSO, DSc (h.c.), MA, FRAeS

As an embarrassingly callow youth in hindsight, I was fortunate to join the fledgling Tornado GR force in the late seventies as many of the Royal Air Force's squadrons relinquished their trusted and much-loved steeds – Jaguars, Buccaneers and the venerable Vulcans included – and began to transition to the wonder jet of its day, the 'electric' Tornado GR1. A product of the perennially Byzantine and frustrating union of Europe's leading military aircraft manufacturing nations, the Tonka, as it was affectionately known to its loyal air and ground crews, arrived to herald a new era for the Service's all-weather ground attack and nuclear strike roles. Advanced navigation and avionics capabilities, the adaptability of 'swing wing' variable geometry aerodynamics and fly-by-wire, advanced technology engines and the all-important terrain following radar and coupled autopilot systems – all pointed towards a step-change in the Royal Air Force's ability to hold the Cold War defensive line against the threat of the Warsaw Pact, albeit a threat that we may now judge probably owed more to political hyperbole than earnest intentions in Moscow.

After two years of being dragged up via my junior pilot bootlaces by the hugely experienced initial aircrew cadre on 27 Squadron Tornados at RAF Marham, I managed to manoeuvre myself into a posting to 17(F) Squadron on the leading edge of the 'front-line' at RAF Brüggen in Germany, where the resident Jaguar squadrons were re-equipping with the new jet. I arrived still relatively young in years and flying experience, but as one of the more experienced operators of the Tornado at that time and possessed of the naked hunger for professional success, status and peers' respect that drives many a young military aviator. It was therefore with a mixture of puzzlement and wary anticipation that I received the news from my, obviously amused, squadron commander and his executive officer that I was to be crewed with a soon-to-arrive ex-Buccaneer navigator who, it was clear, already had an established reputation amongst them and many other of my squadron compatriots. Descriptors such as 'a don in the Buccaneer mafia', 'has "chopped" weapons instructor candidates just by looking at their course photos' and 'a hard party animal' conveyed to me an image of a hard-drinking, once-able, social hand grenade who would face some challenges in transitioning to the modern, technologically advanced Tornado force, of which I was of course already nigh-on a high priest. And so …

In person, Dave Herriot was not quite what I had expected – slight in build, but with a forceful personality and presence well-able to compensate and 'hold a room', aided and abetted by a pronounced Scottish accent that it became apparent could convey old-world charm and latent menace in equal measure! I am very confident that we saw each other initially as a has-been to be tolerated and a naive youth of little obvious ability and even less humility – it became apparent quickly that one of us was wrong… Our 'courtship' was at times fractious, probably unsurprisingly so when Celtic temperaments, testosterone and, shall we say, somewhat assertive leadership styles collided in the highly dynamic and high-pressure 'office' environment of a Tornado cockpit at high speed and low-level over the North German plain! As a constituted crew, we flew together routinely and, given the aggregate experience we offered – me in terms of my Tornado systems' knowledge and Dave in terms of his wealth of weapons and tactical leadership expertise – we were soon to be accorded the privilege of planning and leading complex multi-aircraft missions, including the pre-planned offensive counter-air missions that would be triggered by a major Warsaw Pact incursion into NATO territory. At the time, the *raison d'être* of the Tornado Force was deterrence and the pinnacle of our preparedness and self-evaluation was to be found in the periodic Western Vortex ultra-low and blind flying training evolutions in Labrador, and the iconic USAF Red Flag large-scale live flying exercises in the Nevada desert. Dave Herriot's pivotal role throughout this period, as tactical leader, coach, upholder of professional standards and, yes, sometimes court jester, cemented a place for him in the Tornado Force annals – a place that could only be secured by his unwavering commitment to his profession, to the highest of professional standards and to understanding how, despite the tragic lows that inevitably accompany such a profession at times, to have fun in the process, not least by laughing at himself.

To the extent that I personally made any worthwhile contribution to the development and sustainment of the Tornado Force as it matured into the backbone of the Royal Air Force's ground attack capability, a capability that has been drawn upon continuously in successive operations over a uniquely long period for a single RAF aircraft type, it is a contribution that was moulded and burnished by the example set and personal mentoring provided by Dave Herriot, the epitome of professional military aviator adepts. I can think of none better to chart and recount this seminal period of the Tornado's era.

Preface

This volume follows on from my biography '*Adventures of a Cold War Fast-Jet Navigator: The Buccaneer Years*' published by Pen & Sword Ltd in 2017.

Consequently, Chapter One, 'A Passion for Flying', is a summary of that work. Hopefully, it will allow those who have not read about the first half of my almost forty-year Royal Air Force career to enjoy this volume, with some understanding of what has gone before. It cannot repeat verbatim, or in its entirety, the thrills, spills and alcohol-induced fun that life as a fast-jet navigator on the RAF's Buccaneer Force entailed in the 1970s and early 80s. It will, though, give an insight as to where my career was heading, downwards, when in 1983 I left the Buccaneer Force and headed for my first ground tour, before I then climbed into a Tornado cockpit at the Tri-national Tornado Training Establishment at RAF Cottesmore in 1985.

Whilst I spent only five years on Tornado, those years were an exciting time for the RAF and the Tornado Force in particular. The fall of the Berlin Wall, resulting in the subsequent demilitarisation of Western Europe, and Saddam Hussein's invasion of Kuwait in 1990 all played a major part in my time on the Tornado. But I was not finished with Tornado at the end of 1990, much if not all of my subsequent career was involved with the aircraft. Whether it was in the management of the tri-national Tornado training programme or defining the requirements for new smart weapons for the jet, the Tornado formed a very significant part of my military career right up until my retirement in 2007.

So, for those who enjoyed my *Buccaneer Years* please feel free to jump to Chapter 2. I trust that you will enjoy it as much as you did my first; why else would you be back here! For those new to my Cold War *Adventures* I do hope that you enjoy reading this book as much as I enjoyed writing it.

David Herriot
West Bridgford
March 2019

Chapter One

A Passion for Flying

It all started with a seed. I was thirteen years old, a newly-fledged army cadet in the High School of Glasgow Combined Cadet Force who had a particularly well-developed wayward attitude to my scholastic studies. The school Easter holidays were approaching and I had had an invitation to spend them in London with the family of a friend of my father. However, my parents had no real means of getting me to London unescorted and were not keen to fire me in a southerly direction by either coach, my father's routine transport mode for journeys of that nature, or rail, with the prospect of me getting lost on route. In the end, the only sensible solution was for them to purchase a return air ticket from Glasgow's Renfrew Airport to London Heathrow, where I could be collected by the Wallfisch family and driven along the A4 to their residence in Notting Hill.

To any thirteen-year old the prospect of flying was an exciting one. For me it opened my eyes to a career that offered excitement, camaraderie and a daily 'routine' that very few would ever be privileged to enjoy. As a young child, like a great many boys in the 1950s, I had had a desire to become a train driver. As I grew into my early teens, my career choices matured and thoughts of steam trains were replaced by images of operating theatres and a career as a life saver. There could surely be nothing better than a career in medicine. But I had never flown. I had never experienced the thrill of leaving the Earth behind to soar above the clouds. But I was about to. Having kissed my parents goodbye, I climbed happily up the steps of the British European Airways Vickers Vanguard to find my window seat and prepare myself for the just over one hour's flight south to London.

As each of the four Rolls-Royce Tyne turboprops began to rotate in turn my excitement grew. The smiling face of the stewardess was reassuring, but I felt no fear, only an overwhelming feeling of mounting excitement as the aircraft nosed along the taxiway at Renfrew towards the threshold of Runway 08. Cocooned, with the other one hundred or so passengers who were also heading for the nation's capital, within the hull of the Vanguard, I listened through the Perspex oval window on my right-hand side to the thrum of the four Tynes as they increased to fever pitch their revolutions that would thrust the aircraft into the moist and leaden air over the city of my birth. Before I knew it, the repetitive bounce of the nose wheel on Renfrew's tarmac runway ceased and we were airborne and climbing in a banking turn towards the Southern Uplands and England.

I loved the whole sensation of it all. From the moment I climbed on board to the moment I stepped into Terminal One at Heathrow, it was the most wonderful event that I had ever experienced. I could not wait for the return flight in ten days' time. That flight, and the subsequent journey north, set in train a passion for flying that would last throughout my life. From that moment, sat at 27,000 feet above that green and pleasant land, my career thoughts changed. I was determined to become a pilot; a military pilot and not just any pilot, but a fighter pilot to boot!

My life at the High School of Glasgow was overshadowed by my lack of academic diligence, however. To compensate, I threw myself wholeheartedly into many of the extra-curricular activities on offer and enjoyed sport albeit at a level below that of my elder brother who played both rugby and cricket for the school's First XV and First XI respectively. My natural bent for acting the fool, suited best a number of starring roles in the Glasgow High's Amateur Dramatic Club productions. Acting also provided an adequate excuse for skiving class, as did my latter years in the CCF, where I rose to the rank of Under Officer and filled the post of Corps Adjutant. It was all too easy for a senior teen who had determined to enter the Royal Air Force as soon as he could escape from school. Who needed high academic scores when five O-Level grades were all that was required, as a minimum, to gain Her Majesty's commission? Not me, for sure. At least that is what I had convinced myself by the time I had reached the 5th Form. My mother, however, was not convinced and nor was Dr Lees, the Rector of the High School of Glasgow! My application for a 6th Form scholarship was shunned by the Officer and Aircrew Selection Centre at Biggin Hill. My subsequent application for a Direct Entry commission, submitted during my second last year at school, was likewise dismissed by the RAF, but at least this time I ventured as far as Biggin Hill and completed the whole of the selection process. I was nearly there. Third time lucky? I was. With my Scottish Higher exams behind me and my results known, rather than the poor predictions that David Lees had provided for my last encounter with OASC, I was on my way. My academic results were poor, but I suspect my military success in the CCF and my achievement of the highest honour in school, that of School Captain in my final year, must have swayed the board that I had the potential to lead and had proved myself so at the High School of Glasgow. There was just one sour note in the letter that came with an invitation to join the RAF on a Direct Entry Commission, Type A. I had proved in the aptitude tests that I would make a better navigator than a pilot! Whilst my dream of being a fighter pilot was instantly dashed, the thought of being a military aviator, no matter the brevet to be worn, was too much to resist. The seed had formed roots and a tree was about to grow. As it turned out, after almost forty years of service that included a particularly unfortunate incident when a pilot offered me the controls of a Hunter T7, I am sure that the RAF was correct. Had I attempted and succeeded at pilot training, I would likely have ended up as a Truckie,[1] which in my view has no comparison with the thrill, danger and excitement of being a fast-jet navigator in any war, cold or otherwise!

My officer training course was held under the guidance and stewardship of the Aircrew Officer Training School (AOTS), which in 1969 was located at RAF Church Fenton, near York. Other than the drill sergeants and physical training instructors, the staff instructors were all aircrew. That fact alone had a significant bearing on how my social career developed. There was much more fun around AOTS than I believe that there might have been at the 'College of Knowledge', as the cadet training course at the RAF College at Cranwell was then known. Certainly, during its short history, AOTS produced a particularly strong and very capable cadre of aircrew officers for the RAF who were able, equally, to stand their ground with their Cranwell equivalents. Partly thanks to a couple of light-hearted flight commanders who liked a beer and a good laugh, I thoroughly enjoyed my time at AOTS and developed a mild social irresponsibility that lasted throughout my formative years in the RAF.

Commissioned on 4 July 1969 I departed Church Fenton, via a short holding period at RAF Upwood, for No. 2 Air Navigation School at RAF Gaydon, there to learn the finer points of navigating the 'Super Pig', otherwise known as the Vickers Varsity T Mk1. The Varsity was a slow but reliable workhorse that allowed student navigators to learn their trade without too many opportunities to wander too far from track. We navigated using Second

---

1. A military aircrew expression for those who fly multi-engine passenger or freight-loaded aircraft.

World War navigation aids like Gee and Rebecca and used manual air plot techniques to meander our way through the skies over Devon and Cornwall and north-east England. By the time Gaydon closed and we moved lock, stock and barrel to RAF Finningley in South Yorkshire, students on 133 Course had moved on to discovering the delights of shooting the sun and the stars through a telescopic sextant that was plugged into the ceiling of the aircraft for the duration of our shots. Accuracy now was very much dependent upon pre-flight preparation on the ground and a number of awkward calculations to provide necessary inputs on the sextant's bezel. Finding the correct star in the night sky was crucial, as was the pilot's ability to hold the aircraft steady whilst the star shot was being taken. Wandering far from track was now common practice!

After successfully completing the basic phase, those students that remained on the course, of which I was one, moved forward to undertake the Advanced Navigation Course at Finningley on the Dominie T Mk1. Navigating the Dominie was equally as hard for us learners as it had been in the Varsity. For a start, its cruising speed was much higher and so the preponderance for being 'temporarily unsure of my position' was greater with a concomitant need to make larger alterations to regain track!

It was all good fun and I found that I did indeed have a natural aptitude for the art of air navigation. However, I still had a natural ability to play the fool, drink in the bar and all at the expense of diligent study. This personal weakness often had an adverse effect on exam results, which was affecting my overall grades on the course. A visit to the Vulcan Operational Conversion Unit at RAF Scampton solved all that, however. One look into the rear crew positions of the Vulcan convinced me to work harder. It was common knowledge amongst students at the time that those who filled the bottom rungs of the success ladder at Nav School ended up on the V-Force,[2] strapped into a black hole with no means of escape from a doomed aircraft other than a swivel seat and a push cushion that would throw one out the – hopefully – open door into the aircraft slipstream!

I vowed from that day forth to work harder, came third overall on the course and was rewarded with my first choice of posting to 237 Operational Conversion Unit at RAF Honington. There I was to learn all that there was to know about and how to operate the Blackburn Buccaneer. I had decided at

2. Aircraft of the V-Force were the Vickers Valiant, Avro Vulcan and Handley-Page Victor.

a very early stage in my flying training that I wanted to fly Buccaneers. There was something about the mean appearance and the environment in which it was operated that excited me.

My indoctrination into the RAF proper was with XV Squadron, which had reformed with the Buccaneer S2B at RAF Honington on 1 October 1970. By the time I reached the squadron a year later, however, the unit was operating under the command of RAF Germany at RAF Laarbruch. To say that the aircrew on XV Squadron then were boisterous would be an understatement! Indeed, with just a quarter of a century having passed since the end of the Second World War, the aircrew on XV Squadron were still fulfilling Bomber Harris' stated view that aircrew were entitled to enjoy a 'good party' and to live for today. They had reason to. Only a year into its reincarnation as a Buccaneer squadron, the outfit had already suffered a fatal accident and had lost its first commanding officer as a result.

There were some extremely colourful characters on XV Squadron and one in particular, Barrie Chown, was undoubtedly the most colourful and the greatest entertainer and mischief maker amongst a happy band of brothers. The RAF had nurtured Barrie from NCO Signaller to commissioned navigator. He was the only person in the RAF who had actually flown as crew in both of Mr Blackburn's two best aircraft – the Beverley and the Buccaneer. Barrie Chown, or Wings as he was universally known, not only introduced me to the finer points of navigating and operating the Buccaneer, but also to the more boisterous activities in the officers' mess that became part and parcel of my early years in the RAF. He was an absolute fool, and I mean that in the nicest possible way, when it came to squadron parties or beer calls in the mess. If he wasn't attempting to emulate Douglas Bader with his straight-legged walk, or show us how a one-armed man filled his pipe or counted his change,[3] he would be sucking up beer from glasses with a live cylinder vacuum cleaner strapped to his back. His *pièce de résistance*, however, had to be his fancy dress outfit at a Roman Orgy party, when he came dressed as 'Christ on the Cross', with two six-foot planks forming the cross attached to his back. He was also the only man I know who was banned for life from every single Forte's establishment across the Globe! It was harsh punishment indeed. All he had done, with others, was to steal a golf cart in the middle of

---

3. Imagination required here, but it all had to do with an open zip in his trousers and a finger poking through to tamp his pipe or count the coins in his other hand!

the night and inadvertently drive it into the Forte Village swimming pool, in Sardinia, whilst being chased by security! He was the only person to own up and took his punishment with great fortitude.

'Wings' became a very good friend and was by my side for much of my time on the Buccaneer. Indeed, he was responsible for training me as a Qualified Weapons Instructor in 1976, and recommended me to be the staff navigator on the QWI Course that took part in the RAF's second participation in Exercise Red Flag at Nellis AFB, Nevada in 1978. I have a lot to be grateful to Wings for. He pointed me on the path of becoming one of the RAF's most respected and experienced weaponeers. A path that would eventually define the second half of my almost forty-year career.

With 'Wings' by my side on XV Squadron, I got into far too many social scrapes. I drank rather too much, played the fool more than I should have and, more often than not, ended up on the Boss's carpet regularly, with my hat on and without a coffee cup in sight. Despite all of my transgressions in the officers' mess and elsewhere, however, I etched out a strong professional profile on XV Squadron that marked me out as an above average navigator on the Buccaneer Force. Not bad for a first-tourist who as a group, in the RAF, were historically given a long social leash and encouraged to 'hang themselves' with it. As a result, when I left XV Squadron in 1974, and headed back across the Channel to 12 Squadron at Honington, it should not have come as a huge surprise to me to discover that the squadron executives had been warned about my boisterous behaviour. I need not have worried, however, as having received the 'gypsy's warning' from my flight commander during my arrival interview, he, and his senior cohort, then led the raucous events in the mess at the very first Happy Hour that I attended at Honington; the one that welcomed me into my new home!

I spent four years on 12 Squadron and loved the Anti-Surface Warfare role immensely. Long-range missions out over the ocean at 100ft, searching for and attacking maritime targets was, after all, exactly what the Buccaneer had been designed to do. It was navigator heaven because it required all of our skill to navigate the featureless sea with some pretty antique navigation aids. It was a challenge, but a challenge well worth the effort. My second tour also provided plenty of opportunity to visit some of the extremities of the NATO region. Exercises from Bardufoss and Bodø in Northern Norway and the three Danish bases of Aalborg, Karup and Skrydstrup were regular occurrences, as were deployments to the Mediterranean and the RAF stations of North

Front in Gibraltar, Luqa in Malta and Akrotiri in Cyprus. All visited in the name of one maritime exercise or another. Lossiemouth in Scotland also became a home from home on an annual basis, again to attack maritime forces on exercise in the North Sea and the Atlantic Ocean. Of course, all these locations allowed Buccaneer aircrew, and Chown and Herriot in particular, to display more and more raucous behaviour. Despite it all, however, my scores as a professional aviator were increasing and I was making solid progress with my annual reports and recommendations for promotion.

In 1975 I fell in love. The squadron executives watched, in hope, that the love of a good woman would calm me down. It did to some extent, but it also distracted me from my studies and there then began a sequence whereby I failed regularly the promotion exam that should, all things being equal, have opened the door to the rank of squadron leader for me. I was now getting High Recommendations for promotion, but was banging on a closed door because, annually, I was failing the C Exam.

In 1976 I was selected for the Buccaneer Qualified Weapons Instructor Course and spent the summer of that year studying hard, flying regularly on long days that started at 0600hrs and ended well into the evening. My fiancée took it all in her stride. She was already deep in the throes of organising our wedding, which was planned for 25 September, which was just two days after I returned from yet another wild and wonderful deployment to Lossiemouth, to be bothered about my whereabouts.

It was a great tour on 12 Squadron, topped by the arrival of my son, Christopher, in August 1977 and my successful completion of the QWI Course. I left the squadron on a high in 1978 and headed along the 'waterfront' at Honington to become an instructor on 237 OCU. My final confidential report classed me as an above average Buccaneer navigator, but with only three years seniority as a flight lieutenant I had just scraped into the 'Recommended for Promotion' bracket for the first time. It was early days, but my report did indicate potential for higher rank and so I was satisfied as I settled into the crewroom in C Hangar and began to learn about my new role teaching pilots how to operate the Buccaneer. Another three years and I wanted to be hitting 'high recommendations' for promotion as a very minimum.

Life on the OCU was somewhat different to that on the squadron. It was more stable in that we spent more time at home 'chasing the line' of student throughput. But that, in itself, increased the risk. Whereas, on the squadron, there had been a routine to flying crewed with the same pilot for almost every mission, here on the OCU it was a different pilot every day and the student pilots were, initially, unfamiliar with their environment. They had to rely heavily on the man in the back to guide them through each sortie, from start-up to engine shut down. As a staff navigator, I was now required to become more involved in what was happening in the front seat. I had to be more alert than ever – especially as without a 2-stick Buccaneer I was there with student pilots after they had flown the beast just once before with a brave QFI. He, bless him, had had to monitor the student pilot's actions without any method of overruling him other than with a high-pitched scream.

But I survived and thoroughly enjoyed my three year tour as an instructor and QWI. Before my arrival, 237 OCU had been renowned throughout the RAF as a 'tough school'. It needed to be. The Buccaneer was a great aircraft, but it could catch the unwary and particularly so at slow speed in the final stages of an approach. A number of students did fall by the wayside, but many who passed were highly competent aviators who went on to do great things in the Buccaneer, and beyond, and in their RAF careers generally. My career was now progressing well despite a number of setbacks. During my tour as an instructor, the Buccaneer was grounded twice following two fatal accidents; one of these groundings lasted the best part of six months. I too suffered a personal four-month period on the sidelines with a compression fracture of my thoracic spine, caused by one of the less able students who had already been through the OCU once, had been suspended, but had been reinstated by his personal 'mentor', the AOC. He was an ex-Vulcan pilot with a V-Force approach to crew cooperation and a lack of understanding of how a 2-man crew were meant to operate. He was also very inflexible, which actually made him dangerous! An overzealous application of 'G', not by him, but by his leader, my pilot, was my downfall. I don't blame my pilot who had to take avoiding action when the errant student, returning to the formation having been lost, brought with him a Lightning interceptor determined to get a Buccaneer kill! Unfortunately, at the time of the onset of the 'G' force, I was bent double writing copious notes on my kneepad about the student pilot's ineptitude!

During my period of incapacitation, however, my wife and I were delighted with the arrival of our daughter, Sarah, in March 1979. Conversely, the irritation of failing the C Exam, yet again, and struggling with ISS was a setback to any promotion hopes that I was nurturing. By late summer, however, I was back in the cockpit and fully engaged again with the training of Buccaneer crews.

As the end of my tour approached, in 1981, I received a call from my desk officer at the Personnel Management Agency who let it be known that he had placed me at the top of a short list, of three Buccaneer navigators, for an exchange tour with the USAF at Mountain Home AFB, Idaho, flying the F-111. I was over the moon and so was my wife. She was not overly keen on the hunting, shooting, fishing lifestyle enjoyed by the inhabitants of that corner of the USA, but saw the opportunity that it presented whilst our family was young and below school age. We both knew the potential career benefits that an exchange tour would have on our future. I snapped up the opportunity, but sadly it was not to be. The desk officer changed and the new incumbent was not long in getting me on the phone to tell me that my progress with the C Exam and my poor showing in ISS was enough for him to drop me to second on the list. The chap promoted to first place was struggling 'academically' too, but, and despite my Boss's protests, he went to the USA and I did not!

I was, to say the least, devastated. I had set my heart on three years in North America, but it was not to be. The alternative, it transpired some few weeks later, was an offer to be the first QWI navigator on the first Tornado GR1 squadron at Honington. Great, but it was not as good as an exchange on the F-111 and, worse, it meant another four or five years in Suffolk. Nothing against Suffolk, but Idaho has definitely got more hills.

Undergoing refresher training on the Buccaneer at the time were both the future station commander for RAF Laarbruch and the next commanding officer of 16 Squadron, also at Laarbruch. They were both aware of my disappointment and, desperately in need of some capable middle management flight lieutenants on the two Buccaneer squadrons in Germany, they asked me if they could poach me away from Tornado for one further tour on the Buccaneer in Germany. I discussed it with my wife, who had never been to Germany before, and we agreed that it would be better for our children to go overseas now rather than later and that it would compensate better for the loss of the tour in the States. Offers of 'we'll look after you, David' from the two senior officers sealed the deal and so, with their intervention with my desk officer, we packed our house up and headed across the Channel for one more tour on the Buccaneer.

The decision to do so did, however, have an impact on my career progression. Having slowly but surely improved my promotion recommendations my decision to stick with the Buccaneer set me back again. I had started my OCU tour with a High Recommendation at the first opportunity and followed it similarly at the end of my second year on the outfit. However, the Senior Navigation Instructor, who had written those reports, had been posted and his replacement did not share his opinion. He formed the view that I had turned down Tornado 'just to buy a new duty free car'. Nothing could have been further from the truth and he certainly did not know me if that was his view. I protested to my Boss, the Chief Instructor, but to no avail. The 'Recommended' for promotion stood. Despite my now widely acknowledged prowess as a Buccaneer navigator, instructor and Qualified Weapons Instructor, an Above Average assessment in the air had no bearing on one's potential for promotion.

But for the fact that I was married with two children and a dog, life in Germany was no different from the first time I'd been there as a bachelor almost ten years previously. We still stood nuclear QRA, we still had MINEVALS, MAXEVALS and TACEVALS and we still bimbled around Germany at 250 feet in pretty poor visibility. There were opportunities for me, however, on 16 Squadron. When one of the flight commanders was posted, I replaced the Weapons Leader whilst he was elevated to fill the flight commander post. Being Weapons Leader gave me some element of authority, albeit I did not gain acting rank. The Boss also took me as his navigator, which enhanced my profile. Life was good, my family was settled and I revelled in the role as a mid-level manager on the Buccaneer. The squadron spent much of its time at Laarbruch, but we did participate in squadron exchanges at Spangdahlem and deployed our Buccaneers across the Atlantic, without AAR, to participate in Exercise Red Flag in Nevada. I also enhanced my CV by becoming a co-opted member of the NATO TACEVAL Team, tasked with flying with and evaluating other NATO air forces in exercise combat operations. This was an activity that I continued during my subsequent time on the Tornado GR1. Whilst with 16 Squadron, I flew in Belgian Mirage Vs and USAF F-4Es. I also passed the 2,000 flying hours mark in the backseat of the Buccaneer.

Towards the end of my tour the Boss, concerned about the performance of a young pilot recently arrived from the OCU, gave me up in an effort to improve the young lad's performance. He needed a steady hand to stop him killing himself and the first-tourist navigator, who arrived on the squadron with him, was not the man to do it. I appreciated the opportunity given to me and accepted that, with the squadron commander's pending posting later in the year, it was an opportunity for me to train up a new pilot before my own posting, which was planned for late 1983.

He was a ripshit and required a heavy hand to keep him in check. So, when he breached my flight authorisation on departure from RAF Akrotiri one Monday morning, I had to take him aside upon our arrival back at Laarbruch and point out the error of his ways. I explained to him that when I had said that he was not to fly below the leader during our 'departure beat up' of the airfield, that was exactly what I had meant. The fact that he flew under the leader, who was level with the top of the air traffic control tower, and that I was looking into the tower from an angle of about thirty degrees above the horizontal was unacceptable. I explained that I was in his cockpit to assist his development, but that if he was not going to heed me, there was little point in me being there. He apologised and his indiscretion, on that occasion, remained between us. However, I let him know that if he was ever to do such a thing again, I would report him.

He did! At Wick Airport during an airfield attack during an Exercise Maple Flag work-up sortie. I had no option, but to report him. He was grounded and I found myself without a pilot for Maple Flag! An unintended consequence, but I would rather that he and I survived than be found dead in the Canadian tundra.

Towards the end of the detachment in Canada, where I managed a sortie in a USAF E-3A AWACS and four Maple Flag sorties with other Buccaneer pilots, I was informed by the Boss that my wife had demanded that I return to Laarbruch immediately. I had no idea, and she didn't let me know then or afterwards, why she wanted me to return, but with just a few days to go I agreed that I could not get home any quicker than I could by deploying back to Germany in a Buccaneer some two days hence.

Upon my return to our OMQ, it became clear that my wife was unhappy. She was, needlessly, concerned about my faithfulness when I was away from home, she told me, and seemed overly concerned about our marriage. I did my best to explain that she had nothing to fear and that I was still deeply in love with her. But she was very unsettled, so much so that the squadron executives became aware and allowed me time to try and settle my family and reassure my wife. I did my best, but nothing seemed to quell her distress and so we did our best to complete the few remaining months of my tour and return to the UK in September 1983.

The whole episode had a detrimental effect, once again, on my promotion hopes. I had started my tour with a Spec Rec[4] for promotion, but these had been followed in subsequent years with a High Rec and finally, by my First Reporting Officer, just a Recommended! A complete downward trend and, effectively, it put the kybosh on any prospect of promotion any time soon. Notwithstanding, the new squadron commander had upgraded it to a High Rec and the new station commander had stated:

> '... *the best thing that could happen to the Service would be to promote Herriot in 1984. I say this because he is red-hot professionally and I have no doubt that he will respond 100% to the challenge of increased responsibility*'.

I left Germany in the early autumn of 1983 and headed for RAF High Wycombe. It had been decided that a 'rest tour' was in order to give me time to sort out my family difficulties before I returned to the cockpit and, hopefully, a Tornado one at that. My task at HQ Strike Command was, as a supernumerary officer, to write the Conventional Weapons Employment Manual for the Ministry of Defence.

---

4. Specially Recommended – the highest recommendation and not given lightly.

Chapter Two

'Badger', 'Badger', 'Badger'

Of the ten Principles of War,[1] Concentration of Force and Economy of Effort are probably, but not exclusively, prime. From an Air Power perspective, however, they are most certainly key as no government, no matter how flush they might be for cash, can afford to provide the absolute total resources necessary to cover all bases at all times. Consequently, every campaign plan must be rigorous in its management of its air assets. From a mud-moving standpoint it is imperative that assets, in the shape of both delivery platforms and weapons, are matched appropriately to the target in question. It is not, and has never been, the case that those who task aircraft at war do so on a whim. Specific targets have specific vulnerabilities to specific weapons. The task of the weaponeer is to know and understand those vulnerabilities and match suitable weapons in sufficient numbers to achieve the specific level of damage required against a nominated target. To do this campaign planning staff require a weaponeer's bible and the weaponeer's bible in the Ministry of Defence in 1983 was SD-110A-0300-1G, The Conventional Weapons Employment Manual. It was hopelessly out of date!

On the face of it my task looked simple. Write a book! Write a book about air-to-surface weapons! Include current and future contracted weapon systems! Cover weapons effects! Incorporate a section on weapon effort planning! Finally, make it less scientific and more user-friendly! All of the above was well within my remit as a QWI and as a graduate of the Weapons Employment Course and I had been given two years, on my own, to complete the task. Once done, I was promised a posting to Tornado!

Now hang on just a cotton-picking minute! Was I not the poor unfortunate who had been struggling with ISS and had been criticised for my failings in written English! Yet PMA thought me an appropriate and suitable candidate to write a tome that would be published in large volume, was to be classified SECRET and would be distributed to all squadrons, HQs and government

---

1. The Principles of War are: Selection and Maintenance of the Aim; Maintenance of Morale; Security; Surprise; Offensive Action; Concentration of Force; Economy of Effort; Flexibility; Cooperation; and Sustainability.

agencies charged with the delivery and support of conventionally armed attack weapons from the air!

Irony – pure irony!

I was tasked directly by Ops(OS Wpns)(RAF)[2] in MOD Main Building in Whitehall and worked under his guidance throughout. However, because of a lack of space in MOD MB, I was allocated an office and a desk in the Operational Research Branch (ORB) within HQSTC, situated between Naphill and Lacey Green near High Wycombe. This Buckinghamshire location suited much better my family circumstances and removed any requirement for a daily commute into Central London. Moreover, the ORB was staffed, mainly, by Civil Service scientists who were accustomed to project work and who could lend necessary support and advice as and when it was required. I was one of a handful of RAF officers within the ORB and the only one with a specialisation in mud-moving! This had its advantages and its disadvantages. The prime advantage was that, routinely, I was left to my own devices to get on with my project undisturbed. Most of the others in the department, scientists and air force alike, were of the air defence persuasion and were snowed under resolving issues with the ill-fated Nimrod AEW project, which at the time was undergoing flight trials. I shared an office with Bill Sandiford, a Higher Scientific Officer in the Civil Service. Bill was a man with an excellent mathematical brain and an absolute bonus when I needed assistance with some of the more complex formulae that required explanation in the CWEM. But his focus in the ORB was air defence and so I would, more often than not, have the office to myself when he was out and about at RAF Boulmer putting the trials Nimrod through its paces. There was one other junior officer at the ORB during my tour. Tim Hills was an air defence navigator and was renowned to be the loudest man in NATO. Not just the RAF, but NATO! He could certainly disturb the peace in the tranquil corridors of the ORB and did regularly. He was a great guy, good friend and an excellent drinking buddy with a brilliant sense of fun.

Being the only mud-mover, however, did result in me being asked often to assist the air defenders with their scientific analysis and staff papers. On one memorable day, whilst sat quietly behind my desk minding my own business, one of the less experienced scientists approached and asked for assistance

---

2. Operations (Offensive Support Weapons) (Royal Air Force) – the man in MOD directly responsible for policy for current in-service air-to-surface weapons in the RAF.

with a paper that he was writing. In short, he had been tasked to write a thesis on how British Air Defence assets could best repel a mass attack by Soviet bombers approaching the UK FIR from the Norwegian Sea. His question to me was simple enough. It went something along these lines.

'Hi, Dave, can you help me please? I'm writing this paper and I need to ensure that what I have written is sensible. I'm building a scenario about how Soviet bombers would operate as they approached the UK Mainland for a mass attack.'

He then proceeded to reel off a whole list of heights, speeds, manoeuvres and launch parameters that did not, in the least, sound familiar or plausible to me. Now I am no Russian Air Force tactician, but his philosophy did not seem realistic. So, based on my knowledge of Soviet bomber tactics and my personal experience with four tours on the Buccaneer under my belt, I pointed out to him what I thought might be more realistic. He listened attentively, but made no notes whilst I was talking. Then turned on his heel and left my office with an over the shoulder comment of, 'Oh I'll just put all my original points in as assumptions. It'll be fine!'

And that, my friends, was my first introduction to how some MOD scientific staffs calculate and build their case in air power studies. If it's in the assumptions, rightly or wrongly, then it will get the paper through higher scrutiny.

We were allocated a married quarter very close to the entrance to the HQ, which meant that I had a five minute stroll to and from work and was able to pop home for lunch on a regular and routine basis. Parkwood was a cul-de-sac, which provided a relatively safe place for the children to play either in the front or back gardens. Christopher was enrolled at St John's Primary School in Lacey Green and Sarah followed him there in September 1984. We were well settled and life took on a brand new significance for my family.

I started work on 3 October 1983 and my first task was to scope the project. This I did by identifying the current, but obsolescent volume of the CWEM! I was shocked to discover that the book had last been amended some ten years previously and that it had been written from a scientific perspective by a scientific team rather than an operator. No wonder I had never heard of it! No wonder nobody had used it! No wonder it had fallen into disrepute and never been amended! I determined immediately that if the book was to be usable it had to be readable, user-friendly and set in an eye-catching format with plenty of photographs, where appropriate, and less of the technical drawings that littered the current volume.

First and foremost, I persuaded my Boss in London that I should undertake once again the Weapons Employment Course. It wasn't that I had forgotten what I had learned as a member of the OCU staff when I had completed the course during a Buccaneer grounding some three years earlier. More, that a number of significant inventory changes had happened in the meantime and the WEC was also the best place to refresh my Weapons Effort Planning skills. One week after my arrival at High Wycombe I found myself at the RAF College for the three-week course that was held within the Department of Air Warfare in Trenchard Hall. For me it was a most valuable refresher and set me up well for the task ahead. The syllabus focused primarily on weapons' effects and weapon effort planning and required the students to calculate Over Target Requirements using the American Joint Munitions Effectiveness Manual. The very fact that this high-profile and popular course was using the American equivalent of the CWEM was testament to the poor quality and lack of credibility of the book that I was tasked to improve.

We spent an awful lot of time in class calculating the number of aircraft required, the OTR, to achieve the required Probability of Kill, P_k, against a Soviet target or group of targets. If the target was a bridge, we might be tasked to 'drop a span'. If it was a tank or a group of tanks, we might be tasked to ensure a Mobility Kill or a Firepower Kill, as to destroy a tank with an unguided weapon was a tall order for any air-delivered ordnance and mainly based on a lack of accuracy in the delivery system. Aircraft in dispersal would likely necessitate an outright kill, or a K-kill as it was known in WEP circles, and runway surfaces would require a 'Prevent Take-Off' Kill. Terminology such as Mean Area of Effectiveness for a specific warhead type was an essential part of the equation and whether it related to Blast (MAEB) or Fragments (MAEF) was equally important as blast and fragments would each have a different bearing on the result. The end result, of course, was to calculate just how many aircraft were required to take-off to reach the target and 'kill' it to the P_k required. Based on the theory of probability, the calculations had also to include the number of aircraft that would go unserviceable before take-off, or become unserviceable, or be shot down on route to the target. It was all very complex and the MOD did not possess a suitable manual that reflected its inventory weapons and its WEP needs – we had to rely on an American DoD volume that was designed with MAEFs and MAEBs et al. for specific US weapons. It was a shambles and, frankly, a disgrace that we had got ourselves into this situation. It was my task to resolve the matter.

Importantly for me, the course undertook visits to Hunting Engineering Ltd and British Aerospace (Dynamics) Ltd, which were the two main weapon contractors engaged with the MOD. On the same three-day tour the course visited the Royal Armament Research and Development Establishment at Fort Halstead in Kent. All three locations presented me with the perfect contacts to support my task and featured regularly in my travel itineraries throughout my tour.

The course, however, was not known throughout the RAF as the Whitbread Enjoyment Course for nothing! As you may know, aircrew have a prevalence for social drinking whenever they get together and, without too much pre-study required in the evenings, the Officers' Mess bar in Trenchard Hall was usually awash with various beers, but mainly Whitbread, whenever the WEC was in town. However, with three officers' messes at Cranwell it was not uncommon to visit both York House and College Hall at least once during a course at the College either for a change of scene or to meet up with buddies who were partaking in other courses or activities on the unit. York House was the flyers' mess and College Hall accommodated officer cadets and staff from the Department of Initial Officer Training, a unit and mess that played a very large part in my later career. I decided to avoid it like the plague, however, in 1983! My only previous experience of College Hall had been in 1980 during my first WEC. Rather than visit Hunting Engineering on that course, the company had come to us and we had entertained them to lunch in CHOM after a morning of company briefings and an introduction to their many products. It was all very civilised and typically RAF. Pre-lunch drinks were served in the Ladies' Room followed by a top table luncheon served in the dining room under the huge bronze eagle that supports the College Colour. The formal military setting, with its portraits of great RAF leaders adorning its walls, cried out 'military tradition' from every corner! Its usual clientele were held under significant scrutiny throughout their officer training courses and were prey to the whims of their flight commanders as to whether they might pass or be cast aside back to Civvie Street. We, as students on the WEC, were beyond all that – we were operational aircrew with operational aircrew attitudes!

I had gone for a preprandial pee in the officers' staff toilet and was in full flow when I heard a voice behind me announce: 'Get out of the mess!'

I carried on peeing, there was not much else I could do and I assumed that he was talking to somebody else. He wasn't.

'Did you not hear me? Get out of the mess!'

Having finished urinating and having zipped myself up, I turned around to see that my verbal assailant was a wing commander and he did not look happy.

'I'm sorry, sir,' I responded, 'is there a problem?'

'Yes! You! Get out of my mess!'

'What seems to be the problem, sir?'

'Your hair's too long! I insist that very high standards be set for my cadets in DIOT and your hair is too long!'

'Sir, I'm afraid that I am hosting delegates at a formal lunch and cannot, therefore, get out of the mess!'

The whole thing was ridiculous. My hair was in need of a trim, I admit, but it was not 'long' per se!

'I do not care what your purpose is in being here; you are to leave this mess immediately!'

I had no option. He was insistent and two ranks above me, I had to leave. As I made my way past the Ladies' Room with the wing commander close in my six o'clock, one of the staff from the WEC came out of the Ladies' Room and asked me what was going on. I knew Mick Whybro well from the Buccaneer Force and he was sympathetic to my tale of woe! He was also one rank higher than me. He took the matter up with the wing commander and managed to resolve it as long as I promised to get my hair cut at the Station Barber's that afternoon. I agreed, had my lunch and headed straight to the barber's shop before the afternoon lectures.

You might wonder why I tell this almost inconsequential tale here and why it had such an impact upon my memory. Well the reason is a simple one. The wing commander concerned filled the post of Wing Commander Cadets in DIOT and, if you stick with my story to the end, you will discover that I too filled that role later in my RAF career! That encounter, with one of my predecessors in 1980, moulded very much the approach that I adopted with the officer cadets that were placed under my charge in 1997. It was certainly a country mile from that adopted by the idiot that I met in the toilets that day.

With the WEC behind me, it was further agreed that, before I started on my task, I should undertake the equivalent Air-to-Surface Conventional Weapons Course at the SHAPE-run NATO School in Oberammergau. There was a need to complete both courses quickly and certainly before I set down finally to put pen to paper. Fortunately, the next available course commenced on Tuesday, 3 January 1984 and, with Hogmanay out of the way, I quickly found myself on a flight to Munich on the Bank Holiday Monday for three weeks in a German B&B in the centre of a snow-covered Bavarian village. The course was run by a USAF captain by the name of Bill Nikides and he became a most useful contact later in the project by opening doors for me within the Pentagon and at weapons research establishments in the USA. When Bill was reassigned to an appointment in Denver he wrote me a note thanking me for my friendship. In it he stated:

'Knowing you has been, despite my being easily amused, one of my most rewarding experiences since arriving in Europe. I deeply appreciate your help, but more importantly, your friendship.'

Thanks, Bill. As I look at his note today, written over thirty years ago, it has caused me to stop and reflect a moment on my three weeks in Oberammergau. The course was outstanding in its value to me personally. It provided me with a better understanding of the JMEM process and its origins. It allowed me to compare the effects of the equivalent American weapon and its UK counterpart and it allowed me to mix and compare notes with representatives from across the Alliance. Americans, Belgians, Canadians, Danes, Frenchmen, Germans and Norwegians, as well as another Brit, made up the SHAPE WEC class of January 1984. It was thus culturally strong and there was plenty of opportunity to exchange views and ideas in the local bars in the evenings. Most importantly, however, it gave me the confidence to take my task forward and succeed.

Typically, the course was as sociable as it was professional. Classroom days were full on and having started at 0800 they finished around 1630 hours each day. Of course, in January, in Bavaria, the streets of Oberammergau were paved with a deep and crisp covering of snow and, with the sun rising and setting on our way to and from work, the whole place had very much a Christmas card feel to it all. Early evenings were usually spent in the sauna and spa at the Wellenberg Swimbad, which was just a short walk from our lodgings, before we settled into a quiet meal in town, usually schweinshaxe in the Zauberstub'n washed down by copious quantities of Hackerbräu. Apart from the first Wednesday, which concluded with an evening Meet and Greet Cocktail Party at 1800hrs, all other Wednesday afternoons were designated as sports afternoons!

No sooner had the course started than it stopped to allow the Bavarians to celebrate Epiphany! With the sixth of January falling on a Friday in 1984 this meant a long weekend and the opportunity to ski for three solid days on the Kolben slopes to the south and west of the village. The Kolben had a long chairlift to the summit from where you could ski unhindered back to the village or take various drag lifts to explore the many runs on the mountain's north facing slopes. There were plenty of 'refreshment' stops on route to the bottom and we students took advantage of most of them.

On the middle Wednesday afternoon I, and my fellow Brit, made a plan to take the train to Munich and thence to Dachau. It was a simple transfer in Munich to travel the ten or so miles north of the city to reach the Nazi Concentration Camp there. However, whilst sharing a few beers with one of our young German co-students, an Alpha Jet pilot, he asked us what we planned to do for 'sports afternoon' that week. Not wishing to offend him by stating our true plans, I said that we were going shopping in Munich. He asked if he could join us, as he knew Munich well, and would be able to take us to the best shops. We did our best to duck and dive, but he insisted on coming with us and hosting us in the city. In the end we had to capitulate and I told him that we wanted to take the opportunity to visit Dachau and that we had not wished to offend him by declaring that as our true destination. He was delighted and explained to us that he was definitely coming with us to be our guide around Dachau. He further explained that he had been to Dachau before as part of his officer training at Fürstenfeldbrück. In the education of the modern military officer, the Luftwaffe had added a visit to the concentration camp as an essential syllabus item, to ensure that the sins of Hitler and his henchmen would never be repeated. It was a most amazing, if sombre, visit where his inside knowledge and ability to translate all the descriptions into English for us enhanced our experience ten-fold. An evening in the Hofbräuhaus followed before a rather alcohol-induced drowsy journey on the train back to Oberammergau.

The last Wednesday afternoon was spent on a cultural visit to the Andechs Monastery which sits just to the east of the Ammersee and some thirty kilometres from Munich. The purpose was, on the face of it, to view the 15th Century monastery and meet the Benedictine Abbot who had been Erwin Rommel's radio operator during the Desert Campaign. He, apparently because of his military experiences, enjoyed very much guiding parties from the NATO School around the vast structure and giving lectures on the history of the monastery. He did, however, have not one word of English, we were told, and so a member of the NATO staff came with us to translate.

The tour of the monastery lasted about ninety minutes, was very informative and was much enjoyed, thanks to the efforts of our translator. The abbot spoke quickly in German, but, whilst he was quite happy to engage with anybody who chose to speak to him in his mother tongue, he made it quite obvious that he would have no truck with those whose first language was English. After the 'sermon' we were invited by the abbot to join him in the monastery's keller bar where we were to be invited to sample some of the beer brewed on site. After the abbot had consumed no more than a half litre of the brewery's finest pilsner, he became much more talkative and soon relaxed amongst us all prattling on in English like a linguistic master. It had all been a front and it was, we were told, borne of a life-long devotion to his erstwhile commander in the desert and the battles fought against Montgomery's Eighth Army. Despite warnings to the contrary, I decided that my last beer before departure had to be a dünkel. Sensibly, I opted for a 25cl glass, the smallest available. By gum it was strong and it almost took my legs away from under me. As the coach pulled out of the car park, Rommel's man stood waving farewell to his new found English speaking friends. I knew exactly why it was that he had chosen to live the rest of his life in Andechs – the beer was outstandingly good and it was available on tap all day long too!

Back at High Wycombe my first problem was to overcome the fact that, in 1983, few computers were available to allow everybody in the HQ to be allocated their own. Typing pools were established for just such a task and so, from the outset, all my drafts would have to be handwritten and submitted for typing to the pool of ladies on the second floor. It was a very inefficient method of production and so, very quickly, I set about establishing the case for a stand-alone desktop computer in my office. It took a long time in coming, but there was plenty I was able to achieve in the meantime. I made personal visits to HEL at Ampthill, BAe (Dynamics) Ltd in Stevenage and RARDE in Kent to ascertain just how much and at what cost the two companies and the weapons testing establishment could provide. I checked in with my Boss in MOD and gave him an update on my progress and how I planned to scope the project. He in turn warned me that I needed to be aware that there had been no funding allocated to the project and, whilst my salary would continue to be paid, I needed to scratch around for suitable resources and materials at as low a cost as possible. The most critical point made was that there was no funding available to pay for the publishing of the document! It was typically MOD! Here's a job, get it done, there's no funding! Great!

With promises from HEL and BAe of technical information and photographs in the bag, I started to put pen to paper. Section One was simple enough. All I needed to do was research each of the weapons that were to be included, write a descriptive piece on each, break them down into sub-categories of 'Guided', 'Unguided' and 'Guns and Rockets'. Find a punchy photograph of each and pass my written work to the typing pool for them to put it all into an eye-pleasing format.

Next came a slightly more difficult piece. Now I had to write a section on Weapon Effort Planning, explain the procedures and equations. Provide sample calculations and transpose effectiveness tables similar to the JMEM into my document. Here was the first stumbling block! HEL was the go-to company for providing effectiveness indices[3] in table format. However, the company estimated that to do each of the calculations necessary to create a table against each of the targets with all the appropriate weapons would cost well in excess of £100K per weapon. Because it would require not only theoretical, but also physical testing to achieve the results required for each weapon it would also take them something in the order of eighteen months to complete the table for just one target! Notionally I had been given only two years to complete my task, so things were not looking rosy for the CWEM. More importantly, any loss of impetus could catastrophically kill the project and even delay or cost me my posting to Tornado.

RARDE were unable to assist and BAe were powerless as they did not have sufficient expertise in the field as their prime focus was on guided weapons. Undeterred I kept to my task and busied myself with other aspects of the book. I had to speak with the necessary offices that would ensure that the book was published under strict SECRET arrangements and I eventually got my hands on a stand-alone desktop computer that removed the requirement

---

3. A measure of the extent to which a weapon system may be expected to achieve a set of specific mission requirements. It is a function of the system's availability, dependability and capability.

for the typing pool's assistance. I also knuckled down to complete ISS, which I did on 5 September 1984; my final and overall assessment was graded 'Aircrew A.'[4]

Personally my life had been turned around. My wife had found work as a nursing assistant at a local private hospital, the children were happy in their primary school in Lacey Green, I now had the C Exam and ISS under my belt and my first ACR after just eight months in post had begun to reverse the trend that had left me feeling quite low when I had left 16 Squadron. I had a High Rec for promotion and was marked 'above average' in my ground appointment. Most importantly, perhaps, I found that I had a natural aptitude for project management, was diligent in fulfilling my task and loved working unaided and autonomously. For the first time in my RAF career, I felt as though I was now in control of my own destiny with few if any outside influences to unsettle me along the way.

I called Bill at Oberammergau to ask him if he could suggest any method by which I could short-circuit procurement of the Effectiveness Index tables for my tome. He could not! He used the JMEM, the JMEM was routinely amended and the office that dealt with the JMEM was in the USA at Aberdeen Proving Ground in Maryland, not at Oberammergau. Then there was a flash of inspiration from Bill. He had contacts in the Pentagon who could open doors for me at Aberdeen Proving Ground, if I could persuade my chain of command to find the Travel & Subsistence necessary to get me across to the States. He also recommended that I should meet with JMEM staff at NAS China Lake in California. Bingo!

I flew from RAF Brize Norton on the RAF's regular weekly VC10 shuttle to Washington DC where I was collected by a squadron leader from the British Embassy and shipped to a hotel. After a few office calls the following day in the Pentagon, my British escort then whisked me north-east towards Baltimore and into Aberdeen Proving Ground where, after I was security cleared, I entered a number of discussions with DoD scientists about their JMEM document. The following morning it was a short ride from the Embassy Suites hotel in Arlington to Washington's Ronald Reagan Airport and a flight across the States to Los Angeles. A further two hundred miles north by automobile to Ridgcrest, in the Western Mojave Desert, was followed the next morning by a meeting around a slightly sand-covered table

---

4. 'C' Grade Pass known as an 'Aircrew A' in the flying branches!

in a shack on the airfield with doughnuts, fruit, fruit juice and coffee available for those who might have missed breakfast!

It was all very helpful and informative and the conclusion was that although there were minor differences, particularly in ovoid shape, between US weapons and UK weapons the Effectiveness Indices of each could be directly read across one to the other. Brilliant! With the promise of a letter to that effect to follow, I headed back to Washington, back to the VC10 and back to the UK and the typing pool where the girls were tasked and happy to copy the tables from the JMEM directly into my draft of the CWEM.

The volume stretched to six hundred pages by the time it was complete. I had ensured that it was readable, pictorially attractive and was both useable and user-friendly. It fulfilled its mandate perfectly and it superseded the JMEM in common use throughout the RAF, the Royal Navy and the air forces of Australia and New Zealand, who had requested copies for their own staffs. It had taken me just fifteen months from start to finish for it to roll off the presses. Huntings, who had had a vested interest in its production from the outset, had remained true to me from day one with the assistance that its staff provided. Indeed, the company eventually scraped £10K out of an ongoing project to provide funding for its publication. The new SD-110A–0300–1G was printed, bound and then securely stored in their printing and publication department before it was shipped to HMSO for onward distribution.

In many ways the book reflected my character. I had been tenacious in ensuring that it was completed in time and I had worked scrupulously to ensure that there were no typographical errors within it. I had checked each and every page over and over and over again before I locked it into the final draft for publication. I had also added a couple of humorous Herriot 'identity tags' that I knew those who knew me would spot. The first featured in the Glossary where, as well as identifying *RDP* as a Radar Discrete Point, I included the alternative 'Run Down Period'[5] for the acronym. My other Herriotism related directly to my earliest days on XV Squadron.

I had met Iain Ross at RAF Honington in 1971 when we had both turned up to be among the first students on 237 Operational Conversion Unit. I was a fresh-faced first-tourist navigator straight from Nav School and Iain,

---

5. An aircrew expression that means coming towards the end of a tour where one can begin to relax and run down.

a pilot, had arrived following a first tour flying Hunters with 208 Squadron at RAF Muharraq, in Bahrain. He was an erstwhile Cranwell cadet and I wasn't. His father had been a very senior air ranking medical officer in the RAF, whilst my father had been a bank teller. On the face of it, we had very little in common apart from the fact that we were both Scots. And that mattered. We got on like a house on fire.

I will always be eternally grateful to Iain for guiding me through the Buccaneer conversion course. He taught me an awful lot about flying in fast-jet aircraft and he used his prior experience to help me with the more technical aspects of the Buccaneer airframe. He taught me also much of what life was really like at the very front of the RAF's elite force of operational fast-jet aircrew. We left 237 OCU together and spent the next, very happy, two years crewed together on XV Squadron at RAF Laarbruch. Amongst all that he taught me, he schooled me, and the rest of this happy band of operational aircrew, in a bar game, if you could call it a game, that became a regular feature during our drinking sessions in the officers' mess bar or even in the crewroom over a quiet cup of coffee before flying!

It was a simple enough 'game' that appealed to our puerile senses of humour. In its basic form, and it was basic from the outset, it revolved around being punished physically for passing wind in public! In short, fart and regret it!

A loud fart would attract instant retribution. Anybody within range would start to punch the transgressor until he completed the following 'shout':

'Badger, Badger, Badger! One, Two, Three! (Whistle three times)! One Hundred and Ten!'[6]

It was important to make the call as quickly as possible because, until it was completed, anybody present was allowed to punch and hit you as hard as they could until you were done. Trying to whistle three times whilst giggling and trying to hold a full glass of Heineken was probably the most difficult task, especially whilst being pounded by all those within range!

Of course, trying to sneak one out in the 'silent, but deadly' fashion was a dangerous tactic. You might get away with it if it was odourless, but if not,

---

6. Ridiculously, I have had to place this phrase in quotation marks. Why? Because if my erstwhile Buccaneer pilot, Iain Ross, ever reads it, he will find me and punch me until I have fallen unconscious or he gives up!

the first faint wisp in an adjacent nostril could have a devastating result for the perpetrator.

There were exceptions to the rule. If the gathering was not indoors then a quick call of *'Outdoor Rules'* would suffice, although the sharp witted would still attempt to get a sneaky punch in before that was completed. Farting and running away was certainly not within the rules as Barrie Chown found to his cost at Laarbruch! Having farted, he ran for the cover of the concertina door in the bar and attempted to make the required call from the sanctuary of the Ante-Room with just his head poking through into the bar. Unfortunately for Barrie, a well-aimed, half-full Heineken bottle launched by Nick Berryman caught him square on the forehead, poleaxed him to the floor and left him with a small smiling scar on his forehead forever afterwards.

Apparently, according to Iain, the words in the call related to a Soviet bomber of that NATO designation and its wing span, which was one hundred and ten feet wide! Of course, the problem came when you just wanted to state the name of that Soviet bomber, see how guarded I am being here, in a context other than having just farted! In that instance it was necessary to state just *Quote Badger Unquote* but, again, a sharp-witted individual was allowed to strike you as long as he hit before the word unquote had finished being uttered! There was a plus point to this game, of course. Nobody on XV Squadron ever forgot the wingspan of that renowned Soviet bomber. Now, ask me the wingspan of a Tu-95 Bear? Sorry, I can't help you there!

Consequently, and back with the Conventional Weapons Employment Manual, knowing that Ross would never allow me to get away with printing the name of the Soviet bomber anywhere in my six hundred pages without either the full call or its alternative, I encased it in quotation marks on every occasion that it appeared in the CWEM!

It is good to leave your mark on a professional work, and like Breughel with his little boy peeing in every painting, I had left mine on the Conventional Weapons Employment Manual. I handed over responsibility for the document to the Attack Weapons Specialist at DAW Cranwell, handed back my desktop computer and closed up my office. The CWEM was amended regularly over the next five years, but since the mid-90s, it has once again found itself stuffed at the back of secure cabinets throughout the RAF with no attention or time spared for its upkeep. It was ever thus!

I departed the ORB at the end of January 1985 with another High Rec for promotion, an Above Average assessment in all aspects of my work and support from my chain of command for my request to fill a post as a squadron leader on a Tornado squadron as soon as possible! The trend had been reversed and my career was heading back in the right direction. When I had arrived in Buckinghamshire I had given serious consideration to leaving the RAF at the earliest opportunity, which would have been on my thirty-eighth birthday. I was thirty-five and off to fly Tornado. I decided to stick with the RAF for the time being, and see what happened.

Chapter Three

From Folding Wings to Swing Wings

For the next twelve months I became a weekly commuter to and from our married quarter at High Wycombe. I was due to join 65 Course at the Tri-national Tornado Training Establishment at RAF Cottesmore in May 1985. However, beforehand, there was a need to attend two pre-employment courses at the Aviation Medicine Training Centre at RAF North Luffenham and, eventually, Sea Survival training at RAF Mount Batten.

RAF North Luffenham used to be located between the villages of Edith Weston and North Luffenham in Rutland. However, much to the disappointment of aged aircrew like me, it no longer exists. It was not the fact that we ancients enjoyed being subjected to the rigours of hypoxia or explosive decompression, you understand. No! More for the fact that Rutland is famous for not much apart from being the smallest county in England and the brewer of Ruddles very fine County Ale. A visit to AMTC was essential as a precursor to flying a new aircraft type. I had experienced the unit's three-day course on Aero Medicine as a fresh-faced navigator about to embark on my Buccaneer career and now it was my chance to return to 'Ruddles County' to sample its delights before turning my attention to the Tornado.

A gathering of aircrew routinely calls for a few ales and a night or two at North Luffenham usually resulted in rather more than a few pints of the 'County'. The effect was, usually, no more debilitating than any night spent in any bar in any county in England. However, a night in the officers' mess bar at North Luffenham, before a morning session in the decompression chamber, was more debilitating in one particularly unimaginable way – unless you were aircrew and had been briefed on it beforehand by the medical officer. Strapped in to the chamber, kitted out with flying helmet and oxygen mask, we victims prepared for our first hypoxia demonstration. With the chamber sealed, and the doctor issuing instructions through a radio link to the outside world, the technician gradually began to reduce the pressure in the chamber. Concomitantly, the altimeter in the chamber began to show an increase in height. Nothing odd or uncomfortable was experienced as the chamber 'climbed' through 10,000 feet. However, as the pressure decreased further the effects of the 'County' began to stir in the bowels of those present. Medical guidance at this point was clear and unequivocal. 'Just let it rip, chaps', was the sage advice of the doctor. The relief on my gut was instant and the expressions on the other faces around me indicated that similar satisfying releases had been achieved too. Our eyes smiled knowingly to each other as we continued to breathe in the pure oxygen being piped from the regulators connected to our masks and into our lungs. Our smiles were very quickly wiped from our faces when it was time to remove our masks to experience the effects of hypoxia. Unfortunately, there was neither a drill nor Flight Reference Cards for 'Noxious Fumes in the Cockpit' of the decompression chamber at North Luffenham.

The other task of the AMTC staff was to issue aircrew with their specific-to-type flying equipment. For potential Tornado GR1 aircrew this included a new flying helmet, external G-suit, and life preserver. The first two of these were very similar to those supplied for my Buccaneer tours, but the last was, by far, a much more sophisticated affair. Unlike the torso harness issued to me back in 1971, the Tornado 'Mae West' had full sleeves each with an attachment for arm restraints. It was not that a Tornado ejection was any more hazardous than that from a Buccaneer. It was more that, supported by accident investigation, medical science combined with aviation technology had advanced such to ensure that none of my four limbs would flail should I have to make a prompt departure from a doomed aircraft. In addition, the Tornado had a Command Ejection system, which could mean that a caring pilot might pull the lever without warning to ensure that, whilst I was not the master of my own destiny, I at least stood a chance of surviving.

On the third morning of the course we mustered again in the AMTC classroom to be introduced to flying equipment that might save our lives if we were ever subjected to Nuclear, Biological and Chemical conditions. Back we went into the chamber to undergo all the same exercises that we had completed earlier in the week, but this time we looked far more sinister as, under our flying helmets, we were swathed in a black neoprene hood and sealed, clear visor. In our hands we carried a battery powered respirator that created an overpressure around our fully encased heads! We looked and sounded like something out of a *Star Wars* movie.

The AR5 comprised a single piece rubber hood with a heavy rubber cowling and a neck seal. Incorporated in the rubber hood was an aircrew oxygen mask, a transparent visor, full microphone wiring and switching and a drinking tube. Considerately, somebody had thought it a good idea to fit an anti-drowning valve – I for one hoped it would never come to that! The trick was that, under NBC attack, aircrew would don all this protective equipment in a clean area in the Pilot Briefing Facility before venturing out into the unclean atmosphere to mount their aircraft and go to war! To ensure that the air inside the hood remained clean for the walk from PBF to cockpit a handheld respirator – affectionately known as the 'Whistling Handbag' – provided filtered breathing air until the mask was connected to the aircraft oxygen system. It was a piece of kit that could quite easily induce the most appalling nightmares and the very thought of ejecting into the sea wearing the monstrosity was enough to make the bravest man quake! The Water Entry Drill, which I would eventually have to practise on an annual basis, involved two very difficult twisting actions that had to be executed absolutely correctly else you would drown instantly! All undertaken whilst also having to wear a pair of NBC neoprene gloves and liners! Dexterous action this was most definitely not.

As I reflect on the significant number of times that I, as a navigator,[1] had to fly around the North German Plain wearing AR5 on MINEVAL, MAXEVAL and TACEVAL, I remember the fatigue inducing faff of getting into the cockpit wearing it! Once strapped in the procedures necessary to exchange the O_2 feed from the Whistling Handbag to the aircraft system were almost impossible to complete properly. Peering through a Perspex visor that was situated above a large and protuberant facemask made the task quite difficult. Wearing neoprene rubber gloves, that turned your fingers into something that resembled large black carrots, ensured that the search to locate the join in the O_2 tube increased the task to very difficult. Holding your breath at the same time to simulate and therefore prevent noxious gases entering your airways made the task utterly impossible. Taking it all together, I would be very surprised if any war mission could ever have been efficiently or effectively completed by AR5 wearing aircrew! It was the one piece of aircrew equipment issued that, without exception, every fast jet pilot and navigator loathed beyond all measure. With my AR5 stuffed into my RAF aircrew holdall, along with the rest of the issued equipment, I set off back to High Wycombe for a week at home before I headed south-west to Devon for

---

1. Tornado pilots were excused because of flight safety implications.

another bout of sea survival training. It was early May; at least the sea would be beginning to warm up, if it was not yet at full bath temperature!

I am a non-swimmer! Well, that statement is not strictly true. I am a non-swimmer by choice, would be a bit more accurate. I do not, even after almost seventy years of life, voluntarily wet my body unless I am taking a shower or having a bath. Swimming for me started, or probably better to say stopped, when I was eight years old and my elder sister thought she would teach me whilst on a family holiday in St Andrews. She failed and, in truth, I am sure she attempted to drown me. Whatever it was she did, and after my rubber ring brought me back to the surface after what seemed like an eternity, I vowed never to dip my feet in the ocean or a swimming pool ever again. The RAF had a different attitude, however, which I discovered to my cost when I turned up at AOTS at RAF Church Fenton in 1969. Friday mornings were swimming mornings at the Yearsley Swimming Pool in York. All aircrew must be able to swim a minimum of twenty-five yards and I was no exception. Oh how I struggled to qualify. Every Friday, around midday, I would disconsolately dry myself off in the midst of all my Johnny Weissmuller[2] mates in the full knowledge that I would be back in the pool, in seven days' time, trying desperately to swim its length, just so that I could sellotape a certificate into my flying logbook that would allow me to progress through flying training.

I did it! I swam twenty-five yards on my back whilst the PTI Warrant Officer dangled a long pole above my nose. I grabbed at it and he pulled it away. I grabbed it again and up it went – again! But I made it to the deep end and with some huge relief felt my fingers touch the end of the pool. Admittedly, it was my last chance before commissioning, but I did it and I received my Y-Category swimming certificate just in the nick of time.

However, by the time I finished navigation training at RAF Finningley some eighteen months later, I had lost it; the certificate that is. And despite all my protestations to the contrary, the staff officer at Headquarters Training Command refused to believe that I had ever possessed such a certificate. What is more, he was about to cancel my posting to the Buccaneer OCU unless I could prove that I could swim from one end of the RAF College pool to the other. Needless to say, and with some exceptional coaching from

2. An Austro-Hungarian-born American competition swimmer and actor, who was best known for playing Tarzan in films of the 1930s and 1940s and for having one of the best competitive swimming records of the 20th century.

the RAFC Cranwell PTIs, I eventually managed to crack the distance, on my back. That certificate was glued, sellotaped and stapled into my logbook and there it remains even now. Yet still to this day, whilst I am quite happy in the shallow end of a swimming pool without any form of flotation aid, I refuse to venture to the deep end, no matter the occasion. So Dinghy Drills and Sea Survival Drills throughout my RAF career were anathema to me. I dreaded the annual training, but had to get a 'tick in the box' to satisfy the squadron's Basic Training Requirements. Throughout my four tours on the Buccaneer I developed a Baldrick-style cunning plan. Whether it was swimming pool or North Sea, and despite the PTI's insistence not to, I always 'accidentally', pulled the Mae West inflation valve before I leapt from either the edge of the pool or the back of the RAF Marine Craft.

After a day of lectures on the contents of our Personal Survival Packs, a refresher on our parachute descent drills, water entry procedures and SAR helicopter recovery actions the merry band of RAF aircrew, who were destined to be my playmates on the course at Cottesmore, trotted down to the harbour at Mount Batten to board the marine craft that would, eventually, deposit us overboard in Plymouth Sound! They trotted, I sauntered.

'Just a reminder, gentlemen, stand on the stern, but do not inflate your Mae West until you're actually in the water!'

'You can forget that, pal,' I thought as I pulled the toggle just before I leapt into Plymouth Sound. 'I'm not a Y-Category swimmer for nothing, you know!'

TTTE was established in 1981 as a multinational aircraft conversion unit, based at RAF Cottesmore, tasked with training crews from the RAF, the German Air Force and Navy and the Italian Air Force on the Tornado GR1. The syllabus began with a four-week groundschool and simulator phase, which was followed by approximately nine weeks of flying. Aircraft from the three nations were allocated in ratios relative to their training throughput with the Germans providing the most and the Italians the least. There was no differentiation as to which nation's aircraft students flew and so my logbook shows that in the two months, June and July, that I was a student at Cottesmore I flew in RAF, Luftwaffe and ItAF jets. Three training squadrons formed the Tornado Operational Conversion Unit and each in turn was commanded by an officer from one each of the nations. A Squadron was the 'German Squadron', B Squadron was the 'British Squadron' and C Squadron was the 'Italian Squadron', but all three had a mix of aircrew and students from all three nations. A 'Standards Squadron' was responsible for follow-on training, the training of instructor crews and conducting check flights. Policy for the unit was mandated by the Tri-national Tornado Steering Group, a committee that met biannually and was chaired by the RAF, and funding by the three nations was apportioned 40:40:20 (Germany: Great Britain: Italy). With growing differences in aircraft variants, and in the post-Cold War era, the unit closed in 1999 with each nation agreeing that they would be better served performing their own conversion to type training.

I arrived at Cottesmore on Sunday, 19 May 1985 and met up with my fellow students in the bar. There was a significant number of Germans, both air force and navy, three young RAF pilots on their first tours, a first tour RAF navigator and Capitano Roberto Reggianini from the ItAF. It was a very good mix and the banter and 'war stories' started almost immediately. All of the foreign pilots had come from Starfighter backgrounds and the German navigators had all graduated recently from navigator training in the USA. We were mostly junior officers of flying officer or flight lieutenant equivalent, but the Germans were led by an Oberst and had a couple of majors thrown in the mix. They were a lively bunch – particularly Kolvi Kolvenbach and Rich Thomas! Roberto, who was allocated as my pilot, was a dead ringer for Luciano Pavarotti. He had never seen a navigator before, let alone flown with one. Like his Luftwaffe brethren, Roberto had cut his teeth on Starfighters, though how he managed to fit into one I will never know!

The Tornado was, avionically, far superior to the Buccaneer. With its swing wings it was also streets ahead aerodynamically! We all had a lot to learn on the groundschool and it came at us thick and fast. I was lucky that I had my Buccaneer background to fall back on, but some of the younger navigators found the pace and intensity hard to manage. There seemed to be constant testing of knowledge and we had to know and repeat our Bold Face Drills routinely so that they would become second nature in the case of an emergency. New technologies such as the aircraft's digital inertial navigation system and its Ground Mapping Radar that, unlike the Buccaneer, could pick out a plank across a stream or the corner of a fence around a field were all a revelation to me. I had to learn the idiosyncrasies of the Terrain Following Radar and how it and the GMR et al were inter-linked. TACAN and RHWR installations I was accustomed to, but the complexity of the Tornado system, its feeds to the two TV Tab screens and the Combined Radar Projected Map Display had to be understood. More importantly, it all had to be managed by me in the back seat and, whilst the Kalman Filter would smooth out the errors and place us always on track, when the day came that it all failed I needed to know how to recover the system. Thank God for over 2000 hours on the Buccaneer. There was no need to stop there either! I needed to know how the engines worked, how the hydraulics and electrics worked and, with the complexity of a wing that could be shoved back from twenty-five to forty-five or sixty-seven degrees dependent upon how fast you wanted to go, how the flying controls worked. It was all quite mind-boggling!

'Sorry, say that again! You can land this thing with the wings swept fully back? Are you serious?' Apparently he was being serious and although the airspeed over the fence was extremely high you could put it down on the numbers and stop using the reverse thrust and still leave plenty of runway available should anything else untoward occur! What a beast and Roberto and I were about to put the aircraft and our new-found knowledge into action in the simulator.

The first thing I noticed when I climbed into the simulator for the first time was the consideration that had been given to the occupant, his need to interface with his surroundings and his comfort. No longer was I sat in the ergonomic slum that had been the rear cockpit of the Buccaneer. At no time in its design had anybody thought it a good idea to chuck all the black (they were grey actually) boxes up in the air and screw them in where they landed! Everything was laid out in a neat and eye-catching fashion with a place for everything and everything in its place. Straight in front of me were two Television Tabulation screens upon which most of my navigation needs would be met. Between them sat the CRPMD upon which I would, for the first time in my life, be able to take radar fixes and identify and attack radar discrete targets easily. At a flick of a switch on the CRPMD I could change from radar to map or vice versa and see exactly where I was on the surface of the Earth! A position cursor on my left hand TV Tab showed me exactly where the aircraft was relative to the track that was digitally represented as a route plan on the screen whilst on the right hand TV Tab track and waypoint information was instantly available and clearly displayed before my very eyes. Everything that a navigator would ever need to ensure that he was never temporarily unsure of his position was displayed straight in front of me. Considerately, should I become at all interested in what the man in the front was up to, the designers had very kindly positioned both an altimeter and an ASI above the CRPMD. There was even an Artificial Horizon gauge and an RCDI for my benefit too. Plus, and here they were getting serious, I had my own undercarriage UP/DOWN indicator lights and a Central Warning Panel. In the Buccaneer, the two-man crew were integrated by choice! In the Tornado, the two-man crew were integrated by design.

Advances in safety had also been considered with a Command Ejection System and limb restraints were improved with two restraint points at the ankles and the knees and one on each of the upper arms just below the shoulder! If you decided to leave this jet in a hurry you would do so with all your joints firmly tucked in to the bang seat, which would stop them wildly flailing when you hit the 500kt slipstream! If you failed to disconnect them all, or your Personal Survival Pack lanyard, before vacating the cockpit after a sortie then the only slipstream that you were likely to encounter, and at some volume, would be that coming from the Boss's mouth after he had been informed of your stupidity! It happened!

Below the CRPMD were two panels that ensured that the navigator was fully integrated into the whole digitised system when it came to getting to, and putting bombs on, the target; the Nav Mode Control Panel and the Weapon Aiming Mode Selector. The NMCP and the WAMS. It was a joy to behold in comparison to my previous FJ experience, but there was one major snag. All this kit and caboodle obscured the navigator's forward vision. Even with the bang seat fully extended it allowed only a very limited forward view either side of the CRPMD – I missed the superior offset seating position and free forward vision that had been the Buccaneer navigator's delight.

Nevertheless, the Tornado was a great weapons delivery platform as long as you accepted its limitations, one of which was that, without a bomb bay, ordnance hung underneath the fuselage and wings had a somewhat detrimental effect on its range – certainly when compared to what I had been used to.

Mission planning was undertaken in exactly the same way as in the Buccaneer; we drew lines on maps. But, instead of marking Turning Points on a map, Tornado crews marked Waypoints[3] and Fix Points as well as IPs and Targets, all of which were then measured electronically. Additionally, whilst we followed and planned for traditional tactical routing when VMC, using sixty degrees of bank turning circles, the Tornado had a fully integrated system that allowed us to terrain follow whilst completely IMC! The result,

---

3. Waypoint is a Turning Point but just with a fancy name!

in planning terms, was a whole new collection of plastic rulers and a whole new consideration of what effect the angle of bank applied by the pilot made to the actual turning circle achieved in the air. Whether it was a singleton, a pair, a four-ship or greater sortie plan, it all had to be drawn out on a half million map beforehand. That would be sufficient for the average navigator! Give me a map, a stopwatch, a competent pilot and a clear day and I can take you anywhere. Not so with the Tornado! Not only did the pilot need to know where we were going, but so did the computer! Map drawn, it was spread across a large electronic table so that all the details thereon could be transferred by a relatively simple scanning process into what looked very much like a Sinclair Spectrum on steroids! OK I'm exaggerating, but you get the idea! The Cassette Preparation Ground Station, or CPGS as this monstrosity was known, was at least six feet tall and encased inside a rigid, but transportable metal container. It relied on a five-inch floppy disc to boot it up with the necessary information to plan a route and was connected to a dot-matrix printer that produced an almost unreadable printout on a flimsy roll of paper! Thankfully it had a basic computer monitor screen built into it and a QWERTY keyboard upon which to type the needed inputs and confirm the scanned route. Its biggest snag was that it was a relatively slow process and, for large formations, it could take much more than the available time to produce a coherent plan upon it. It was, nevertheless, every Tornado navigator's friend and master. It was a good friend, but it could be a monstrous master. The old computer adage of 'Garbage In equals Garbage Out' became very well understood on TOCU at Cottesmore. Any glitches on the map, any finger trouble on the keyboard, any electrical surges at a critical scanning point could be devastating for a formation leader. However, when it worked well it was a godsend and the cassette tape that it produced on completion of the scan transferred all the required detail into the aircraft's Main Computer during engine start. A couple of subsequent TV Tab button presses and, hey presto, the navigator was ready to taxi for take-off! If the tape failed, the whole process of Waypoint after Waypoint, Fix Point after Fix Point and Target after Target had to be entered manually using the alphanumeric buttons under the TV screens! It took ages and quite often delayed take-off considerably.

Roberto and I successfully completed nine simulator sorties at Cottesmore between 16 May and 7 June 1985. The first four missions were sufficient to allow us to familiarise ourselves with our cockpit drills, but the last five were full mission familiarisation sorties with emergencies thrown in. Twelve days later I got airborne on my first trip in a Tornado GR1 with a staff pilot who put the Tornado through its paces for me and, for the second time in my life over the North Sea, I broke the sound barrier.[4]

The syllabus included twenty-four more sorties which were flown over the next five weeks. Each was designed to enhance my understanding of the Tornado and scaled to introduce me to all facets of its operation. Sixteen of these were flown with various staff members and the remaining third with one's allocated student pilot. After an initial five singleton navigation sorties using all the various aspects of the 'system', the syllabus moved up a gear with an introduction to formation flying and then the weapon system. No weapons were dropped whilst at TOCU, but a full understanding of the system had to be proved before us Brits moved on to the RAF's Tornado Weapons Conversion Unit at RAF Honington.

Roberto and I got airborne together for the first time on 8 July and we very quickly clicked! Despite his concern about his unfamiliarity with flying with somebody 'in the boot' and his worries about weak English, he proved very quickly that he was a very competent pilot. I very much enjoyed flying with him and it was evident from the outset just why the ItAF had selected him to be an instructor on C Squadron at Cottesmore upon completion of the course.

On we went intermingling staff trips with subsequent crew trips. Formation practice, TF sorties, night flying, night TF and complex attack sorties, where we had to put the whole package of training together and complete a realistic mission into the borderlands of England and Scotland. None of the sorties lasted much longer than eighty minutes because none were flown with anything other than internal fuel. At the end of the course what impressed me most overall about the Tornado was just how accurate the navigation system was. Others I know, particularly those who had not come from a fast jet background, struggled to master the concept of actually being able to see out and navigate from feature to feature. They comforted themselves in the back seat by 'following the green writing' on the screens in front of them and often lost the tactical picture as a result. However, for me, looking out was second nature and my biggest problem was to remember to use the kit for what it was designed to do!

---

4. The first had been in a TF-104 of the Royal Danish Air Force whilst on detachment at Aalborg with the Buccaneer during my tour on 12 Squadron.

I was never a great fan of night flying, but the Tornado certainly made my task easier. Like many FJ aircrew, I always worked on the principle that if birds do not fly at night why should humans! However, with Roberto in the front seat, there was an added incentive to get airborne at night and complete the sortie successfully – he made a mean *Spaghetti Aglio e Olio*,[5] or Spaghetti GTX as he referred to it, in the crewroom afterwards, and all washed down with a few post-night flying beers.

Socially TOCU was fantastic fun. There was a definite party atmosphere around the place and each nation did its utmost to outdo the others whenever an excuse was available to organise a party. The Germans, I have to admit, were best at it and it was not uncommon to see a C-160 Transall sat on the ASP disgorging barrel after barrel of Löwenbräu for the next party organised by the Luftwaffe and Deutsche Marine. It's July! Let's have an Oktoberfest! I liked their German logic! My regular weekend commute meant that I was not always present when the best parties happened but, because of the timing of my course, my wife and I did manage to get to the Cottesmore Summer Ball in 1985. It was a grand affair and enhanced greatly by the multicolour dress uniforms of the three nations and their efforts to outdo each other on the food front!

Roberto's wife had remained in Italy whilst we were under training so he routinely and quite regularly came home with me for the weekend, took over our kitchen and cooked us extravagant Italian meals at High Wycombe. Even after we had gone our separate ways, he would quite often leave his car at our house whenever he popped home to Modena to see his family. He and his family eventually moved into a married quarter at Cottesmore, where he occasionally hosted us. We remain firm friends to this day.

With a High Average report under my belt and thirty-one hours on Tornado, four and a half undertaken whilst the birds were in bed, I waved Cottesmore goodbye in early August and headed off for a family break in Brixham, where my in-laws now lived, before I reported to Honington for Course 32 on the TWCU, which was due to commence on the twenty-eighth. Having flown with the Cottesmore Station Commander, Group Captain 'Sam' Goddard, twice during the course he wrote a ringing endorsement on my final report:

---

5. Main ingredients: six cloves of garlic, quarter-teaspoon of red chilli flakes and half a cup of olive oil!

'From personal experience I can confirm Flt Lt Herriot's good performance on the Course. He is also a good social leader although he has always "made briefings on time"!!!'

Whatever could he have meant by that!

Back home after a very pleasant two weeks in the sunshine of the south Devon coast, I repacked my car and headed off back to Honington. The route from High Wycombe to Suffolk was very familiar to me as my parents had abandoned Glasgow in 1980 to be closer to their four children who were all based in southern England. In spite of my warnings of our peripatetic lifestyle, they had chosen to buy a bungalow in Ixworth, near Bury St Edmunds. Despite being painfully homesick for Scotland they were, on the whole, happy there as they had more contact with their growing band of grandchildren. My arrival at Honington would ensure that I was able to spend more time with them before we, once again, headed overseas to Brüggen to join the Tornado Wing there.

Honington had grown considerably since I had left it in 1981 to head to 16 Squadron. Extensive work had been undertaken to improve the airbase to accommodate Tornado and the dispersals on the north side of the airfield had been hardened to protect squadron aircraft from air attack. The officers' mess too had been doubled in size to accommodate the large throughput of Tornado crews on the TWCU. The bar had been open two hours by the time I 'Warned In' to the mess on my arrival. Having found my room in the annex, I grabbed a tie from my bags and headed off to the bar.

It was a typical pre-course gathering of like-minded souls. Many of the staff members had assembled there to greet the new arrivals and I quickly fell in with some of my chums from the Buccaneer Force who had got to Tornado before me, including Gordon McRobbie who was now the CI. Gordon and I had flown the Buccaneer together occasionally on XV Squadron and had, notably, got lost in Bavaria when he first arrived on the squadron and I was tasked with showing him 4 ATAF! I say we got lost – that would be unfair on Gordon! I got lost and he managed to find us again much to my relief. He was a real gentleman aviator and I looked forward to renewing our acquaintance.

After a short groundschool programme and one simulator familiarisation ride I was airborne on the TWCU Familiarisation sortie with my old 237 OCU staff mate, Frank Waddington. He's the guy who I was flying with in 1979 when I damaged my back whilst writing copious notes on my kneepad about a wayward student pilot on the Buccaneer OCU. Frank's the guy who snapped 5G when that wayward student pilot arrived back in the formation with a Lightning interceptor on his tail whilst I was writing on my kneepad to build a case at the debrief that might eventually get the wayward student pilot suspended from training for the second time. That was the day my head hit my knee under the onset of the 5G and compressed the T4 vertebra in my spine that resulted in some four months off flying![6] The banter level in the now familiar Tornado cockpit had not diminished and the rapport, front to back, was just as I remembered it.

The course continued throughout September, October and November and each weapons phase was introduced with a Phase Brief and a simulator sortie before I was let loose in the aircraft with first a staff member and then my allocated student pilot, Paul Comer. The sorties usually included a short low-level phase before or after a range detail to practise either Laydown, Loft or Dive bombing; three missions of each discipline. Four night sorties were included, sadly without the reward of *Spaghetti Aglio e Olio* afterwards, as were four Air Combat Training sorties. ACT was a brand new ballgame for me. It had been the practice with the Buccaneer to get low and fast to evade detection by fighters – you could not do much else given that it was ill-equipped aerodynamically to turn and fight even if it had had the weapons to do so. The Tornado was different. It had the weapons and the manoeuvrability to turn and fight, albeit avoiding detection and maintaining the track to target was, like the Buccaneer, the primary aim.

ACT was a good exercise to prove aircraft handling and combat awareness. It ensured that the navigators understood the imperative of good look out and exercised their airmanship and their understanding of air combat in a high stress environment. Communication front to back was vital in ACT and with the pilot having the responsibility to handle the aircraft effectively, the navigator, whilst assisting him verbally with his task, had also to monitor systems and aircraft safety. With wings sweeping forward and back and 'burners' being used to improve position or overcome a possible defeat there was a lot for the navigator to comprehend and prove under the constantly changing high 'g' manoeuvring. It was also inordinately good fun! The course climaxed with one dedicated TF sortie followed by five complex operational

6. The full story is available in *Adventures of a Cold War Fast-Jet Navigator: The Buccaneer Years (Pen & Sword 2017)*.

sorties which brought together all aspects of the training and concluded with bombs on target at one of the UK Air Weapons Ranges on the east coast. Only three months after arriving at Honington and with a further thirty-five hours on Tornado, I was ready for a squadron and yet another Combat Ready Work-up programme.

Paul and I had been posted together to 14 Squadron at Brüggen but, after some internal wrangling between the three Brüggen squadrons, my posting was changed to be the QWI navigator on 17 Squadron. Before I could take up that role, however, I had to convert my Buccaneer weapons instructor qualification by completing the two-week Tornado QWI Groundschool at Honington. It was a tall order! Unlike my peers on the course I had only sixty-six hours on the Tornado and, despite my vast experience as a Buccaneer QWI, my knowledge of the Tornado, to say the least, was extremely scant in comparison. Consequently, I found the two weeks tortuous and failed the final exam paper at my first attempt. The story of my life and I could almost hear the Rector at the High School of Glasgow, who had had little faith in me as an academic wizard, saying, 'I told you so'! However, the staff recognised that I had been placed in a difficult position and I was certainly pleased to be offered a re-run of the exam, which I then passed.

I left the TWCU with an Above Average rating and headed back home to spend December with my family and to start preparations for a family move back to Germany. I was due at Brüggen just after New Year, but without a married quarter instantly available, I had to leave my family in the quarter at High Wycombe until such time as a house became available in Germany.

Chapter Four

The Black Hand Gang

On 6 January 1986, I once again found myself on board the trooper bound for RAF Wildenrath. With all my flying kit having been sent ahead I was ready for the next phase of my flying career, but this time on a new aircraft type. Having settled myself into my bachelor accommodation in the Brüggen officers' mess, I headed to the bar to meet up with my new squadron mates who had gathered there to welcome me. The squadron had been located at Brüggen since 1 September 1970, operating first Phantom FGR2 and then Jaguar GR3 aircraft in the Strike/Attack role. It had only been operating Tornado GR1 for some nine months by the time I arrived and formed a third of the Brüggen Tornado GR1 Wing; the other two squadrons being 14 and 31. The officers' mess was thus a lively affair with each of the three squadrons trying to outdo each other in both drinking and singing – it was, I felt upon my introduction, no different to my first experience of Laarbruch some fourteen years previous. It was going to be a good tour and I could not wait to get stuck into flying, once again, over 2 and 4 ATAF.

No. 17 Squadron was known at Brüggen as the 'Black Hand Gang'. The name had come about because the squadron badge was a gauntlet, chosen to symbolize armed strength and its previous operation of the Gloster Gauntlet fighter in the 1930s, and the fact that it was lodged in 'Black Sector' on the north-east corner of the airfield. The squadron motto is *Excellere Contende* which translates as 'Strive to Excel'. Although it has had some short periods of downtime since its formation on 1 February 1915, the squadron is still active 103 years on as the RAF's Test and Evaluation squadron for the Lockheed Martin F-35B Lightning II.

When I arrived in January 1986, the squadron was commanded by the irrepressible Grant McLeod, whose favourite expression was 'just come for a quiet chat on the patio'. One never knew whether his invitation was a good or bad omen as his face would never flicker whilst he was saying it. If it was followed by his other renowned catch phrase about 'cutting the mustard' then things could be about to go from bad to worse. Grant was an ex-Jaguar pilot, but I could not hold that against him because, like me, he was a Scot.

I was programmed to fly my first trip on the squadron on the eighth, with the Boss, who planned to reacquaint me with the North German Plain and some laydown bombing at Nordhorn Range. I therefore had just one day to read and sign all the necessary flying orders, ASIs and Hot Poop[1] and complete as much of the station arrival procedures that I could. It was a hectic start, but nothing that I had not seen before and nothing that particularly fazed me. Importantly, however, I needed to make my number with the Families' Officer to identify just how long it would be before my family could join me at Brüggen. It was a promising first encounter as it quickly became apparent that a married quarter, albeit a top floor three-bedroom flat, at 12 Dürerstrasse in Elmpt, had already been allocated at the beginning of February.

I had been paired with Flying Officer Phil Wright as my pilot for the initial stages of the combat ready work-up. Phil had been one of the first tour pilots on my course at TTTE and had also been with me through the TWCU at Honington. We had not flown together previously, but found ourselves airborne on 9 January 1996 exploring 2 ATAF and Nordhorn Range, which was for him, if not for me, a brand new experience. The weather in January in northern Germany had not improved since I had last experienced it in my time with the Buccaneer. However, unlike my previous time stumbling around the North German Plain in poor weather, we now had the advantage of TFR in the Tornado to advise us where the unseen Osnabrück Ridge was in the low level mist, and assist us in its avoidance. Unfortunately, the weather in Germany in January 1995 soon deteriorated beyond safe low-level flying limits and the squadron was forced to programme Hi-Lo-Hi missions to the UK's East Coast Ranges to allow us to continue with our CR work-up. Towards the end of the month, with the weather at Brüggen often well below safe landing limits until mid-afternoon, lunchtime 'land-aways' at Leuchars and Honington became the order of the day.

The LCR and CR work-up programmes were no different to those that I had experienced twice before in Germany on the Buccaneer. All three Tornado squadrons, along with their sister wing at Laarbruch, stood Strike QRA and it was imperative that I achieved that qualification quickly so that

---

1. Hot off the press information required to be understood and signed for by all squadron aircrew.

I could take my share of being incarcerated in 'Q', for twenty-four hours at a time, to react should the Cold War explode into Armageddon!

At the end of January I was granted two weeks leave to head back to the UK and collect my wife and children and install them in Dürerstrasse. Chris was eight and Sarah almost seven, so both were enrolled at Barnes Wallis Primary School situated on the Brüggen camp. For me it was but a short drive from Elmpt to the squadron and, for the children, it was a journey by school bus that picked up and dropped off almost outside our front door. The flat was not ideal, but at least we were all together again as a family.

Returning to the squadron in mid-February my next two sorties were in the dark! The first a night Loft sortie at Wainfleet Range, followed four days later by a jaunt round the 2 ATAF 'Nite C' route. Night flying around Germany was restricted to a minimum height of 1500 feet and was cast in a number of preordained routes that allowed deconfliction from other fast jet traffic doing similar and from civilian aircraft operating above and below that height. There were two routes used commonly by RAFG Tornados from both Brüggen and Laarbruch, with a common entry and exit point for each route. The 'Nite C' route followed an anti-clockwise circuit around 2 ATAF that incorporated a simulated attack at the RAF's Radar Bomb Scoring Unit, situated atop the Osnabrück Ridge, followed by a live bombing run at Nordhorn Range before recovery back to home base. The other route, used regularly by the two Tornado Wings, was the 'Nite Bene', which followed a circuit over the Benelux countries before a bombing run at Vliehors Range on the Dutch coast. By the end of February, Phil Wright and I had been separated in order to accelerate me through the LCR work-up process and I thus found myself flying with a number of different pilots throughout March and April.

The month of March was spent in the sunshine of Decimomannu, in Sardinia, for the squadron's Armament Practice Camp. It was an intense month of concentrated weaponry sorties to the local air-to-ground range at Capo Frasca. I had been to Frasca many times during my Buccaneer years and was very familiar with the set-up. However, never before had I conducted strafe on APC and each of the short sorties all finished with a strafe detail. Virtually every sortie that I flew in the eighteen flying days of the APC involved Laydown and Shallow Dive bombing with Strafe to conclude. It was a very high workload for both pilot and navigator as there were a number of switch changes to be made in the cockpit between each event. To screw any of them up would result in a humiliating dressing down from the debriefing QWI, one's name appearing on the 'Pigs Board' and, undoubtedly, a need to buy beers for the rest of the formation. As I was one of those tasked with giving humiliating dressings down, I could not afford a 'Switch Pigs'!

The weather back at base began to improve in April and, out of my eleven sorties that month, I flew with eight different pilots. The sorties were all designed to bring me up to LCR as quickly as possible, so they included day and night Loft at Wainfleet Range, Evasion with Laydown and Dive Bombing at Nordhorn, Loft at Vliehors and a 'Nite Bene'. The squadron also participated in Exercise Mallet Blow in April 1986. Mallet Blow was a quarterly exercise designed to test the air defence of the UK and involved aircraft from a number of NATO air forces, including routinely the USAF, RDAF, Luftwaffe and the RAF. The exercise was always well supported as it tested not only the skills of the personnel and aircrew manning the UKADR, but also the evading skills of the attacking force and their ability to penetrate to their target and deliver weapons on allocated targets on Otterburn Range. It also tested the attacking forces EW skills and equipment, as each mission was required to route through the RAF's EW Range at RAF Spadeadam.[2] Towards the end of April, I spent a couple of sorties flying with Iain McNicoll in the lead of a five-ship formation tasked with rehearsing and then undertaking a formation fly-past for the RAF Brüggen Officers' Mess Cocktail Party that was held on 2 May. To find myself at the front of a formation that was tasked with accurate flying and precision timing, after just four months on the squadron and with just a meagre one hundred and twenty-five hours on the jet, was an honour indeed. I knew at that point that I had made the grade on 17 Squadron.

Flying with pilots who were already CR accelerated me through the process and, on 20 April, I was declared CR in the nuclear strike role and thus qualified to share the load in QRA. With that award came the traditional requirement to drink the 'Squadron Op Pot'! If you are not experienced in the ways of RAF FJ squadrons then those three words might suggest to you that it was a quiet soiree amongst like-minded souls where a celebratory drink or two were shared amongst friends. You would be wrong! The 17 Squadron 'Op

---

2. RAF Spadeadam is a Royal Air Force station in Cumbria, close to the border with Northumberland. It is the home of the 9,000 acre Electronic Warfare Tactics Range, making it the largest RAF base in the United Kingdom.

Pot' was a large vessel, filled to its brim with noxious fluid, predominantly of the amber frothing variety, but not exclusively, that had to be downed in one, whilst those who had already achieved the exalted status of being operational watched and cheered with amusement as we poor unfortunates gagged at the prospect. Once emptied, the ewer had to be placed upside down on one's head such that there could be no cheating and, at best, only the dregs ran into your hair and down your neck! I was never a great one for schooner races, but with the challenge set I had to prove that I was fit to be a member of this elite group of individuals – so down it went not in record time, but with only a small amount of the foul concoction spilling over the front of my flying suit. With the pot now upside down on my head I fought back the urge to throw the whole lot back up and was cheered by my fellows for my achievement. I then watched with glee as the next poor unfortunate was faced with his challenge!

As one of only three QWIs on the squadron, the APC in March had presented something of a challenge to me. I had not long qualified on type and had, very recently, completed only two weeks in groundschool converting my Buccaneer qualification to a Tornado one. My confidence as a Tornado QWI was not that high at the time. Nevertheless, my previous role experience and strength of character, so it says in my report, helped me play an effective part on the APC where, apparently, I became an effective film and weapon debriefer. Indeed, it would seem from my flying assessment report, written just six months after my arrival on 17 Squadron, that such was my impact on the squadron that it was decided that I should be the next Weapons Leader on the outfit!

After the formation fly-past on 2 May, I was permanently crewed with Flight Lieutenant Tim Anderson. It was made clear to me by Grant McLeod that he had decided that Timo and I were to be brought on as four-ship and six-ship leaders and so from early May 1986, just as it had been with Iain Ross on XV Squadron, few other pilots' names appear in my logbook other than Anderson.

Tim was a comparative youngster on only his second operational tour in the RAF; I was on my fifth. His first tour had been on Tornados with 27 Squadron at RAF Marham and, from there, he had been posted to 17 Squadron along with his navigator from 27 Squadron, Flight Lieutenant John O'Shea. They had been the first ever first tourist crew to be posted to Tornado and had done outstandingly well on that tour. They had both been on 17 Squadron for about nine months by the time I arrived.

In mid–May the squadron deployed for Exercise Winter Vortex to Goose Bay in Labrador to undertake Operational Low Flying training. Although we were able to practise ULL over small areas of the UK, this deployment to Canada allowed us to fly complete missions, and test our tactics and evasion manoeuvres, down to the realistic operational height of 100 feet as soon as we left the airfield boundary. The only way that we would survive in war was if we flew as low as was safe to do so and had exercised our tactics to their fullest extent. So, in the sentiment of the rather emotive 'Welcome to RAF Brüggen' board, at the station's main gate, which read 'Our Task in Peace is to Train for War', a detachment to Goose Bay allowed us to do just that.

In the 1940s the permanent Canadian airbase, near the town of Happy Valley in Labrador, was constructed. In October 1944, the British government finalised the negotiations that established a ninety-nine year lease at Goose Bay, which allowed British aircrew to operate and train there. In response to lessons learned from the Vietnam War and the growing sophistication of Soviet anti-aircraft radar and SAM technology, other NATO nations began looking for opportunities to train at ULL. With a population of around 30,000 and an area measuring 294,000 km,[2] Labrador made an ideal location for OLF training. In addition, Labrador's sparse settlement and with its local topography being similar to parts of the Soviet Union the deal was sealed. By the mid-1980s CFB Goose Bay had grown to become the primary low-level tactical training area for several NATO air forces.

Notwithstanding its sparse population, however, complaints were often received about FJ aircraft at ULL interfering with salmon fishermen's lodge parties in the lakes and rivers north of the base. These complaints were taken seriously and when a lodge was known to be active large 'avoid' circles were placed as NOTAMs on all navigational planning maps and were adhered to. They were so few and far between that it had little impact on what we were trying to achieve anyway. Of more importance than disturbing the fish was the concern of the local Inuit[3] who protested that military flying operations in close proximity to the ground was adversely affecting wildlife, namely caribou, and affected their traditional way of life. If a herd was on the move large swathes of the countryside would have a flying embargo in place to allow the caribou to migrate as peacefully as possible. Occasionally, if they

---

3. A group of culturally similar indigenous peoples inhabiting the Arctic regions of Greenland, Canada and Alaska. Commonly referred to as Eskimos by Europeans.

had wandered off their predicted track you would see them from the air, but that, I am afraid, was unavoidable – we did our best to keep the peace with the indigenous population of the area.

The flying was fantastic. I had flown over Alberta during Maple Flag exercises in the Buccaneer, but the sheer ability to be at 100 feet and 450 knots straight after take-off from Goose Bay was extremely exhilarating. The vast expanse of unpopulated landscape, high conifers, deep lakes and river valleys was outstandingly beautiful. The fact that every sortie included a 'Bounce' and a couple of SAP targets ensured that you had to have your wits about you from beginning to end. It was truly training in peace as we would fight in war and, of the ten sorties that Timo and I flew out of Goose Bay, we led seven of them. Upon our return from Goose Bay I was declared fully CR and with that had to down another basinful of a disgusting brew!

The squadron training programme was full on, but there was still ample time in the calendar for socialising in the officers' mess and at dinner parties on the married quarter patch, none of which was any different really to the parties that we had had at Laarbruch. The squadron had an eclectic mix of ages, experience and aircraft backgrounds. There was a preponderance of ex-Jaguar pilots who had been at Brüggen in their previous guise and had returned immediately upon completion of the Tornado conversion courses. There were also some who had already completed a tour on the Tornado in the UK and were embarking on another in RAFG and there was a clutch of fresh-faced pilots who were on their first operational tour in the RAF. Amongst my fellow navigators, there was a considerable number with two-seat experience, but a large percentage who had come from the V-Force. This mix, in front and back seat, did mean that there was a significant supervision issue for the squadron executives as they strived to ensure that the squadron was ready for the inevitable TACEVAL as the wing built up to its full AE and UE. Too many of the V-Force navigators were 'dyed in the wool' and required a great deal of encouragement to change the manner in which they navigated to one that was all too familiar to those of us who had come from Buccaneers and Phantoms. Getting them to stop 'following the green writing' and get their eyes out of the cockpit was an uphill struggle but, with encouragement and cajoling, not to mention a bit of mild ridicule at the sortie debrief, standards amongst the navigators did improve. They had to, the squadron was due to deploy back to Goose Bay in October to conduct a further bout of OLF before deploying further west to Nellis AFB for Red Flag 87/1.

My career seemed definitely to be going in the right direction at last. Buoyed by my reports from my ground tour and with positive assessments in my flying, airmanship and leadership just six months into my tour on Tornado I was keen to continue in that vein and elevation to the role of Weapons Leader, albeit without the rank, had been a positive move in the right direction. I became a flight authorizing officer in the middle of the summer and, having completed a short six sortie phase of ACT in September, I was anointed by the station commander as one of only a few navigators qualified to be an Air Combat Leader.

With the winter and spring in Germany being unpredictable weather-wise, the summer months were reserved as 'exercise season'. Exercises such as Ample Gain, Blue Moon, Cheerful Challenge and Central Enterprise routinely filled the flying programme.

Central Enterprise, NATO's largest air exercise, was an annual 2 ATAF and 4 ATAF exercise operated over the most congested airspace and densely inhabited expanses of Western Europe. Contributing air forces routinely included those of the United States, the Federal Republic of Germany, the United Kingdom, Canada, the Netherlands and Belgium in a coordinated wartime scenario. Occasionally the French Air Force, which in the 1980s had non-integrated status in NATO's multinational military structure, would also participate. The exercises were routinely very well organised and the missions required a lot of planning, but they did not always provide extensive feedback to the units as to their success or failure. It was, in essence, a command and control exercise for NATO headquarters' staff. We, the participating forces, were mere pawns in the plan, necessary to achieve the outcome. To sum it up, the training routine was a little stilted, but the flying was good and the participation of AD forces also provided some realistic training.

Ample Gain sorties were tasked by the ATAFs and were designed to test the turn-round facilities of other NATO airfields. In simple terms this meant that a crew who were programmed to fly an 'Ample Gain' mission were to land at a specified airfield, hand their aircraft over to the local Visiting Aircraft Squadron (VAS) technicians and leave them to prepare it for a further sortie. The first knowledge that the VAS personnel would know of their impending task was when the visiting aircraft called up the airfield on the radio and announced that they were making an approach for an Ample Gain. Blue Moon and Cheerful Challenge were Air Defence exercises, the former designed to exercise those units based in and around the Jutland peninsula and southern Norway.

Labrador in the fall is somewhat different from Labrador in the spring! We flew by RAF VC10 direct to Goose Bay from Brüggen and, after a weekend settling in, Timo and I were airborne on 6 October leading a pair on a re-familiarisation sortie in the low flying areas, followed by loft bombing on the local range. The following day the pressure began to build and before long we were leading six-ships of Tornados conducting ULL with evasion thrown into the mix. The RAF had a long history of success on Red Flag and 17(F) Squadron was not about to let the side down.

There was time however to enjoy the odd glass of Molson's in the officers' mess bar where you could pass from room to bar to dining room and back again without ever having to go outside. The extremes of temperature were such that in winter the whole area would be snowed in and to venture outside was to guarantee a severe refrigeration of your soul from the searing wind and the below zero temperatures. In the summer, if you could avoid the blackfly, it was actually a very pleasant place to visit. In winter, with the sea frozen just the other side of Happy Valley and thick snow everywhere, the Canadians had very sensibly built tunnels between all the buildings to ensure that its troops never had to catch a cold, let alone frostbite. So our evenings were spent playing shuffle board, watching movies and drinking beer. If the weather eased it was possible to venture into Happy Valley to sample the delights of an alternative drinking establishment – one had to be careful though as not everyone in Happy Valley was happy and the local Inuit were sometimes not keen to share their bars with the men who made their caribou scatter!

Weather-wise, our first week at Goose Bay had been a very successful one. Temperatures had been relatively high for the time of year and we had even managed to play a round of golf on the scrubland course on base on the Sunday. However, as Jerry Gegg and I wandered back from the golf course to the bar for a beer I pointed out a permanent sign to him that adorned a lamp post beside the main road on the airbase. It said: 'Snow chains are required during the snow season. The snow season commences on 13 October!' It was Sunday, 12 October, when we woke the following morning there was a clear three foot of snow covering the landscape. So don't tell me that you cannot predict the weather, Met Man! They can in Canada! Snow or not, the efficient Canadians had the runway cleared in no time and after a check of the braking conditions Timo and I were once again at the front of a six-ship for ULL, evasion and loft bombing.

The snow did not abate, however, and it was often a struggle for the Canadians to keep the runways clear – so alternative entertainment had to be found. Not difficult when aircrew are bored, congregated and beer is available on tap! One of the best japes executed in the snowbound Goose Bay that October was the smothering of the Boss's 'Mini' in a snowbank suitably sculpted to ensure that the snowbank took the exact form of his vehicle. However, just to cause confusion to its owner, another snowbank, without a 'Mini', was carved alongside the original! Well we were bored!

With work-up complete our next task was to fly the Tornados from Goose Bay to Nellis AFB. This was achieved in three legs that first took us down the St Lawrence Seaway, past Montreal and across the US border into Griffiss AFB in New York State. Refuelled and lunched, Timo and I continued west in a three-ship across the southern Great Lakes, over Illinois and Iowa and on to Nebraska where we night-stopped at Offutt AFB. The following morning, we handed over our Tornado to another crew and climbed aboard a C-130 for the last leg into Nellis.

Red Flag was designed by the USAF post-Vietnam to exercise aircrew through their first ten combat missions. Analysis of air combat results from the Vietnam War proved that if aircrew survived their first ten missions then they would likely survive the war. Thus Red Flag provided not only an expanse of sparsely-populated desert to the north-east of the city of Las Vegas, where aircrew could operate down to 100 feet, it also provided a tactical area that was brimful of Surface-to-Air Missile simulators, Smokey SAMs[4] and captured Soviet missile systems. All these systems were active and capable of targeting low flying aircraft and whilst none were armed, the sight of a Smokey SAM leaving the rails and heading your way was enough to turn the adrenalin pump from moderate to extreme. Typical Warsaw Pact targets were also either mocked up in the desert or, if it was an airfield for example, scratched out of the desert to full scale. Some targets were cleared for live weaponry. Above the desert floor, an unlimited expanse of airspace allowed for full combat manoeuvring that was monitored by the US company's, Cubic, Red Flag Measurement and

---

4. The Smokey Sam Simulator includes single- and four-rail launching pads, an AN/VPQ-1 radar set and GTR-18A smoke generating rockets. When launched, the GTR-18's rocket motor produces a distinctive white plume, providing a realistic simulation of the launch of a surface-to-air missile.

Debriefing System. The 64th Aggressor Squadron, based at Nellis AFB, flew Northrop F-5E Tiger II aircraft that were painted in camouflage schemes identical to those observed on Russian-manufactured aircraft and were marked up with Soviet Red Stars and other typical Soviet Air Force motifs. The aircrew who flew these aggressor aircraft were schooled in Soviet doctrine and tactics and flew their aircraft just as if it was a Mig-21 Fishbed. To supplement the 'Red Air' Aggressors, air defence squadrons from the USAF, USN and USMC were drafted into Nellis for the period of a Red Flag to oppose the attacking 'Blue Air' of which we, in our Tornados, were a part. The flying was demanding and it required absolute concentration.

Each sortie would start with a fairly benign departure from Nellis and a climb out and cruise at about 15,000 feet through a designated corridor into the Nellis Range complex. Once clear of the corridor, the formation would descend to low level to be at 500 knots and 100 feet as we approached the 'gate', or start point of the exercise, which on Red Flag was known as Student Gap.[5] All missions were deconflicted by space and time at Student Gap so it was critical that you hit your allocated time slot. Routinely a five minute 'trombone'[6] would be built in to allow either a slow down or a catch up in case of a problem with the departure from Nellis.

From Student Gap it was eyes out, ears open and hard aggressive flying. At such speed and flying so low, pilots had to focus ahead and rely on their navigators to warn them of any hazards such as HT or telephone cables, for example; advise them of EW alarms on the RHWR; keep them updated on other aircraft positions in the formation; monitor the rear quadrant from two o'clock round to ten o'clock for opposing fighters; describe navigational features; give clear and precise directions with regard to the route to be flown; and scream for evasive action to be taken if intercepted or if locked up by one of those Soviet SAM systems that were spread strategically across the desert floor. It was hard work! It was made easier by the light years visibility in the prevailing weather conditions, which meant that navigation was ordained mainly by flying at ULL to the next mountain ridge where the pilot would

---

5. The start point for the combat stage of the mission.
6. A low level leg, shaped like the extending tube of a trombone, would be built into each mission. It was usually five minutes outbound and similarly inbound and marked with one minute marks. This allowed the lead navigator to adjust his timing early or late in order to depart the 'gate' exactly on time.

turn onto the next heading by 'ridge rolling'[7] to reduce as much as possible the time that the aircraft was skylined! Contact with the 'enemy' would result in a call of 'Buster'[8] and, probably, a call of 'Counter' or 'Break'[9] either to port or starboard, but always towards the threat in an effort to reduce his firing options.

Red Flag in a Tornado was very similar to that flown twice before by me in a Buccaneer. But now I was the Weapons Leader and an authoriser with all the responsibility that that entailed. As was the norm on Red Flag exercises, the squadron was broken into constituted formations of six crews that would fly every mission together for the duration. Each six-ship would have at least two six-ship lead crews amongst its construct and at least one other four-ship lead crew to cope with tasking that might involve two four-ships at the same time. Timo and I were delighted to be appointed as one of the two six-ship leaders and flew all of our nine Red Flag missions as either leader or Number 2. There was a down side to this nomination, however. Some of the other pilots and their navigators had taken it upon themselves to assume that we were being favoured undeservedly by the squadron hierarchy and took to calling us 'Supercrew' as a result. I had experienced similar feelings to them when I had been a young navigator on my first Buccaneer squadron and had seen people, who I felt might be no different to me, being pulled out for stardom! Over the years one realises that not everything in life is fair but, given that all those pilots I knew and who were treated in this fashion went on to become air marshals and knights of the realm, it is clear that true stars shine brightly from the very beginning – well, at least in the Royal Air Force.

The exercise finished on 6 November and, as was its way, the last sortie was a massive Balbo[10] of aircraft, attackers and defenders, all looking for a brawl between Student Gap and the targets to its west. The last day ended with the traditional votes of thanks from all the various visiting detachments

---

7. At the crest of the ridge the pilot rolled the aircraft almost inverted and pulled the stick back to allow the aircraft to dive towards the ground before rolling the wings level and continuing at ULL. To do otherwise (a pull up and push over) would mean that the aircraft would balloon above the ridge line making it vulnerable to both ground and air defences.

8. Internal radio call by any crew member in the formation to alert others to the fact that a fighter was on our tail. On hearing the call all pilots 'bustered' to max speed, usually 580 kts.

9. 'Counter': a max rate turn towards the threat. Break: a max permissible 'g' turn towards the threat.

10. Between 1 July – 12 August 1933 Italo Balbo, Minister of the Italian Air Force, led a flight of twenty-four flying boats on a round-trip from Rome to Chicago, Illinois. As a result, the term 'Balbo' entered common usage to describe any large formation of aircraft.

at the mass debrief and, as the Brits and the only foreigners taking part, it was expected that we would do something out of the ordinary to entertain the crowd. We did. I had with me the words of the 16 Squadron song[11] that Paul Dandeker and I had composed a few years earlier and, with a quick amendment to the title and the verses, I led the assembled throng in:

> *'We're Seventeen Squadron, we're on detachment*
> *And we're having lots of fun,*
> *Drinking beer and playing hard*
> *And bronzing in the sun*
> *But we've got a lot of work to do*
> *And I'm sure you'll all agree*
> *Tha-at this is the life for you and me!'*

It went down an absolute bomb! The Americans loved it and, with Timo leading the assembly with a pointer across the words, written on OHP slides, they all joined in when and where they could, but particularly with the chorus:

> *This is the life! Travelling!*
> *See the world!*
> *It's sixteen forty-five and still no rain!*
> *Travelling!*
> *See the world!*
> *This is the life!*

They kind of lost the plot when we repeated the chorus in French, after every other verse, but that was more because they could not stop laughing rather than that they did not understand the language!

> *'C'est la vie! En voyageant!*
> *Voir le monde!*
> *Il est seize heures quarante-cinq et pas de pluie!*
> *En voyageant!*
> *Voir le monde!*
> *C'est la vie!*

---

11. *Buccaneer Songbook (Reading Room Publishing 2008).*

Of course, we had changed the words of each of the verses to remove the 16 Squadron Decimomannu happenings and replace them with events that had been exposed during each of the mass debriefs on Red Flag.[12] The Americans, love 'em or not, are not at all worried about laughing at themselves and that rendition of that song at Red Flag confirmed that fact!

Having cleared our operational accommodation on the Friday and tidied up our work spaces we handed the jets over to another Tornado Squadron and headed home by VC10. It had been a great month in North America, but we were all glad to be home and our families were very pleased to see us.

I arrived home to receive the news that having reached the top of the frozen list I had been allocated a three-bedroomed house in Am Kastel. Despite the allocation of the top floor flat, I had asked to remain on the housing waiting list in an effort to secure a house instead. Am Kastel was further into the village of Elmpt, but not much further from the Brüggen main gate than the blocks of flats. Its advantage was that it had a reasonably sized back garden, large living space, was in a cul-de-sac opposite the Schloss with a large expanse of grass opposite where both British and German children could play together, unmolested by traffic. We packed up Number 12 and moved to Number 8 all in one day and were well established by the time Christmas 1986 hove into view.

If I was night flying, I always enjoyed taking Chris and Sarah to catch the school bus in the morning and, if able, I picked them up in the evening too. One day, Sarah stepped off the bus with a mouse in a cage! I was taken aback – I am not very keen on rodents of any kind. She explained that a boy in her class was going home to England and that his mother had told him that he could not take the mouse with him. Her story continued that the class teacher had suggested that a 'names in a hat' selection process should take place and that had duly been undertaken. Sarah's name had not been first (or second or third, for that matter) out of the hat, but, when the lucky dip winner had been announced, the owner had exclaimed that he did not want the winner to have it, but that Sarah was to have it instead. She needed no further bidding and here she was standing on the pavement complete with her 'prize'! We walked home silently and I was pleased to see that her mother was equally aghast when she too realised the situation and heard how it had all come about! Neither of us was prepared to tolerate a mouse in the house

---

12. See Appendix for the complete lyrics and for a further two songs that I had a hand in writing.

and so, after long explanations of what is fair and what is not fair, I marched Sarah and the mouse to a top floor flat where she very reluctantly handed the mouse in its cage over to its excited and jubilant new owner. I say jubilant, but I speak only of the child here. His mother was, like us, aghast at the prospect and tried to forcibly push the mouse back into Sarah's willing hands explaining all the while that her son already had a hamster. I was insistent! It was a lesson in life for both of them, I stated. Her lad had won it fair and square and I did not think it would serve any purpose, as a lesson in life, if Sarah were to deprive him of that honour!

We won the battle and, it transpired, the war too! About two weeks later I bumped into the lad's mother at the bus stop whilst I awaited my offspring's return from a gruelling day at Barnes Wallis First School.

'Oh by the way,' I asked her, 'how are you getting on with the mouse?'

'Oh the mouse!' she replied, 'We don't have it any more!'

'Oh!' I queried.

'No!' she responded, 'the mouse managed to escape the other night and wandered into the hamster's cage. The hamster took exception to its arrival, unfortunately, and bit its head off!'

Oh well, you can't win 'em all! I never knew that hamsters were that territorial! To appease Sarah we purchased a hamster, which she named Darter.

With its sophisticated Nav Attack system and its multitude of computers, radars and the like, the Tornado was a highly capable all weather aircraft. Unlike the Buccaneer and its predecessors who would shut up shop and head for the bar when the weather got a bit ugly, the Tornado Force was truly an all-weather strike/attack force. Operating in the nuclear strike role as singletons, in cloud, at low-level by day or night, with the navigator checking for obstacles and marking his targets and waypoints using his GMR and the pilot using the TFR with the autopilot engaged to follow the contours whilst completely IMC, was not a difficult task. It was not my favourite pastime in the air, but it was feasible and relatively safe because we practised it and we had worked with the system so often that we could justifiably put our faith in it as a singleton.

It was a bit of a different kettle of fish, however, when the time came to put conventional bombs on a target that required a large OTR of aircraft to achieve the required P_k. If you have been paying attention earlier you will realise just what I am talking about. Getting six aircraft through to a target in gin clear weather under enemy fire is one thing, however the prospect of getting six aircraft through to a target at low-level in cloud or fog, by day or by night, whilst being fired upon, is something completely different all together. But we trained in peace as we would fight in war and so a method of doing just that had to be identified, practised, practised and practised again to ensure that we could fly multi-aircraft formations under IMC conditions – and survive!

The advantage, of course, was the outstanding accuracy of the Tornado avionic system coupled with the excellent planning tool, the CPGS. The latter allowed you to plan two parallel tracks just two nautical miles apart and then download the route onto two separate cassettes for subsequent uploading to the aircraft detailed to fly either the right or left track. Subsequent aircraft in a formation were then detailed as 'left' or 'right' and took copies of their allocated route on cassette out to their aircraft for upload. In this way a formation of up to eight aircraft could penetrate through to the target in the most awful meteorological conditions. As long as everybody followed their allocated track and maintained forty seconds separation fore and aft there was no possibility of hitting another aircraft. It was only essential to maintain the timeline such that each aircraft arrived exactly on its allocated Time over Target. The Tornado navigation system did the rest and, with Auto-TF selected, the TFR ensured that nobody bumped into hills, pylons, masts etc. It didn't matter if you never ever saw a wingman or your leader as long as you stuck to the plan. It was an outstandingly clever way of ensuring that we could get through to our targets in all weather conditions and deliver the right number and type of weapons on the target successfully. Cross-over turns were, of course, a no no, but by flying squared cornered turns, or threepenny-bitting as it was known, aircraft could maintain their position in a formation and ensure that sufficient electronic EW coverage was available to protect our six o'clocks. Judicious planning by the navigators would ensure that any loss of position after a threepenny bit would be compensated by a similar turn in the opposite direction the next time around!

The Tornado's weapon inventory had not changed from that that I was accustomed to in the Buccaneer. We still practised conventional shallow dive, laydown and loft bombing as well as strafe, rather than rockets, with the two 27mm Mauser cannons in the nose of the aircraft. As well as our commitment to SACEUR's nuclear response option, we flew the same operational missions as we had in the Buccaneer, Option Alpha being our first task once the flying phase of any exercise was underway. However, in 1987, rather than 1000lb retard bombs, the Tornado's primary war load for an OCA target became Hunting Engineering's JP233. Thus, once the conventional phase of any exercise got underway, squadron aircraft were time generated with two JP233 weapons on the shoulder stations under the fuselage. JP233 had been developed collaboratively with the USA, but in 1982 the Americans withdrew from the programme for financial reasons. Initially, it was the MOD's intention that the weapon be fitted to both Jaguar and Harrier as well as to Tornado, but in the end, given the size of the weapon and the fact that the Jaguar and Harrier could only carry a foreshortened one each, the weapon was procured only for Tornado.

It was a massive weapon weighing something in the order of 3,000lbs. Each JP233 was divided into two sections and each section held submunitions that would deny access to a runway surface and achieve a Prevent Take-off Kill, or PTO_k in weapon effort planning terms. Within the rear section were thirty SG357 two-stage runway cratering submunitions, each of which weighed fifty-seven pounds. Upon release, each of the submunitions deployed a retardation parachute that guaranteed the correct striking angle was achieved for successful runway penetration. SG357 munitions were 'Reverse Follow-Through Bombs' and were shaped like a bottle of Corona beer. At the tip of the narrow end was a telescopic stand-off proximity-sensor that activated a shaped charge warhead that occupied the rear bulbous section of the 'beer bottle' and was designed to open the concrete surface of a WP runway. The longer, smaller-diameter forward section consisted of a cylindrical high explosive charge with a hollow cavity running through its centreline. On impact, the fuse initiated the shaped charge, which created a molten metal jet that travelled through the centre of the forward charge and then penetrated the concrete runway surface to create an underground chamber. Once fractured, the smaller charge was laid within the chamber where it would detonate, creating a crater and heave to the runway surface. If all thirty submunitions detonated successfully, thirty craters with heave would render the runway surface unusable and a PTO_k would have been achieved.

The HB876 munitions were the nasty element of JP233 and were designed to prevent airfield repair teams from repairing the craters. Designated as anti-personnel mines they were actually more than that. Housed in the forward canister of JP233, the two hundred and fifteen submunitions were dispensed at the same time as the SG357 and created a 'no go' area that covered nineteen acres! These mines too were fitted with a small parachute to ensure that they floated gently down to earth and covered the requisite area. The munition was designed with a Misznay-Schardin Plate[13] and the cylindrical case of the mine was made from dimpled steel. A coronet of spring steel surrounded the base of the munition and was held taut against the sides of the mine until such time as, after landing, a small explosive charge jettisoned the parachute and released the coronet, thus springing the weapon into an upright position with the Misznay-Schardin Plate pointing vertically upwards. If left undisturbed HB876 was designed to detonate at pre-set intervals. On detonation small steel anti-personnel fragments would spread, rather like a hand grenade, in all radial directions. However, if anybody or anything interfered with the weapon, it would tilt toward the interference and fire its preformed slug of molten steel into the shovel, bulldozer blade or person with devastating results.

JP233 was intended to overcome all the inaccuracies of stick-bombing against runways or airfield surfaces. Its biggest flaw, however, was that to achieve a PTO_k the delivery aircraft was obliged to fly straight and level along the entire length of the runway, offset slightly for any crosswind component, at 500 knots and 100 feet until all the submunitions had been dispensed. For a WP airfield this meant that you had usually to fly straight down the throat of the SAM-3 system placed exactly to deter you from doing just that! Not ideal, but it was the weapon of the new age and so our eight-ship operational OCA missions were designed exactly to do just that and suffer the consequences accordingly!

January 1987 brought me my first station MINEVAL at Brüggen and on Day One, Timo and I were up front leading the OCA eight-ship across 2 ATAF to our airfield target in Jutland. Over the next three days we were back and forth to Jutland to attack Eggebek, Husum, Schleswig and Leck in four-, six- and eight-ship formations. Exactly one month later we were at it again at Husum, but this time the mission was flown with the navigators dressed in AR5 – not a happy experience, but at least this time we were Number 4 in a

---

13. A characteristic of the detonation of a broad sheet of explosive which expands directly away from its surface. Unlike the blast from a rounded explosive charge, which expands in all directions, the blast produced by an explosive sheet expands primarily perpendicular to its plane, in both directions.

four-ship and so my role was less taxing even if it was an exhausting exercise trying to 'Check Six' cocooned in my black neoprene hood!

TACEVAL came and went successfully in March and in April the squadron found itself back in Decimomannu for yet another APC; this time with me solely responsible for its success or failure as Weapons Leader. It went astoundingly well. I had built a ten sortie flying syllabus that would allow crews to develop their weaponry skills and at the same time test them in their knowledge and understanding of the weapons system. Unfortunately, or maybe fortunately, Timo and I did not win the bombing competition, but we gave it a damned good try. Having ensured that all crews managed to get away for a weekend ranger, once it was all over Timo and I took advantage of leading a four-ship to Ghedi AFB in northern Italy for a long weekend before we headed directly back to Brüggen on the Monday morning. We spent the weekend in the Hotel Eden in Sirmione, with views across the stunningly beautiful Lake Garda. I'll say no more, just go and see for yourself!

Not long before we left Brüggen for Decimomannu, Jim Squelch and I were summoned to Grant McLeod's office. No indication of why we were required was given and, as we walked from the PBF to the 'soft' building where his office was, we surmised about what we might have done and how deep the shit might be that we had to be in! We were none the wiser after Grant had told us that the station commander wanted to see us both and that we 'best bring our hats'! He drove us down in his Mini with both Jim and I looking quizzically at each other as the imagined metaphorical pile of poo just increased in volume. Along with the Boss we were eventually summoned into the CO's office by his PA, saluted smartly and waited for a gale force wind to issue from John Houghton's mouth; he did not look particularly happy and we were still totally oblivious as to what we might have done!

Slowly his face broke into a smile as he passed forward two blue letters. I could not believe my eyes. I had been a flight lieutenant for thirteen years and was fast approaching my thirty-eighth birthday that brought with it an option to leave the Service or transfer to become Specialist Aircrew. I knew what a 'blue letter' meant. I had been disappointed for a number of years that I had not received one. I had been devastated when my reports on the Buccaneer OCU and 16 Squadron had hammered a nail into my career coffin, but that was all behind me now.

'Congratulations,' said John, 'you are both to be promoted to squadron leader on 1 July.'

I was speechless and after a round of handshakes and smiles all round, we jumped into Grant's car and raced back to the squadron to tell our happy news to the rest of the team. As we left his office, the CO called out that he'd be in the bar at 1700hrs – I needed no further bidding! At lunchtime I rushed home to Am Kastell to break the happy news to my wife and explain to her just why I might need a lift home later!

May and June 1987 saw the squadron undertake an intensive ACT phase to work up crews, new and old, before our planned deployment back to Decimomannu in October to use the Air Combat Manoeuvring Instrumentation,[14] ACMI, facility. It also prepared crews mentally for the Wing's live AIM-9G firings at Aberporth Range, off the Welsh coast, in July that year. As an ACL, I was fully engaged in air combat sorties throughout the two months, predominantly as a wingman working up pilots in 1 v 1 scenarios. The exercise season also continued throughout June with the squadron participating in Exercises Central Enterprise and Ample Gain, the latter from Automatic Terrain Following Radar sorties into France for lunch.

With my uniform re-ranked, Tim and I headed to RAF Valley, in Wales, on 2 July to preposition and be loaded with a live AIM-9G Sidewinder. Valley was the home of the Strike Command Air-to-Air Missile Establishment. The unit's role was to support aircraft involved in live firing exercises on Aberporth Range and to analyse and catalogue the results of every air-to-air shot taken against airborne targets. I had been to Aberporth before to fire a TV MARTEL from a Buccaneer, but on that occasion, unless there had been a misfire, it was an in and out mission from and to Honington where I was based at the time. This was different. This time, squadron crews rotated through Valley to have the live missile uploaded to their Tornado and to be briefed and quizzed on the 'On Range' procedures. Whilst the firing was planned to take place under a benign pre-planned profile, the missile still had a lethal kill capability and so everything had to be done by the book and perfectly. The missiles in question, G-models, were time expired too, which gave the sortie an added edge. With a time expired missile, whose components and batteries are beyond their 'sell by date', unexpected problems can, and often do, arise. Operationally, the Tornado GR1 was equipped with the more

---

14. A three-dimensional live tracking and recording system that provides rangeless, real-time training, monitoring and debriefing for aerial combat. It presents capabilities for an objective training and assessment via real-time monitoring, recording and replaying of missions for briefing and debriefing of combat aircrews.

capable AIM-9L, but for our purposes on this bright and sunny Thursday in July 1987, an AIM-9G would do very nicely, thank you.

Unlike the Buccaneer, Tornado GR1s had been built from the outset with the capability to defend themselves and the Sidewinder, albeit an early model, was sufficient to deter an aggressor even if it was routine practice for crews to try and avoid contact with fighters, just as we had in the Buccaneer. However, Tornado also had a much more sophisticated jamming system and its outboard wing pylons were each taken up with either a Skyshadow ECM pod or a BOZ Chaff and Flare dispenser pod. So with two JP233s, one Skyshadow, one BOZ, two under wing fuel tanks and two Sidewinder missiles the Tornado was a pretty potent ground attack aircraft.

For some reason that my aged brain refuses to recall, I did not fire my AIM-9G with 'Timo' Anderson in my front seat. After the STCAAME team had briefed us on our mission, I flew my first sortie to the range as 'chase' for, I assume now, Tim Anderson's firing. In my front seat was a young pilot who had not long arrived on the squadron from his first tour as a 'creamed off[15] QFI'. Steve Hillier[16] was an able pilot, but lacked experience on Tornado at the time, which may have been why I was put in his back seat for the Sidewinder firings. Whatever the reason, and it does not matter now, after a quick hop to Aberporth to monitor Tim's firing, Steve and I were back at Valley preparing for our own firing, with Tim as chase, before the bar opened that same night. It all went very smoothly. With our switches set for an air-to-air firing, our adrenal glands working overtime and the Jindivik target drone spotted in our right one o'clock, trailing its flare for the Sidewinder to lock on to, Steve started to track the target through the Head Up Display whilst we waited to hear the distinctive growl in our intercom headphones that would indicate that the missile had seen the target through its infrared seeker. With a 'Clear to Fire' from the range controller and a squeeze of the trigger from Steve, the missile left the rails with astonishing speed and accelerated to Mach 2+ as it headed for the flare towed behind the Jindivik. In a blink of an eye it had covered the separation distance, struck its target and allowed me to claim my one and only ever Fox 2[17] kill!

---

15. An RAF expression that identifies a pilot who, immediately after flying training, has been assessed as having above average instructor potential and who has been diverted to the Central Flying School's Qualified Flying Instructors' course and a first tour as an instructor.
16. Went on to become Chief of the Air Staff.
17. Indicates launch of an infrared rear-hemisphere air-to-air missile.

During the summer months I liaised with my new desk officer at PMA about possible postings in my new rank. Having not long taken delivery of a new Volvo 240 Estate, I was keen to remain in Germany and avoid having to pay import tax on it. I need not have worried. The posting plot played into my hands and it was agreed between PMA and Rocky Goodall, the new station commander, that I would take over from Steve Parkinson as STANEVAL(Weapons) in December 1987 for a further three years at Brüggen and three more years flying Tornado.

In late August, as part of my farewell to the squadron, I was tasked with a weekend ranger to RAF Akrotiri in Cyprus along with OC Ops Wg, George Clayton-Jones, and Mike Dineen who was then STANEVAL(Flying) working in Ops Wing HQ. I was crewed with Steve 'Ramco' Cockram for the weekend and the plan was for the two aircraft to deploy via Gioia del Colle, in southern Italy for an overnight stop to refuel the aircraft. More importantly, a night-stop would qualify us for subsistence allowance in Italy that would, if we were careful, provide us with sufficient funds to get us through an expensive weekend in Cyprus for which, routinely, we would have to rely on our own funds. We stayed in a local hotel just off base, dined in a quiet local restaurant and repaired to our beds quite early knowing that we had an early start and needed to conserve both our energy and our funds for whatever might lay ahead at the eastern end of the Mediterranean!

Arriving at our aircraft the following morning we were astounded to discover that we had a flat battery! Gioia was an Italian AFB that operated Tornados. The Italian groundcrew had been adamant that we should leave the 'After Flight' and 'Before Flight' checks of the aircraft to them, and that we had done. Despite our possession of certificates that said we had proved that we could do it, common sense said that they had to be more proficient in putting the aircraft to bed than we were. How wrong can you be! The team that looked after ZD742 for Ramco and me failed to disconnect the battery and every Tornado aircrew, and groundcrew man, should know that with the battery connected the flaps will creep, which in turn will flatten it! We were stranded. I cannot remember now whether the Italians did not have a spare battery or whether it would take all weekend to recharge it, but we were going nowhere! As we waved OC Ops and Mike Dineen off from dispersal I began to wonder just how we were going to cope with a weekend in Puglia without suitable funds having been allocated in advance by OC Accounts at Brüggen.

For a start we had nowhere to stay and for seconds there was little or no night life in downtown Gioia del Colle for two likely lads from 17 Squadron.

Aircrew from the local Tornado squadron came to our rescue. A quick telephone call to the Riva dei Tessali Golf Hotel, near Taranto, secured two rooms in a beachside retreat for our weekend and a taxi was laid on to take us there. Whilst we waited for the taxi I used one of the few Eurocheques that I had with me to secure initial funds and off we went!

We checked in and took our bags to our rooms. Whilst I was unpacking and changing out of my flying suit there was a knock at my door and a somewhat perplexed Ramco entered to ask me if I had seen the room tariff and the menu prices. I had to confess that I had not, but was shocked when he told me just how much this weekend was going to cost us. I started to scratch my brain and then came up with a sparkling idea that, hopefully, would work – it was our only option as the Lire that I had withdrawn from the bank would buy us not much more than a meal and a few beers let alone pay for three nights in this posh establishment with its private golf course and beach!

I rang reception and asked if they could put me through to the British Embassy in Rome. It was already 1630hrs, but I was hopeful that, at the very least, the security staff had not left for the weekend. A very polite English speaking lady answered the phone and quickly connected me through to the Air Attaché's office. The phone rang and rang and much as I wanted to hold on forever it soon became apparent that nobody was going to answer. Eventually, the lady came back on the line to inform me that the Air Attaché had already gone home for the weekend, but that the Naval Attaché was still in his office. She put me through to a very understanding RN commander who, having listened to my tale of woe, reassured me that he would sort it all out. In essence, his plan was that we should charge everything that we did or had in the hotel to our room numbers and he would pick up the tab. All he needed me to do was give him the receptionist's telephone number and he would square it away with the management. So that is what happened. His last words as I put down the phone were 'but don't kick the arse out of it, squadron leader'!

So that's what we did. We ate all our meals in the hotel and we didn't kick the arse out of it. I paid cash for all our drinks and hire of beach loungers and we relaxed in the sun-drenched Gulf of Taranto all weekend. It was a great weekend and just as much fun as any weekend in Cyprus. We welcomed the other crew back to Gioia on the Monday and with a revitalised battery headed back to Brüggen with sore heads, suntans and not quite so empty wallets after all – well, certainly not as empty as the crew who had headed further east!

By now both Christopher and Sarah were boarding in Stamford in Lincolnshire. Chris was at Stamford School and Sarah was at Stamford High School, the equivalent independent girls' school in the town. Chris had already been there a year and Sarah had not long started at the beginning of that autumn term. We had chosen Stamford because of the high proportion of RAF children who attended both of the schools and felt that, in that regard alone, it would be something of a home from home. One of the pilots on the squadron, Gordon Reekie, also had a daughter at the school and so we decided, with the squadron's blessing, to take a Tornado to Cottesmore for the weekend, entertain the three of them, and fly back on the Monday morning. All was approved and we set off for a low-level sortie across Belgium and the Channel and landed at Cottesmore just in time for Happy Hour on the Friday night. We entertained the two girls, and Chris, over the Exeat weekend and then did the whole thing in reverse on the Monday morning.

At 250 feet and 420 knots over Belgium we struck a fairly large bird which, from the smell penetrating the cockpit, had ventured down one of the engines! We quickly diagnosed that we would have to shut down the engine and, after going through the initial checks with Gordon, I set about looking for a suitable place to land in the single-engined configuration. Liege/Bierset was not too far distant and it was a base that I was familiar with from my time with the TACEVAL team when I was on 16 Squadron. We landed uneventfully and taxied into a dispersal behind the unit's Follow Me wagon. A quick call to the squadron reassured us that a team was being dispatched from Brüggen to carry out an engine change and that we should find ourselves some overnight accommodation and be prepared to bring the jet home the following day. Somehow we got ourselves inveigled into attending a squadron party on base! And somehow we managed to become involved with two invited guests; one was the Chief of the Vice Squad and the other the Chief of the Drugs Squad in the local city's constabulary. These two gentlemen were drinking quite heavily, but both volunteered to drive us into Liege to our hotel when the time came to leave our hosts.

For some reason that escapes me now, we allowed ourselves to be driven independently of each other! I was allocated the passenger seat in the drugs car and Gordon was allocated the same in the vice car. With blue lights flashing and sirens blaring, I suspect to head off any cop who thought their driving a bit erratic after the beer call, we shot off in an easterly direction towards our beds for the night. It was more like a race with each driver trying to outdo the other. As we reached the outskirts of the city the blues and twos were cancelled and at a more sedate pace we circled through the streets of Liege towards, we thought, our hotel. However, unbeknown to us in the drugs car, the Chief of Vice had decided to give Gordon a guided tour of the Red Light District. We squeezed down narrow street after narrow street past some quite attractive and scantily clad girls, visible through plate glass windows, until my driver let out a shriek and a word I recognised from my days of studying O-Level French at school.

'Merde!' he cried, and then in English, 'I don't believe it; he's not taking us down there, is he?'

'What's the problem?' I enquired.

'This next street is not for the faint hearted,' he told me, 'there is not one prostitute here that is under the age of sixty-five!'

He was right. As we meandered down the cobbled street a host of skimpily clad grannies beamed out at us from behind the large windows. I'd seen many a call girl in Amsterdam and Hamburg in my younger years, but I had never ever seen anything like this before! I can only guess that some people like that kind of thing! A quiet night in Liege followed and by lunchtime the following day we were back at Brüggen with our re-engined jet.

The following week I found myself outbound Lufthansa from Dusseldorf to Milan. The purpose of this jaunt was not, as you might think, to visit Milan Fashion Week, or to visit the opera in Verona. No, with my pending move to STANEVAL and acknowledgement of my previous experience, I had been seconded once again to the NATO TACEVAL Team to evaluate the 154th Squadron of the 6th Stormo[18] at Ghedi; the ItAF's first operational Tornado IDS squadron. Once again I found myself outbriefing to fly with foreign pilots in foreign formations, but at least this time I was flying in an aeroplane that I was familiar with.

The weather in Italy during the first week of October 1987 was perfect for low-level flying and I had the pleasure of flying once, on each of the four days of the exercise, as TACEVAL Chase, with four different Italian pilots. It was an eye-opener! As a navigator, I had been accustomed to flying

---

18. Wing.

with pilots who were comfortable flying with somebody in their boot. Unfortunately for the ItAF, until the advent of Tornado, they had never even heard the word being used in their FJ aircrew lexicon, let alone had they had the delight of meeting a navigator. These Tornado pilots at Ghedi, just like Roberto at TTTE, had all come off Starfighters where they had relied upon their own skills to successfully execute their missions through to the target. Moreover, they had never had the thrill of having somebody in their rear seat telling them what to do, when and how! Thus, when the Tornado arrived in the ItAF inventory, with it came a bunch of baby navigators fresh from training at Mather AFB in California. They had little or no FJ experience and, other than TTTE, the ItAF had little understanding, equipment, or an effective training programme to enhance their experience before they hit their squadrons. Thus the erstwhile Starfighter pilots ruled the roost and the novice navigators had a steep learning curve to overcome in an environment that treated them as second class citizens!

It became very obvious very quickly to me, stuck in the back seat for my first chase ride on 5 October, that the pilots of 154 Squadron treated the Tornado like a Starfighter with wings that swept and an avionic system that they did not fully understand. Whilst all the targets that the formation was tasked against were all overflown, had bombs actually been dropped, none of them would have been damaged because of the pilots' lack of understanding of what the Tornado's avionic system could do to assist them. Thankfully the station hierarchy were aware of the problem and asked me to lead the film debrief for every mission during the TACEVAL; they were keen to learn.

In virtually every sortie, from the film debriefs, it became apparent that the navigators were very capable radar operators and all, using the correct techniques, held a perfect radar lock on the target with the correct height sensor selected for a Phase One attack; over the hills of Italy that had to be BARO.[19] However, when their pilots saw the target ahead of them they all selected Phase Two in their cockpit and simulated the release of the weapons visually. What this did automatically was select Rad Alt[20] as the height sensor thereby giving the Tornado avionics no chance of resolving a weapon release solution over the undulating terrain. The instant result was something known as 'tromboning'! I pulled no punches at the debrief and, in the politest

19. Barometric Height Sensor.
20. Radio Altimeter.

possible way, let the pilots know that their actions in the cockpit and their lack of faith in their navigators' abilities was hampering their operational capability and lowering their scores in the evaluation.

I was also astounded at the flagrant disregard that crews had for the Italian population unfortunate to live underneath their flightpath. In the UK and in Germany, RAF crews took the utmost care to avoid flying over cities, towns and villages. We usually took sufficient care to ensure that if we fell upon habitation inadvertently we would either skirt around it at the last moment or pull up over it rather than blast across the top of it at low-level. Not the ItAF! They planned no avoidance of towns and only avoided airfields and vertical structures, I can only assume, because both could be hazardous to their health. On all four sorties that I flew out of Ghedi that week we rocketed around the length and breadth of Italy at 200 feet and 500 knots totally oblivious to the fact that we had just roared over the centre of a large town or village and had another beckoning on the next hillside. I can only imagine that it was a cultural issue, as to be an air force pilot in Italy is, I understand, something akin to being a Centurion in the dim distant days of the Roman Empire! Certainly, their status is assured for life after they retire because, as Roberto once informed me, if you were lucky enough to reach the rank of *tenente colonnello*[21] in the Italian military then the day before you retired you would be promoted to *generale di brigata*[22] and live the rest of your life on that full salary! So they got something right!

My last task before leaving 17 Squadron was to head back to Decimomannu to the ACMI facility for a dose of ACT and Dissimilar ACT. The detachment lasted only two weeks, but the flying was intensive, even if the sorties were quite short. Under Wing Tanks were dispensed with to allow us to utilise the Tornado's flight envelope to its full and we often flew three sorties each day to and from the ACMI Range to the west of the bombing range on Capo Frasca. Operating at medium altitude we practised 2 v 1 and 2 v 2 combat manoeuvring with each aircraft or pair taking it in turn to be the evading or the fighting formation. Just as it had been on Red Flag and with the same AIS Pod strapped to the aircraft and a growling, but inert, AIM-9L on the opposite side we fought each other until either range control called a kill, which required the 'dead' aircraft to bug out for a short period before it was

---

21. Lieutenant Colonel.
22. Brigadier General.

'regenerated', or somebody called 'Knock it Off' because they had either had enough or needed to re-orientate their personal gyros. Occasionally, if something went badly wrong or an aircraft had an inflight emergency then the call of 'STOP, STOP, STOP!' would result in everybody rolling wings level and maintaining their heading until the problem was resolved.

On the middle weekend I was lucky enough to head off to yet another Italian city, Naples, for a weekend ranger and to sample yet more pasta and pizza washed down by copious quantities of Dreher beer!

Back at Deci on 2 November and the training continued apace as more and more of the squadron pilots qualified in ACT. I was very happy and, as one of the few ACL navigators, was filling my boots in the rear cockpit. The last three days of the detachment raised the temperature further as the DACT phase commenced. Over those days, I crammed in six sorties to the ACMI and fought against USAF Aggressor aircraft and F-15 Eagles. The constant manoeuvring, the high ambient temperature and the need to swivel as best you could in the ejection seat to monitor the six o'clock whilst still monitoring all aspects of the weapon system, aircraft systems and ECM gear made these long and tiring days in the cockpit. Coupled with a long and purposeful mass debrief at the end of the day meant that the first Ichnusa rarely touched the sides when we got back to the Pig and Tapeworm.

It was through contact both professionally and socially with our F-15 buddies that a few of us managed to organise an early escape from Deci back to Brüggen. It wasn't actually an early escape as we left after we were supposed to, but it was earlier than most of the squadron who were delayed because of fog at Brize Norton in Oxfordshire. It had been the plan all along that we would return to Brüggen by VC10 and leave the Tornados at Deci for one of the other Brüggen squadrons to carry out their ACMI. The VC10 was due to arrive, with the replacement squadron, at about lunchtime on Friday and return with 17 Squadron personnel on board that afternoon. Upon our return from our last lunch at Enrico's snack bar, we received the bad news that the VC10 was fogged in at Brize Norton and that it was unlikely to arrive at Deci before Saturday! Despondently we kicked our heels for about an hour, until a few of us decided to wander over to the F-15 squadron to waste some time there before the bar opened.

Over a coffee we told the fighter pilots of our plight and following a few moans and groans from us and some sympathetic rumblings from the fighter jocks, one of them suggested a solution to our travel plans. Every Friday, a USAF C-130 passed through Decimomannu on its way to Zaragoza in Spain. Why, he suggested, didn't we jump a ride on that and then pick up the 'redeye' C-141 Starlifter which left Zaragoza for Frankfurt-Main AFB at 0400hrs on the Saturday morning.

It would never work! Even if the USAF authorised us as passengers, it was highly unlikely that the new 17 Squadron commander would take the risk of letting some of his aircrew wander off through Europe unsupervised and on some other nation's aircraft! But it did work. Everybody with a vested interest in our wellbeing ticked the Yes box. So I and half a dozen 17 Squadron aircrew found ourselves slumming it in the back of a USAF freighter C-130 heading north-west away from Germany to an American airbase one hundred and sixty miles north-east of Madrid! We had no overnight accommodation booked, but thankfully the Officers' Club Happy Hour was in full swing just as we landed! Of course we had no dollars, but we cut a strange dash in the bar with our British pattern flying suits and were soon being plied with beer as one USAF man after another wanted to find out why we were at Zaragoza and just how we had managed to cadge a lift with the USAF. Waking from our slumbers on settees in the lounge at 0200hrs a vehicle whisked us back to the flight line and, before too long, we were back in Germany and, still wearing our flying suits, on a train bound for Mönchengladbach where RAF MT had promised to pick us up and take us home.

I flew my last trip on 17 (F) Squadron on 30 November and packed up my office and headed four hundred yards east to Ops Wg HQ! My flying kit I left where it was as my new role required me to fly with all four squadrons and nowhere on Brüggen was as convenient as the flying clothing section in the squadron that I had just left.

Chapter Five

Setting Standards

My office in Ops Wing HQ was just capable of accommodating two desks; one for me and one for my partner in crime, Mike Dineen. Mike held the position of STANEVAL(Flying) and was already established in post when I arrived from 17 Squadron. The handover from Steve Parkinson was over and done with pretty quickly and was peppered with the words 'Mike will keep you right on that' and 'Any questions, ask Mike!' And so without much ado, and a few beers in the bar to say farewell to Parky, there I was responsible for the standardisation of all the weapons and weapon delivery aspects of the Brüggen Tornado GR1 Wing!

Through the window of our office we both had a good view of the airfield! For me the view was of passing interest as aircraft taxied twenty yards away either to or from the runway. However, for Mike, as the senior QFI on the unit with responsibility for the flying standards of the Wing's aircrew, the view was imperative and he used it often to his advantage when he felt it appropriate to investigate and/or chastise those who either taxied too fast or did not abide by the orders and procedures laid down for the airfield's safe operations. I too had to become accustomed to shouldering the responsibility of my new position and rank. I had, in my previous operational flying tours, been a very strong member of the 'Junior Junta'[1] in the past, but with elevation to the rank of squadron leader and the authority invested in me as STANEVAL, I had become part of the 'management' with direct access to the station commander.

My task was not too different from that of being Weapons Leader on a squadron, a role I had fulfilled on both 16 and 17 Squadrons previously. However, I now had to ensure that I integrated with each of the squadrons equally, showed no bias towards any one and adopted a diplomatic approach to each when and if problems occurred in their management of their weapons training programmes and plans. I was tasked with maintaining the proficiency of the squadrons' weapons instructors, the evaluation and monitoring of

---

1. A cabal of junior officers on a squadron.

Wing aircrew weapon delivery techniques and taking the lead of the Wing Tactics Cell to ensure that each of the four squadrons was singing from the same hymn sheet tactically.

Within my remit was also the task of being the Wing Special[2] Weapons Supervisor with responsibility for training all Strike qualified crews in the handling, operating and delivery procedures for nuclear weapons. Whilst each squadron had its own designated training team, it was my responsibility to ensure that the aircrew of each of the four squadrons were trained, prepared and practised in nuclear safety and security procedures; were capable of fault diagnosis and rectification; understood the theory of nuclear weapon effects and their effect on crew safety; comprehended nuclear theory; had a full understanding of the aircraft weapon release system; and were able to complete, under scrutiny, the external and internal weapon system checks and procedures. All of this had to be mastered by me and all Strike declared aircrew before each and every one of our annual visits by the Royal Air Force Armament Support Unit (RAFASUPU), based at RAF Wittering. With eighteen crews on each of the squadrons this amounted to a training programme that included practical demonstration by some one hundred aircrew each year. Not a small task and, along with the necessary upkeep of training records, it was one that focused my mind constantly throughout my tour. Failure in any aspect by any individual could have a devastating effect on a squadron and the Wing's operational declaration to SACEUR. The RAFASUPU visit, along with TACEVAL, were the two major events on the Station's calendar and were always at the forefront of the station commander's mind! It was up to me to ensure that we did not fail when the RAFASUPU Team came to stay!

There was also a considerable amount of staff work to attend to as STANEVAL. Statistical analysis of weapons results across the Wing had to be maintained and I had to engage with the squadrons with regard to any proposed tactics changes or weapon delivery adjustments as the result of any of the many software upgrades to the Tornado's complex computer-driven weapon system. By coordinating and agreeing our Wing tactics, had we ever gone to war, all seventy-two crews on the Wing would have been operating from the same set of tactical SOPs. To achieve success in the latter I had to liaise with, and be the Wing POC for, the Tornado Operational Evaluation Unit and the RAF's Central Tactics and Trials Organisation. It was all quite

---

2. Nuclear Weapons.

time consuming and with my innate habit of making sure every 'i' was dotted and 't' was crossed, this staff work routinely took up much of my time in the days spent in the office.

However, there was also time for flying and it was not long before I found myself airborne with some of the young pilots who had recently arrived on the Wing. Unfortunately and initially, however, the early months of 1988 were typically 'dunkel' when it came to the weather in North-West Germany. Consequently, throughout the first three months of the year I only achieved just under half the number of hours required by the NATO Standard. Although my hours had been cut, the variety of flying was good, if restricted in the main to just two of the squadrons, 17 and 14, on the base. As well as the foul winter weather there were a number of desk-bound tasks that kept me in the office rather than in the air over those first few months in post. It is part of my character that once I start on a task I sit it out until it is complete and, I know, that that too would have kept me away from the flight line despite my natural instinct to go flying! There was also the circumstance that it seemed natural to head back to 17 Squadron to fly rather than spread my wings beyond that comfort zone. It would be fair to say that both 14 and 17 Squadrons, occupying the south-east and north-east dispersals at Brüggen respectively, were more forthcoming with offers of flying than were 9 and 31 Squadrons at the further end of the airfield. I needed to change that before I fell into the trap of being seen to favour my old comrades over other units.

Towards the end of March I received a call from the NATO TACEVAL Team requesting my participation once again for the Tactical Evaluation of an Italian Air Base operating the Tornado GR1. Unlike my previous experience with the team at Ghedi, where I had flown Italian jets with Italian pilots, this time I was invited to bring my own aircraft and my own pilot to Gioia del Colle – the base where Steve Cockram and I had been abandoned with a severe dose of flap creep on our way to Akrotiri for a weekend. This time there would be no chance of a quiet sojourn at the Tessali Golf Hotel near Taranto. It would be full on flying and, with in-briefs and debriefs, would last for six days that would encompass a weekend too.

Mike Dineen and I flew south in ZD707 on 6 April and were accommodated with the rest of the team in a small hotel in Gioia del Colle town that had been commandeered as the TACEVAL Team's HQ for the week. On Thursday the seventh and Friday the eighth we flew two sorties each day chasing the Italian crews tasked with airfield attacks on the three Italian air bases of Grosseto on the Tuscan coast, Sigonella in Sicily and Cervia north of Rimini by the Adriatic. The fourth and final sortie was against military forces conducting landings in Sicily. The flying was exciting and, with Mike up front, I was able to relax and concentrate on the job in hand – assessing the Italian four-ships and their effectiveness. Whilst I wasn't directly engaged in Italian cockpits as I had been the last time, it was clear that the crews of Gioia's 36th Stormo had got the message about not overflying towns at 200 feet and 500 knots! Their's was a far more considerate and conciliatory approach to their population and, whilst not every pilot had realised the potential of the Tornado's error-saving computer-driven weapons system and the value of having a good navigator in the boot, film debriefs were much improved from those I had experienced at Ghedi some six short months prior.

With the exercise debrief over and the air base chain of command informed of the unit's scores and its success in passing the TACEVAL, Mike and I spent a very relaxing weekend with the regular TACEVAL Team members, which included a visit to the unique and ancient cave-city of Matera.

Back at Brüggen, I spread my wings solely with 31 Squadron in May, but still found it very difficult to achieve anything like the required number of hours to meet the NATO Standard. I know that some of this was of my own making and that I tended to concentrate on staff tasks to the detriment of my flying. However, I was also aware that the squadrons had their own problems with aircraft serviceability and had a need to meet their own individual flying requirements and to train new crews to LCR, to get them into QRA, and CR status. Nevertheless, in nine months, by the end of September 1988, I had only managed to fly with a 9 Squadron pilot four times! That was not a good record, but there was a definite reluctance on their part to pick up the phone and offer me any flying at all! Indeed, from memory, I recall that they had only done so on those four occasions when they were stuck for a navigator and had resorted to asking me to dig them out of a hole. Things did not really pick up with 9 Squadron throughout my tour and routinely amongst the 14, 17 and 31 Squadron entries in my logbook in any one month there is only ever one sortie flown with a 9 Squadron pilot. I have no real explanation for why this might have been. Yes it was the furthest squadron from my office and I know that, as the 'new boys on the block' at Brüggen in October 1986[3] they did not immediately integrate with the three squadrons

---

3. Although IX Squadron was the first RAF squadron to equip with Tornado GR1, its early years (1982–86) were spent at RAF Honington.

already established there. Despite my calls seeking flying opportunities I found them, to all intents and purposes, to be a 'closed shop'. Even in the bar at Happy Hour they kept themselves very much to themselves. On 17 Squadron I had put that down to the fact that they had lived an autonomous existence at Honington and, therefore, found it difficult to conform to a Big Wing concept. Their insularity had the potential of creating difficulties when it came to the development of new tactics and pan-Wing tactical mission planning. However, as STANEVAL, I needed to have access to the squadron and so it became a hearts and minds exercise for me from the outset of my tour. Unlike the other three outfits at Brüggen, however, I never really felt welcome on 9 Squadron.

With the arrival of August came the opportunity to participate on another TACEVAL visit. This time the Luftwaffe base at Oldenburg was the target of the NATO team and so I headed north by car to join the team at their hotel outside the base. Oldenburg at the time operated the Franco/German Alpha Jet. Built by a Dassault and Dornier consortium, the Alpha Jet was a light attack jet and advanced jet trainer, primarily used by the Luftwaffe in the Close Air Support role. It was a fun jet to fly and over two days I flew three sorties in this mini-fighter bomber! The first sortie was flown with a USAF exchange pilot on a routine 'round the houses' chase mission as Number 4 in a four-ship. However the second sortie, flown with Hauptmann Fiedler, involved weaponry at Vliehors Range on the Dutch coast. Vlieland Island is one of the West Frisian Islands and covers just over one hundred and twenty square miles. Topographically it is long and thin, being just less than twenty kilometres in length and only three and a half kilometres at its widest point. The fatter western end is predominantly sand dunes and forms the restricted military area that makes up the gunnery and bombing range. On the north-westerly attack heading, flying in a Buccaneer or a Tornado, it is inevitable that the majority of the range pattern will be flown over the sea. It was therefore a new experience for me in the Alpha Jet to discover that, no matter what weapons we were delivering that day, the turning circle was such that we never actually went 'feet wet!'[4] And what a capable aircraft it was as a weapon delivery platform. In that short fifty-five minute sortie with a twenty minute slot on Cornfield,[5] Hauptmann Fiedler and I conducted CBU, Glide, Skip and Dive bombing profiles and released practice weapons on each pass and then followed that

---

4. Fly over the sea.
5. Vliehors Range radio callsign.

with Rockets and then Strafe attacks. It was all part of the pilot's TACEVAL qualification and it was a great privilege to be in the back seat and witness him doing so! The last sortie was a Hi-Lo-Hi airfield attack against the USAF base at Hahn where I, in the back of 40+33 flown by Major Schultheiss, was sat as Number 3 in a seven-ship of Alpha Jets to observe what was happening and comment later about the effectiveness of the sortie.

If the Alpha Jet was nippy it was no comparison to my next participation with the TACEVAL Team at the Dutch Air Base of Volkel, which was a mere hedge hop across the River Maas from Brüggen. Volkel operated F-16 Fighting Falcons and, following very much the same routine as previously, I was invited to join the team in November of '88 to do what now was becoming second nature for me. Of course, my role with the various TACEVAL Teams was not just one of flying in the back seat and commenting on what happened in the air. I was a full member of the team throughout the TACEVAL and had to observe and report back on every aspect of the Wing's operational performance. The days were long and the evenings longer. Days, which usually started at about 0600, turned into nights with the debriefs finished by around about 2100 hours. A quiet couple of beers before bed and then the routine would start all over again the following morning.

I was only invited to fly in the F-16 once during my time at Volkel and it happened on 29 November with Kapitein Bert Haasakkers. The sortie was a relatively simple OCA mission against an airfield in Germany and J-649, the squadron's two-sticker, was allocated as the chase aircraft in the Number 4 slot in a four-ship. The mission went smoothly with little out of the ordinary to report until we started our recovery back to Volkel. NATO SOPs are designed to ensure the survivability of friendly aircraft under hostile conditions and no more so than during recovery to a friendly airbase protected by trigger happy SAM and AAA located on and around the airfield. A unit TACEVAL was, to all intents and purposes, war without any bullets flying! Although that was not the case in May 1982 when, on an exercise mission out of Wildenrath, an RAF Phantom inadvertently fired a live Sidewinder missile against an unsuspecting RAF Jaguar – and shot it down![6] Other than that accident exercise flying was fairly benign generally.

---

6. The Board of Inquiry determined that the master armament switch in the Phantom had not been taped in the 'safe' position and the pilot inadvertently rendered one of the two main safely switches 'live'. The Phantom's pilot and navigator were court martialled and found guilty of offences of neglect, for which they received severe reprimands.

So our four-ship recovery to Volkel on that Tuesday in late November followed exactly the procedure that the F-16 squadron would have adopted had we actually been at war. The four aircraft split from their tactical formation and began individual straight-in approaches to Runway 24. The whole recovery was conducted under silent procedures and each aircraft slowed down to approach speed and avoided any violent manoeuvres that might unnerve the men manning the airfield defences. The first two aircraft had made it safely onto the ground when suddenly, over the previously silent radio, came a frantic call of 'Airfield Attack Red, Airfield Attack Red, Airfield Attack Red! All Volkel aircraft on recovery divert immediately to Eindhoven!' Again! Perfect practice and clearly a TACEVAL inject to see just how aircraft in the recovery would respond. So after one and a half hours strapped to the rear bang seat of J-649 we and the Number 3 aircraft turned silently away from Volkel and headed for a normal fully controlled radar approach to Eindhoven. Safely on the ground Haasakkers taxied J-649 towards our awaiting marshallers. Now out of the exercise scene whilst the two aircraft were turned round we relaxed and chatted over a coffee in the local squadron crewroom whilst we contemplated and put together a plan for getting back to Volkel when the dust had settled. We couldn't relax for too long as the aircraft would be required back at base for re-tasking. However, we needed to be refuelled with a limited, but safe, quantity that would require us to burn some of it off to get below maximum landing weight.

'Dave, have you ever done a vertical climb after take-off?' my pilot asked me.

Despite having often seen Lightning pilots showing off with its zoom climb capability and remembering my desire to fly in one as a young air force aspirant, I had never ever had the thrill of doing so myself.

As Haasakkers lifted the aircraft clear of the runway he allowed the aircraft to settle and level as he raised the undercarriage. What happened next was quite out of this world. After only the merest of seconds that allowed me no moment for thought he pulled smoothly back on the stick and, with the full afterburner already pushing us forward, we thrust vertically upwards. The bang seat in the F-16 is reclined at an angle of thirty degrees to the vertical which improves the g-tolerance for the pilot by reducing the vertical distance between the heart and the brain. The effect on somebody who had never experienced this before was quite surreal as I lay back looking forward. As we raced towards the sun I could hardly compose myself! At 20,000 feet we levelled off our climb with a roll off the top and settled as we waited for our wingman to join us.

'Split for combat go!' and with that command to our Number 2 we raced away from him for about sixty seconds before turning back to search the skies for him to start a dogfight. I had done STRIPRO in a Buccaneer where we routinely tried to evade the fighters by bustering out at low-level to get away from them. I had done the same in the Tornado and had also done plenty of 1 v 1s in my capacity as an ACL. But I had never had the excitement of conducting 1 v 1 in such a manoeuvrable fighter and in one capable of pulling a sustained 9G! It was outstanding fun and one of my happiest memories of my time with the TACEVAL Team. All too soon we were down to fuel minima and on recovery back to a benign Volkel where all was quiet after the drama of the airfield attack!

Back at Brüggen, the Wing was busy preparing itself for its annual visit from the Tornado Standardisation Unit. Colloquially known as 'The Trappers', the TWCU sent a team of QFIs, QWIs and Instrument Rating Examiners to each of the RAF stations that operated Tornado GR1s every year. The TSU's task was to test and examine all aspects of each squadron's training standards and records, both in the air and on the ground. Although the squadrons were responsible for their own training records, neither STAN(F) nor STAN(W) were immune from scrutiny. By the time of their visit, Ivor Walker had replaced Mike Dineen as my office buddy and had spent much of the time whilst I was swanning around Volkel making sure that all the squadron's training records were up to date. We were in a good place. On 6 December 1988 Ivor and I flew together as 'Bounce' against a 14 Squadron three-ship of Tornados each of which had a TSU man on-board. The very next day, I was airborne again, but this time with Simon Dobb, my friendly trapper, in my front seat. Simon had been a young first tourist pilot on Buccaneers when last I had flown with him, so we knew each other well. The sortie, which was flown as Number 2 in a three-ship conducting low-level evasion around the North German Plain, went fine, as did the whole of the Trappers visit to Brüggen that year.

The New Year brought with it the customary north European fog and so flying in January and February 1989 took place either in the middle atmosphere doing ACT or over the UK. Indeed, in January, I was lucky enough to spend a night at Lossiemouth with 31 Squadron who had deployed there to undertake some heavy bombing work with inert 1000lb bombs on

Tain Range. Over two days, I managed to fit in five sorties, three of which were with the squadron boss, Pete Dunlop. I also was given the opportunity to put my money where my STANEVAL(Weapons) mouth was by lofting four 1000lb ballistic bombs at the Tain target; two of them in a stick. It was great fun and a good spell of concentrated flying. And, of course, a night stop at Lossiemouth with its late-night Bothy Bar was never an opportunity to be missed!

At Happy Hour one Friday night at Brüggen I found myself engaged with Rob Wright who had taken command of 9 Squadron sometime after I had moved from 17 Squadron to Wing HQ. After a couple of glasses of Heineken in Rob's company he asked me why it was that I rarely ventured to the south-western corner of the airfield. I did my best to explain to him that it was historic but, in the end, it came out that prior to his arrival his squadron had seemed to present a cold front to the rest of the Wing and that I did not feel particularly welcome. Accordingly I did not, routinely, seek opportunities to fly with them. He was quite taken aback and vowed to resolve the matter with his executive officers forthwith.

Not too long after, he rang me in my office one day and, out of the blue, asked me if I would be prepared to run a detachment for him at Namao Air Base in Canada. He explained that one of his flight commanders, who was already tasked with the job, was operating 'below par' and, whilst the others were engaged preparing for Maple Flag, he needed a reliable man to take over the Namao detachment. He finished by stating that he knew that he could trust me to do a good job of work for him. I had known Rob Wright since my days as an instructor on the Buccaneer OCU when he had converted from Phantoms and then became a flight commander on 208 Squadron at Honington. We liked each other and respected each other's professionalism. I was delighted at the prospect of taking a detachment to Canada and, more so, because it was the first real approach from 9 Squadron towards me as STANEVAL.

Exercise Griffon Bat took place at Namao, near Edmonton in Alberta, over eight days in April 1989. Its purpose was to utilise Tornados that were 'homeless' between 'Flag' exercises and to give experience to the younger element of both 14 and 9 Squadrons' aircrew who were not qualified or experienced enough to fly on Red Flag or Maple Flag. I flew six sorties on the exercise, five of them in the Maple Flag training areas and one an exhilarating sightseeing mission through the Canadian Rockies. The sortie was finished off with a 'flyby' over the home of my good friends, Mike and Siobhan Gault. Mike was an ex-RAF doctor, who had been a great friend on my last tour at Laarbruch, but who had emigrated to Alberta in 1985. Our arrival overhead, I discovered when I spent the weekend with them in Drayton Valley later, caused much amusement to them and dismay amongst their neighbours, many of whom had been invited for a barbecue to meet the 'visiting' airman! On the last sortie out of Namao we flew the aircraft north to Cold Lake Air Base and the 'youngsters' and I headed back to Germany courtesy of an RAF VC10. I was most grateful to Rob Wright for giving me both the honour and the experience of leading a detachment of aircrew on such an endeavour. It was a steep learning curve for me and, whilst I had support from other executive officers within both squadrons, the ultimate responsibility for the success of the exercise was mine.

Back home life was as routine as ever it can be on an operational RAF station. MINEVAL exercises once again featured regularly in the calendar, but now I found myself not at the forefront of Option Alphas, but fulfilling the task of Night Force Commander in the bunker; effectively being the station commander on the night shift. It sounds grand and exalted, but nothing could have been further from the reality. My shift started at 1700hrs and ended at 0700hrs the following morning. My role involved the monitoring of aircraft generation tasks from the 'Bridge' and responding to signals received and inputs from the Directing Staff. I also had responsibility as the prime decision maker for the whole unit, although there were few serious decisions required in the dead of the night. When the time came, I had to ensure that the unit responded appropriately to all exercise injects that related to the generation of Strike loaded aircraft, most of which started in the quiet hours. It was a humdrum experience. It had its moments and I had to be alert, but around 0200hrs I often found myself dozing off in my chair only to be awakened with a start by the teleprinter machine chattering away behind me or the clarion ring of a telephone within the Ops Room. I had to be alert because at 0700hrs Rocky Goodall, the station commander, would arrive in the anticipation of a concise, but clear handover of just what had been happening overnight.

The social life at Brüggen was no different to that experienced at Laarbruch, in my two previous tours. The focus for all officers was, routinely, the officers' mess and there were always regular suppers or dinner invitations dropping on our mat. Unlike my experience of life in Germany on my first tour as a

High-spirited Buccaneer QWIs: Graham Seaward; Rip Kirby; Author; Mal Prissick; and Ivor Evans. Red Flag 79-1, 20 October 1978. (*Crown/HQ STC*)

The detested Aircrew Respirator (AR5). (*Author's Collection*)

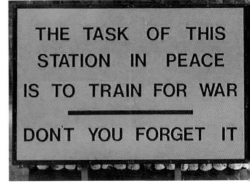

The welcome to RAF Brüggen that left you in no doubt as to why you were there! (*Author's Collection*)

The author with his Italian pilot, Roberto Reggianini. TTTE Cottesmore, 29 May 1985. (*Crown / TTTE Cottesmore*)

The Tornado Office. (*Crown / Rick Brewell*)

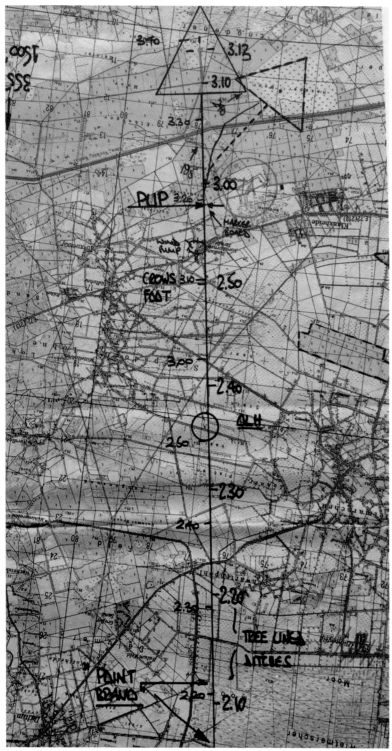

Nordhorn Range target map showing: Strike Target; Dive Circle; avoid areas; pylons; recognisable navigation features; timing marks (mins:secs) from Initial Point; and distance (nms) to go. (*Author's Collection*)

17 Sqn Tornado GR1, 'CZ', ZD742 at low-level over Germany. (*Crown / Rick Brewell*)

The author strapping in to 2-stick Tornado GR1, ZD743, (note the lack of a TV Tab on the port side) for a Laydown, Shallow Dive and Strafe sortie on Frasca Range. Decimomannu, Sardinia, 18 March 1986. (*Iain McNicoll*)

No 17 (F) SQUADRON
ROYAL AIR FORCE
BRUGGEN

OPERATIONAL STATUS (ATTACK) CERTIFICATE

Certified that _____Flt Lt D R Herriot_____ has qualified for
the award of COMBAT READY status in the Attack role
in accordance with Section IV of HQ RAF Germany Annual
Training Syllabus for Tornado Strike / Attack Squadrons.

Date _____11 June 1986_____

_____Wg Cdr
Officer Commanding No 17 (F) Sqn

17 Sqn Combat Ready (Attack) Certificate. Presented to the author on 11 June 1986. (*Author's Collection*)

OC 17 Sqn, Grant McLeod, finds his `Boss's Mini' after the `Junior Junta' prank in the snow. Goose
Bay, Labrador, 15 October 1986. (*Iain McNicoll*)

'Alternative entertainment had to be found' – Impromptu dining-in night – From the left: Jerry Gegg; Author; Gordon McClymont; and Geoff Coop. Goose Bay, Labrador, 17 October 1986. (*Iain McNicoll*)

The bearer is entitled to play one joker per detachment. On being played to the Duty Exec, this card must be forfeited thus obtaining a guarantee of no retribution.

By the Authority of

OC 17 Sqn

17 Sqn Joker Card (Obverse). (*Author's Collection*)

17 Sqn Joker Card (Reverse). Jokers were issued to all squadron aircrew, but could be played only once per detachment if the owner was suffering from the excesses of the night before and felt unfit to fly! (*Author's Collection*)

Fully Swept!' At low-level in 67° wing sweep. (*Crown / Rick Brewell*)

Red Flag Headquarters Building, Nellis AFB, Nevada, 30 October 1986. (*Iain McNicoll*)

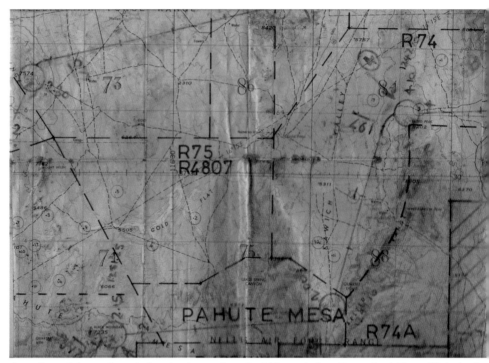

A section of the navigator's low-level map for a Red Flag mission. Dreamland (Area 51) is in the bottom right-hand corner. (*Author's Collection*)

Tornado GR1 at 'high-level' heading for Student Gap. 'From Student Gap it was eyes out, ears open and hard aggressive flying.' (*Iain McNicoll*)

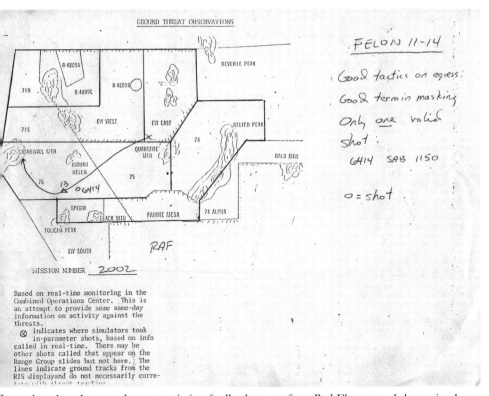

A rough and ready, same day, post-mission feedback report from Red Flag ground threat simulators for Felon section (4-ship RAF Tornado GR1). Good sortie – only one shot taken, unsuccessfully. (*Author's Collection*)

17 Sqn aircrew taking a break from the rigours of Red Flag. Jimbo James, Stringy West, Timo Anderson, Osby Osborn, Author, Brian Trace, and Nigel Huckins. Did I really like that 'porn star' look? Universal Studios, Los Angeles, 1 November 1986. (*Author*)

17 Sqn aircrew choir practice. Paddy Roberts, John O'Shea (partially hidden), Jerry Gegg, Jim Squelch, Author. Red Flag, 5 November 1986. (*Iain McNicoll*)

A powerful force of men and machines. The Brüggen Tornado Wing in 1987. Some six months after this photograph was taken I moved from 4th rank to 2nd rank. You can just see me in front of the tip of the starboard wing tip. (*Crown/RAF Brüggen*)

The four squadrons of the Brüggen Wing. 31 Sqn; 17 Sqn; 14 Sqn; and 9 Sqn (top to bottom). (*Crown/Rick Brewell*)

Exercise Griffon Bat, Tornado GR1 over the Rocky Mountains. Namao Air Base, Alberta, 20 April 1989. (*Author*)

'Al-armed to the teeth!' Two 31 Sqn Tornados fully loaded with Air Launched Anti-Radar Missiles (ALARM). (*Crown/Rick Brewell*)

Two 9 Sqn Tornados loaded with 8 x 1000lb bombs. Aircrew were often tasked to fly in this fit to simulate the weight and flight handling characteristics of JP233. (*Crown/Rick Brewell*)

Tornado GR1 dispensing a full load of JP233 during weapon trials. JP233 was one of the 'new weapons' to feature in the Conventional Weapons Employment Manual. (*Hunting Engineering Ltd*)

JP233 Reverse Follow Through Bomb (SG357 submunition) about to impact its trials target. (*Hunting Engineering Ltd*)

The nasty side of JP233. HB876 area denial submunition. (*Hunting Engineering Ltd*)

Wedding Blessing. Wg Cdr & Mrs D.R. Herriot, Christopher, Helen, Hannah and Sarah. RAF Cranwell, 12 February 1994. (*Author's Collection*)

Back with my first love. 'Farewell to the Buccaneer'. RAF Lossiemouth, 25–27 March 1994. (*Jo Herriot*)

Tornado with Storm Shadow (aka Conventionally Armed Stand-Off Missile/SR(A)1236). (*MBDA*)

Typhoon with Brimstone (aka Advanced Anti-Armour Weapon/SR(A)1238), plus ASRAAM, Meteor and Paveway 4. (*MBDA*)

flying officer, as a squadron leader I had moved up the social scale. As a junior officer I had only ever been invited for drinks at the station commander's. Now, on the first rung of the senior officer ladder, I was welcome across the Brüggen CO's doorstep for supper! Routinely, we would hold supper or dinner parties at our house which, by now, was on base. Having moved up a rank, I was entitled to a Type 4 OMQ rather than the 3-bedroom Type 5s that we had occupied in Dürerstrasse and Am Kastell; 70 Salmond Road fitted that bill and our requirements perfectly. It was a large 4-bedroom semi-detached property with a grassed garden to the rear, a paved patio to entertain on, a walk-in attic on the third floor which provided ample storage and a vast cellar perfect for stowing full beer crates and at an ideal temperature for hoarding copious quantities of Mosel and Rhein wine.

Directly behind our quarter lived the Woodroffe family. Rick and Liz Woodroffe had three boys, the youngest of whom was a similar age to Christopher. The common grass area between the two properties was an excellent location for the four boys' games, and Sarah, when she was brave enough to join in, and they played there together to their hearts' content. Rick, an Englishman, was OC PMS[7] and prior to his time at Brüggen had spent most, if not all, of his RAF career serving in Scotland. He was, in his mind, as much a Scotsman as I was! During the Five Nations[8] rugby competition, Rick would fly the Scottish Saltire from a makeshift flagpole sticking out from an upstairs window. Viewing rugby matches on the now available BFBS Television channel in Rick's OMQ meant that, as well as the copious quantities of beer consumed, 'mein host' demanded that every try scored had to be washed down with a large tot of malt whisky and, when that dried up, brandy! Rick was a lively character and when his thirty-ninth birthday almost coincided with my fortieth it seemed absolutely sensible to arrange a joint birthday party on the lawn between the two houses. It was a common practice, and a much enjoyed theme by the majority, that parties should be Fancy Dress! So, whilst our preparations focused on the quantities of beer and wine required, not to mention just how many BBQ sets we would need to cater for the numbers, the main effort in our early deliberations was the 'theme'. It didn't take us too long to come up with the idea of a Beach Party! Late May in Germany is usually very balmy and can often be quite

---

7. Responsible for the administration of all personnel matters on the unit.
8. Italy was not yet a member of this illustrious group of rugby playing nations.

warm late into the evening. We had the necessary sun umbrellas and plenty of garden furniture for the drunks to park themselves upon, once the alcohol took hold and their knees began to buckle. Moreover, with over twenty-four years as a Beach Boys fan, I had a collection of vinyl records that would keep the mood appropriate to the occasion. Add to that a tax-free Pioneer stereo system, with some of the largest speakers ever to grace a living room, and you can see that we were set up for the event. Then Rick, with all his contacts within the station infrastructure, came up with the bright idea of actually creating a beach! Ten tons of sand was duly delivered and the game was on!

At 0200hrs, the RAF Police patrol car stopped outside our house and two 'whitecaps' ventured round the back and approached the remnants of the party. There were about twenty people left and the party was, technically, still in full swing! Beer was still being consumed, wine bottles were still being opened and laughter and dancing to the loud music still filled the night air. I approached the first corporal to ascertain what their issue might be.

'Sir, is this your party?' he asked. Technically it was mine and Rick's, but I felt it appropriate not to beat about the bush and confessed.

'We've had a complaint about the noise, Sir.'

'Oh really, corporal,' I replied. 'Sorry about that, didn't realise the time. I'll turn the music down!' All the time thinking to myself: 'which miserable bugger of a neighbour had complained about the noise.' We had often been kept awake by the noise coming from parties on the married patch and we had invited all the close neighbours so I was perplexed as to why somebody might complain about our thrash.

'We've had a complaint, Sir, from the local German police in Elmpt! Apparently, they can hear your music in the local town!'

A very slow and drawn out 'Ah' was all I could muster initially. I had had no idea that my Pioneer system was that powerful! However, in our planning for the party we had failed to take into consideration that just ten yards from the epicentre of the party was the perimeter fence and that through the trees behind the fence and just some four hundred yards beyond were the first few houses on the edge of Elmpt.

'Right! Thank you for letting me know, corporal. I will turn down the music immediately and ensure that everybody has gone within the hour.' It made no sense to upset the locals. They suffered enough noise from Tornados in reheat on departure without Rick and me adding to their pain at 0200hrs on a Sunday morning!

The officers' mess organised some terrific parties too and we were routinely regular attendees at all of them and at Saturday Steak Nights. My wife and I were honoured when 'the mess bachelors' invited us to attend a fancy dress party in the mess one Saturday night. In typical bachelor style, the party was designated as 'come as somebody famous and dead'! I elected to go as The Unknown Soldier and my wife opted to be Eva Peron! We arrived shortly after the appointed hour and, as we entered the reception area, were confronted by two officers dressed in lounge suits, bowler hats and each carrying an umbrella and a copy of the *Financial Times*. Gary Brough and Simon 'Shifty' Young were two of 31 Squadron's characters and were the ringleaders in organising the party. Nothing unusual there other than that their suits were tattered, their shirt collars were detached from the shirts and the umbrellas had no material whatsoever! Now add that their bowler hats were split open and on fire and you might begin to realise just how 'dead' they were meant to be. It was just a few weeks after the Kings Cross Tube Station disaster in 1987 when thirty-one people had lost their lives and a further one hundred had been badly injured. The party was a roaring success and not one person mentioned anything about just how sick-minded our two organisers had been. That's Air Force black humour for you!

My wife and I also took up Bridge and met weekly in the mess in an effort to master the art of the game. Here we hooked up with others, some of whom became good friends, and two of which, Brian and Liz Cole, we ventured to Berlin with for a long weekend. Unlike my first trip, on my first tour, through the Iron Curtain with Iain Ross in his Citroen Dyane, we decided to travel in luxury on the British Military Train that plied the route from Braunschweig in West Germany to Charlottenburg in West Berlin, via Marienborn and Potsdam in the eastern sector. Routinely the Train OC was a British Army Warrant Officer and on our trip to Berlin it was no exception. As we settled ourselves into our comfortable seats in the officers' section of the train he soon introduced himself, relieved us of our passports and travel permits and invited us to partake of a preprandial drink. We each chose a G&T and then had another whilst we perused the dinner menu. There was no charge for the alcohol and, indeed, the whole journey to and from Berlin and everything that came with it did not cost us a penny.

Known as The Berliner, the British military train travelled daily between West Germany and East Berlin from 1945 until 1990. Its prime purpose was to maintain access to Berlin through Soviet occupied East Germany.

However, it also provided a mechanism to repatriate troops and families from east to west, or allow a day trip for families based in West Berlin to the west, unencumbered by the security rigours imposed by living in the divided city. Any British military personnel stationed in West Germany were at liberty to use the train if they carried the required and approved clearances and paperwork. The journey took just under five hours to cover the short one hundred and forty-five miles to Berlin. Most of this was spent standing still in sidings whilst engines, drivers and guard were ceremoniously exchanged from western to eastern and back again as the train progressed either eastbound or westbound. After boarding, all the train doors were locked, an armed guard was placed on board and the OC Train took on the mantle of 'mein host'! Dinner on board was exquisite and all was washed down with large helpings of wine from a comprehensive wine list. Engine exchanges took place at Helmstedt and Potsdam and at Marienborn the OC Train, along with his interpreter, met privately with a Russian officer who stamped the paperwork that he extracted from his briefcase. When dinner was over, we were invited to indulge in a glass of port, and whilst we stood stationary in Potsdam while the engine was swapped back before we entered West Berlin, we were encouraged to partake of a 'Potsdamer Port' by the warrant officer. All in order to show the communist shunters and trackmen outside our window 'just how decadent people from the west could be'! With wheels rolling again, and shortly before we drew to a stop at our destination in Charlottenburg, he once again insisted that we drink one last port in celebration of the fact that we were back in the free world again! I do not know about the other three, but I was quite plastered by the time I rolled off the train in West Berlin and it took all my concentration to manhandle our large suitcase the few blocks to our small gasthof booked for the weekend. It was just after 8pm.

After a very pleasant sightseeing weekend in Berlin, which included a military bus tour into East Berlin where we enjoyed a good lunch and some exceedingly cheap[9] shopping, it was time to head back westward on The Berliner. Coincidentally it was the same warrant officer in charge of the train and without the encouragement to drink heavily during the morning's journey homeward we were able to strike up a conversation and enquire about his regular contact meetings with the Soviet lieutenant on duty at

---

9. Prices were depressed anyway but with 7 Ostmarks to the Deutsch Mark at the time we felt like millionaires; shopkeepers were often inclined to seek US Dollars in payment but we had none.

Marienborn. I asked what sort of relationship he had with them and whether it was stilted and formal. He replied that it was with some, but not with all and began to tell us a tale of one meeting with a Soviet who had a strong understanding of, and some empathy with, the British Army man.

According to his tale, the Soviet officer had asked him if he had ever been to the NAAFI, which was a very easy question to answer. What serviceman has never been to the NAAFI? Indeed, it was the NAAFI at Rheindahlen where most of us had bought our stereo systems and all large military conurbations had an equivalent within its wire. The warrant officer had replied in the affirmative and the Soviet had responded with a request for him to purchase a Panasonic Video Recorder for him. The Briton had looked at him askance and indicated that it would cost him quite a lot of money to do so. With that, the Soviet officer pulled a wad of Deutsch Marks, which were not readily available in the East, from his pocket and counted out fifteen hundred of them, which he passed over. Slightly shocked, the train commander took the money and promised to bring a video recorder from the NAAFI the next time he was on duty.

He did. However, as the train headed west through East Germany he suddenly realised that he could not march down the Marienborn platform with his briefcase in one hand and a Panasonic box under his other arm. He therefore walked along the train until he found a private soldier asleep in a compartment with his feet on the seat opposite. Apparently the ensuing conversation went something like this:

'Soldier, wake up!'

'Yes, sir! Sorry, sir!' he blurted as he quickly removed his feet from the seat opposite.

'Going home, lad!' It was not a question more of a demand.

'Yes, sir!'

'Empty your case out!' The soldier emptied all his belongings on the seats in the compartment and the warrant officer was next seen marching along the platform with briefcase in his right hand and the soldier's case in his left, which concealed the illegal contraband.

The Soviet's face was evidently a picture when he handed over the video recorder and he was even more dumbfounded when the train commander handed him back three hundred Deutsch Marks in change! So much for the Cold War! So much for East/West hostility!

In early July 1989 I had participated in Exercise Garlic Breath (who chooses these names?), which was another period of In-Service AIM-9 firings on Aberporth Range for the RAF Germany Tornado Wings at Laarbruch and Brüggen. As STANEVAL(Weapons), I once again found myself at the forefront of the plan with responsibility for the successful firing of the Wing's allocation of missiles. To do so, I pre-positioned at RAF Valley in Anglesey to oversee the crews, aircraft and sorties as they rotated through from Brüggen over the fortnight allocated. Having fired one previously, I was not assigned a missile, but on three occasions I flew as chase crew with a fully armed missile should the primary aircraft or missile go unserviceable. It was a great two weeks with a different group of aircrew passing through the officers' mess bar each night, which played havoc with my liver and kidneys but, since I was never one to shy away from a party, I never once made an excuse to absent myself and joined in determinedly with a succession of drinking bouts!

Similarly, each squadron at Brüggen had an annual allocation of live 1000lb bombs to drop. However, although there were a couple of continental ranges where this could take place the weather was almost invariably unsuitable on the pre-planned date. Strike Command, however, had an exceptional facility at Garvie Island Range. The uninhabited island, which is just two hundred and fifty yards long, sits off the north coast of Scotland and approximately four miles east of Cape Wrath. It was a bit far for a Tornado to get there and back from Brüggen without refuelling! Consequently, I proposed an across-Wing solution that would involve me and a turn-round party of groundcrew of all trades pre-positioning at RAF Machrihanish, near Campbeltown in Argyll, that would receive aircraft post-range or pre-range, turn them round and send them on their way again. I chose the name Exercise Gopher Hit. Partly because it seemed like a good idea, had a modicum of mystery (as evidenced by Exercise Garlic Breath above) and partly because it was a play on words of an oft used expression amongst aircrew at Brüggen in response to a query as to whether one should or should not take some sort of decision or action – 'Yeah, go for it, mate!' The plan scored a major hit for me across the Wing and all four squadrons signed up to my plan. It was hard work at the Machrihanish end as we had to cope with four waves of four aircraft per day and often in quick succession as we usually had a four-ship from the range crossing paths with a four-ship from another squadron on its way to Garvie. It was great fun, however, and the groundcrew responded brilliantly to the challenge. We closed the detachment with a round of golf at Machrihanish

Golf Club where the first hole is described as 'The Famous Drive Across the Atlantic'! My golf was such that I chose to ignore the Atlantic and take a long stroll around its shoreline. It is a classic links course, but its pot bunkers are lethal with some of them offering a reverse exit as the only possible way out! It did nothing for my confidence as a golfer, although in those days I was nothing more than a casual participant in a game that I now enjoy thoroughly in retirement even if I am still no bloody good at it! The detachment was deemed so successful that its format was copied and taken up by the STC and RAFG Tornado bases and became the norm for the whole Tornado Force.

Rocky Goodall was an outstanding commanding officer and he and his wife were very welcoming hosts. I don't think he ever missed a Happy Hour at Brüggen and was very much one of the team. A man to be looked up to and an outstanding leader who went on to become a 3-Star officer and was Chief of Staff at HQ AIRNORTH at Ramstein AFB in Germany. He was knighted by Her Majesty the Queen in her Birthday Honours List of 2001. A Hunter and Harrier pilot before he took command of 16 Squadron flying the Tornado GR1, he had an innate ability in the air and strong tactical awareness. He was an outstanding pilot and a master at air combat. He was thus no pushover when it came to 1 v 1. Well that is until he met Flying Officer Kieran Duffy on 25 July 1989 over the Ardennes in Belgium for just such a mission!

As an ACL, the squadrons often relied upon me to take their new boys on 1 v 1 sorties as part of their ACT work-up training. So I briefed the station commander and Kieran on what was required, what the rules of the game were and what was and was not allowed. We talked about minima for combat. Minimum heights, minimum speeds, use of reheat including when reheat was not permitted and, of course, weather minima. I briefed the 'Knock it off' rules and I briefed the action to be taken if somebody had an emergency and had to call 'STOP, STOP, STOP!' We all understood it, we had all done it before, but it was Kieran in my front seat and his usual navigator, Norman Dent, in Rocky's rear seat who had to prove in the air that they had what it took to fight the Tornado.

Over Belgium, Kieran called 'Split for combat' and with that command Rocky turned his Tornado through 180 degrees to give the two aircraft some twenty miles of separation before we both turned back in to sight our 'enemy'! With a call of 'Tally' from one or other the fight was on whether the other could spot his opponent or not. If the call was 'Judy', it meant that somebody had located the other on their radar; the fight could proceed, but no full engagement was allowed until Tally had been declared by one. The weather conditions above cloud were excellent and we achieved a significant number of successful engagements in the allotted hour for the mission. Kieran put in an outstanding performance, albeit I caught him cheating with his use of afterburner on a couple of occasions. It soon became apparent that he was gaining the upper hand against the CO and fight after fight he managed to get onto Rocky's tail for a Fox 2 shot. I don't recall us ever getting into Fox 3[10] range as the CO was alert to the threat and managed to bug out before he was caught out. All too soon we were down to fuel minima and so I called 'Knock it off' and we reassembled ourselves for descent and recovery back to base.

The weather had not improved since we had departed and, in fact, had closed in. Although Kieran and I were the formation leader, it was inappropriate with his White Card instrument rating for him to attempt to lead the CO in a pairs GCA at base. So we handed over the lead to Rocky and, with both aircraft settled in the descent, we closed onto his wing before we entered very thick cloud. Our hope was that by sticking on his wing he would lead us safely onto the runway, but as the approach continued it became apparent that we were way outside of Kieran's limits and so took an early decision to divert to the Luftwaffe base at Jever which was Brüggen's selected Number One[11] diversion for the day. It was colour-coded BLUE at the time and forecast to remain so.

As we transited on our own at medium level across Germany and under the control of Clutch Radar I pointed out our good luck to Kieran. He was so elated by his combat success that he had not, for a second, considered the implications of us having waxed the station commander's backside in air combat. I knew only too well that, by the time we got back to Brüggen that afternoon, Rocky Goodall would be back behind his desk in SHQ and far too busy with the next thing on his agenda to be bothered about some smart ass flying officer and his rather long in the tooth STAN(W) in his rear seat. Nothing was ever said! Very sadly, Kieran Duffy and Norman Dent were killed on 13 January 1991 when their Tornado GR1 crashed during a

---

10. Guns kill.
11. The Number One diversion is the weather diversion for an airfield, it is usually some distance away and chosen because of its superior weather conditions on the day. The Number Two diversion is closer to base and used if a situation arises where the home airbase is declared 'Black' (runway blocked) and aircraft need only have sufficient fuel to divert to it, normally the nearest airbase.

low-level training flight in Oman. It was just five days before the coalition Counter Air campaign got under way during Operation Desert Storm.

The children came home regularly from boarding school for the major school holidays. I had volunteered to take responsibility for coordinating private coach hire at the beginning and end of each term to get the Stamford mob to, and from school, to Luton Airport to connect with the scheduled Britannia Airways Trooping Flight to RAF Wildenrath, where parents would meet them before driving them home. Half-term holidays presented more of a problem but, if I wasn't detached, we would endeavour to get over to the UK, collect Chris and Sarah and head off to my parents-in-law's home which, by now, was in Brixham in Devon. Generally they were happy times and, for me, my career was at last slanting upwards at about ten degrees as opposed to its downward death spiral at the end of my tour on 237 OCU. We were happy as a couple. We had a good social life surrounded by good friends. We missed our kids, but then so did all the other Mums and Dads at Brüggen whose children were at boarding school. We were no different to anybody else and life was normal. Well as normal as it can be when one is committed to a full career in the Royal Air Force.

My annual medical came due, as it always did, around the time of my birthday. It was linked to the month of your birth, so we aircrew always knew when it was coming and some would crash diet in the months leading up to it in order to present a sylph-like physique to the MO! I had never had an issue with weight but, like every other pilot or navigator I know, I was always concerned about the eyesight test and the hearing test. To fail both or either could have a devastating effect on one's medical category. A reduction in one's medical category below A1 G1 Z1[12] for aircrew was, at all costs, to be avoided. A drop from A1 could mean a temporary or permanent grounding with a concomitant loss of Flying Pay!

Shortly after the Beach Party I received notification that I was to report for my Annual Medical. At the appointed date and time, I arrived with the usual apprehension at the SMC and made my presence known to the medical orderly behind the frosted glass window. After a short wait, I was ushered into a side room where I provided the standard urine sample before having my eyes tested. Failing eyesight was, perhaps, the biggest concern for any

---

12. Medical categories that depict one's suitability for employment in the Air, on the Ground and in Zones of the World. Measured on a scale of 1 to 5 where 1 indicates fully fit and 5 can result in medical discharge from the Service.

airman, but although I knew that my vision was no longer 20/20 my memory had never failed me. A quick glance at the bottom line of the chart as I strolled past it left me secure in the knowledge that once again the eye test would be an absolute breeze!

'Sir, could you cover your left eye and read the second bottom line please from the left?'

Uh oh! The second bottom line? Surely she meant the bottom line! Surely! Oh well here goes!

'D, T, L, N, E, um N, A, C'

'Thank you, sir, now cover the right and read the same line backwards please.'

Hmm. Why can't I just read the bottom line – A, Z, P, B, D, V, Q, L – I've got that one memorised!

'OK. C, A, H, E, N, L, T, O'. Great! Thank God that's over! But now it was time for the audio booth! Rather than having to rely still on the Biggin Hill consulting room whisper, in the 80s advanced technology had provided the quacks with a semi-soundproofed audio booth and an automatic monitoring process to test aircrew hearing. There could be no lip reading now! Into the booth I went, headphones on, my back to the medical orderly who sat at a control panel outside and who could monitor my every move through a glass window behind me. I picked up the trigger button and waited. After a few seconds I heard an easily audible beep in my left ear. Moments later there came another slightly higher in pitch. Then another, and another, and another. Each one slightly higher in pitch than the last. Then a pause. Had I heard one? Had I missed one? Oh hell! Press it anyway. Oh! There was one! Hell that was faint! And on it went until the orderly cut into my ears and told me that we were now moving over to the right ear. The same ordeal! As the pitch got higher and higher I began to doubt whether I had heard or missed yet another. It usually got quite frantic in that padded box as to fail one's hearing test could have a limiting effect on one's flying career. Over the years I had tried to develop a knack whereby I timed in my head the gaps between the beeps that I could hear and then extrapolated them to the ones that I thought I had missed! Goodness only knows whether it worked or not, but the MO never had any complaints about my hearing in all the years that I attended routinely for my aircrew medical. An ECG followed and with the preliminaries complete I took a seat in the waiting room and awaited my moment to meet with the doctor.

'How do you feel about your eyesight?' he asked me after he had debriefed me positively on all other aspects of my medical circumstance.

'I am happy with it,' I said, 'but as I get older I do feel that I am not getting the spots in the air that I used to!'

'How do you mean?'

'Well it used to be that I was one of the first in a formation to spot other aircraft, but I'm being beaten off the mark by some of the younger guys and that's not too great in my position as STAN(W).'

'Fancy seeing an ophthalmologist at Wegberg?'[13]

'That might not be a bad idea', I responded, 'and it can't do me any harm.' So an appointment was made for me at the ophthalmic clinic two weeks later.

Wegberg was an easy twenty minute drive from Brüggen, but it did require an afternoon off work to attend the appointment. I was summoned into the consulting room and was met by a large Germanic figure who spoke to me in heavily accented English.

'Ach zo, skvadron lader, yoo are conzernt with yore eyesight!'

'Not exactly concerned,' I muttered, 'more that it's not as good in the air as it once was!'

'Vas ist yor edge?'

'Forty,' I replied after I had worked out what he meant by my 'edge'.

'Ach zo!' he answered. 'Yoo muss be navigator!'

I smiled and asked him how he had worked that out; there was nothing on my medical record to indicate that that was the case.

'Navigators', he said, 'Zay come to see me at forty! Pilots! Zay are more vain, zay come to see me at forty-two!'

What an astute man and without further ado he tested my eyes thoroughly, compiled a prescription and ordered me some 'Aviator-style' air force issue spectacles with appropriate lenses to correct my vision. In addition, I received a pair of corrective 'Aviator-style' sunglasses and two spare lenses each in a pouch marked 'Left' and 'Right'! I was fully equipped and ready to fly again and beat the best with my early spots! I was also ready to go to war in my gas mask with the 'Left' and 'Right' lenses locked in place! Needless to say, I never bothered with these enhancements as they were just too bloody fiddly to fit and I didn't actually have a problem with my sight on the ground.

---

13. RAF Hospital Wegberg served those military personnel based in the Nord-Rhein Westfalen area of West Germany.

When the children returned to Stamford after the summer recess in 1989, I quickly realised that my planned participation in Red Flag the following spring would clash with their Easter holidays. I had a serious dilemma. I saw little enough of my kids and to be away for the best part of a month and the whole of their time at home would not sit well with me and certainly would cause friction within the family. My wife had become somewhat withdrawn at home and it was clear that there was some resentment towards the time I spent at work and on my various deployments. A three-week stint for me in Nevada when Christopher and Sarah had just come home was not going to help the situation! I found an ally in my opposite number at Laarbruch.

Phillip Duncan and I had routinely compared the performance and competencies of the seven Tornado squadrons in RAFG. He, as STAN(W) at Laarbruch,[14] filled exactly the same role as I did at Brüggen, albeit he had one less squadron's load of aircrew to manage. We had built a good rapport and often visited each other to review progress and discuss tactics. At one of these meetings I happened to mention my Easter holiday problem to Phil who, after a few moments thought, came up with a perfect solution. Good as it was it would need the sanction of higher authority at Laarbruch and at Brüggen and possibly at HQ RAFG also, but it was a sound idea and one that extended our Wing 'cross-fertilisation' tactics discussions into the air. We each proposed through our chains of command that to swap STAN(W)s for a Red Flag exercise would allow insight into how each of the two Wings operated and improve the operational flexibility and capabilities of both Wings.

Nobody on the two units or at HQ RAFG needed convincing and so, after a number of briefings with XV Squadron at Laarbruch, I found myself at RAF Leuchars in January 1990 undertaking yet another Red Flag Work-up programme. My pilot for this new adventure was an erstwhile Jaguar pilot by the name of Ricci Cobelli who, like me, was a squadron leader. Despite not knowing each other beforehand we got on well in the cockpit. After a shakedown singleton sortie with Nigel Risdale, Ricci and I flew seven work-up sorties together in the ULL flying areas, designated for the task, in Scotland. The first was a singleton mission through the Scottish Borders. The planned low level route back to Leuchars took us up the Tweed Valley towards Peebles, which was the birthplace of my father. As we scorched up

---

14. The Laarbruch Tornado GR1 Wing at the time comprised XV, 16 and 20 Squadrons.

the valley I told Ricci that we were about to overfly the castle where my grandfather had been born. Rounding a bend in the river he saw Neidpath Castle before him on the northern bank. As we shot over the top of it at 250 feet and 420 knots, he was clearly impressed that somebody he knew, and was now sat in his back seat, had once owned such a pile! I didn't have the heart to burst his bubble by telling him that my great grandfather was the gamekeeper and that his son had been born in the servants' quarters! We led six 100 feet missions successfully over five working days and left Leuchars on 24 January ready for Red Flag in early March, which would allow me to be back home when Chris and Sarah arrived at Wildenrath off the trooping flight.

XV Squadron and I deployed by RAF transport aircraft to Nellis AFB at the end of the first week of March 1990. Having left my staff work behind I was certainly ready for some excellent flying and looked forward to some continuity too. I flew seven sorties on the exercise, five of them with Cobelli. On all, bar two, of these sorties we were loaded with inert 1000lb bombs to attack Tolicha and Mount Helen airfields and the simulated Soviet tank regiment deployed in the desert. The flying was fantastic, but, this being my fourth, I was an old hand at Red Flag and found nothing much new to learn other than that, it is never a wise move to attempt a reattack in a hostile environment when you failed to release your weapons at the first attempt. Despite my protestations to my man up front, he insisted that we go round again to save the embarrassment of taking our weapons home. Had it been for real, this memoir would not have been written.

Socially I was fully integrated into the detachment and partook fully, once again, in the delights of Las Vegas. The Detachment Commander was the Laarbruch Station Commander, Gordon McRobbie, whom I had known well from my first Buccaneer tour in Germany, he was an outstanding character with a very friendly and open approach. The squadron commander was John Broadbent, who had been a fellow staff navigator with me on the Buccaneer OCU and the Project Officer was Gordon Buckley, who I did not know well, but was clearly from the same 'fun' school as me. They all looked after me exceedingly well such that I felt very much a part of the XV team. Trips to the Hoover Dam, soirees in casinos and golf on the Nellis course were all part of the social routine on that Red Flag. When a team mentioned that they were going to play golf at Pahrump at the weekend, I jumped at the opportunity to join them.

The town of Pahrump sits some sixty miles west of Las Vegas along Route 160. The journey takes about eighty minutes and the road is mostly straight, with dry desert stretching for miles on both sides, apart from a five mile portion that cuts through the southern end of the Spring Mountains. The road through the mountain pass requires some skill to negotiate the bends and gradients. There were six of us in the group and without our own golf clubs it seemed to make sense to all pile into Gordon McRobbie's rented Cadillac; three in the back and three on the front bench seat. I climbed into the back and we set off westwards. After our descent out of the pass the road straightens and, until the turn off for the golf course, has few if any bends on it! We were motoring fast when all of a sudden 'McRobs' hit the brakes hard and let out an expletive! The blokes beside him in the front gripped the dashboard tight whilst we, unsighted in the rear, craned our necks to see just what had caused this sudden stop! We had skidded to a halt with our nearside wheels off the tarmac surface and ground into the dirt of the desert. After a 'what the fuck!' moment, McRobs composed himself and set off back on the road, but hot on the tail of the idiots in the car that had thought it a good idea to turn onto our carriageway right in front of us whilst we were doing probably more than we should have been. We caught up with them at a petrol station and all six of us got out of the car. We pointed out the error of their ways to them, accepted their apology and set off sedately back towards Pahrump.

On the way back to Vegas I was again in the back and, after a couple of beers and a brandy, was resting against the offside door. We had a timeline to meet as we needed to get back for a pre-booked show date in town! Unfortunately, some bright spark pointed out that, just south of Pahrump and about eight miles south, off the '160' was the world renowned Chicken Ranch bordello! Tight for time or not it seemed a perfect opportunity for a team 'photoshoot' with the brothel in the background; nobody dissented! There was, however, only one road in and one road out so, photograph over (that's all it was, folks, honest), Gordon Buckley, who was now driving, headed the same eight miles back north towards the '160'. We were now a further thirty minutes late for our engagement! 'Buckers' put his foot down and the 'Caddy' with its precious cargo of six aircrew that included the Staish,[15] a squadron flight commander, the Project Officer and Brüggen's STAN(W) headed back

---

15. Station Commander.

to the city at high speed. After twenty miles or so the canyon through the Spring Mountains appeared on the horizon and just as we approached the top of descent a Highway Patrol wagon hove into view. Without any warning, the patrolman switched on the vehicle's 'Blues and Twos'! He'd got us with a Fox 1.[16] As he peeled round behind us 'Buckers' began to slow to a halt such that as the 'Smokey' caught up with us we had come to a complete stop at the side of the road. He wound down the driver's window.

'Sir, have you any idea what speed you were doing?'

Gordon Buckley attempted a response tentatively and as best he could. 'Seventy, officer!'

I knew that was not so, because from my side of the vehicle I could see the strip speedometer clearly and it had registered no speed whatsoever! It had registered no speed whatsoever because it was completely off the scale at the far right hand end of it – just one long white strip with no black showing! This was not looking good.

'You, sir, were doing one hundred and ten!' drawled the officer and before Buckers could respond he drawled 'Ha' you ever seen a body that's been dragged outta the desert because he was doing one hundred and ten, sir?'

Our errant driver confessed he had not and without hearing him the officer continued 'Cos ah have, sir, and let me assure ya-all in there that it ain't a pretty sight!'

We were all intelligent people; we really did not need him to tell us that sort of information. Thankfully nobody sniggered and nobody thought it a good idea to interject. We all sat mute, although somebody in the back did mutter that we might miss the show at this rate!

'Can I see your driving licence, sir?'

At one of the last briefings at Laarbruch Gordon Buckley, as the Project Officer, had given us all a stern warning that we would all be expected to be available to drive a rental vehicle at any stage of the deployment. Accordingly, he had continued, woe betide any member of the officer corps who did not bring their driving licence with them to Las Vegas.

'I don't think I have it with me, officer!'

'Sir, would you please turn this vehicle around and follow me back to the station!'

---

16. Air defence speak for a missile shot from in front!

Winding the window up and insisting to us that he'd left his licence in his hotel room, he turned the car back towards Pahrump and followed the 'Smokey' for about five miles away from Las Vegas! Chatter in the car was nervous and high. Speculation was rife as to what might yet befall us and Buckers in particular. Offers of assistance or just company inside the Highway Patrol station were rebuffed as we pulled into the car park just off the '160'. Gordon looked a forlorn character as he followed the patrolman inside! Aircrew morale is never very low and when it takes a knock like this it doesn't stay down for long! Soon, whilst Buckers was receiving his sentence, laughter and banter began to break out in the vehicle which did not help our errant driver when he returned to the vehicle with a glum look on his face. Calls of 'Get in, we're going to miss the show!' and 'Was that painful or what?' were dismissed by him as he finally got to the open window.

'It's not over yet,' he told us. 'Has anybody got any cash?' he enquired.

'Why? What's the damage?' we chorused back to him.

'Seven hundred and fifty dollars!' he moaned, 'and I've only got a couple of hundred!'

A quick whip round secured the necessary amount and after a further trip into the patrol station we were back on the road and motoring at a more steady pace towards Vegas.

The heavy fine had been split into two parts. First, with a speed limit of fifty-five miles per hour on the two-lane Route 160 he had been fined ten dollars for every mile per hour above the limit. Second, for not having his driving licence, which he now confessed he had left in Germany, he received a fine of two hundred dollars that could be recovered if he managed to get his driving licence to a local police station before he departed the USA. Although the detachment was almost over Gordon's wife managed to get his licence to him with squadron aircrew who were coming out to replace us on Red Flag. With now a very short turn-round time, he rushed to the local police station, recovered the two hundred dollars and repaid his debt! We decided to write off the three hundred and fifty that we had contributed towards the speeding fine, as we had all been a party to it. And we had made it to the show, despite everything having contrived to prevent us!

Despite the exchange with the 'Smokey' the whole exercise was an outstanding success and it proved to me the value of sharing tactics and ideas not only on the ground, but also by actually putting them into practice in the air. The Laarbruch Wing learned a great deal from my bringing Brüggen ideas to them and the Brüggen Wing did likewise after Phil's participation on its Red Flag over the Easter period. Little did we know then just how important this cross-fertilisation would become in less than twelve months' time!

When I joined the RAF in 1969 I signed up for a career that would last to my thirty-eighth birthday with the option of continuing to the age of fifty-five if both I and the RAF wished that to be the case. I had always wanted to have a full career and had actually been brought up on the principle of finding a 'job for life'. I certainly did not want to leave the RAF, but the lack of my promotion to squadron leader by the mid-80s had focused my mind somewhat. Without promotion by my thirty-eighth birthday came only two choices: leave the RAF and seek an alternative career; or, if it was offered, accept Specialist Aircrew and continue flying until the age of fifty-five and acknowledge that I would most probably remain a flight lieutenant for the rest of my days. The letter of offer of promotion had come just a few days short of my thirty-eighth birthday and had diverted me away from both options. With that letter came an offer of a full career with all the promotion opportunities available to me. I knew full well, however, that my arriving 'late on parade' for promotion would limit my career ceiling. Nevertheless, I determined that my earlier misguided youthfulness was behind me and that I now needed to knuckle down and prove my worth as a senior officer to my chain of command.

The next step on my newly established springboard of a career was to attend the Basic Staff Course at the RAF Staff College, RAF Bracknell. I had been applying routinely to attend the course but, and despite strong recommendations in my annual assessments to do so, I had not yet found a period in my professional diary when I could be released from the Wing. With my return from Red Flag came the good news that a window of opportunity had been found and that I had been accepted to attend a course. Number 138 BSC was over and done with by late May 1990 and I was awarded the symbol 'qs' in the Air Force List. Not unlike my final report from the ISS Course, I suspect my effort merited an 'Aircrew A'[17] score. Certainly, whilst my report for written skill and spoken skill has no negatives in it there are definitely a few 'althoughs' and 'usuallys' peppered throughout it. Apparently my final

---

17. C-Grade pass.

paper was 'disappointing'. Oh well! A win's a win in my book and another career tick had been added to my CV.

On 2 August 1990 Saddam Hussein invaded Kuwait and instantly the world began to ponder the implications of the land grab by this despotic dictator who had, for many years, been committing genocide against tribal and religious entities within Iraq who did not share the same religion or religious views as his Sunni followers. His genocidal al-Anfal Campaign was primarily against the Kurdish people in northern Iraq and took place under cover of the final stages of the 1980 to 1988 Iran-Iraq War. The Iraqi government's systematic campaign targeted the Kurdish minority specifically between 1986 and 1989. In an attempt to ethnically cleanse Iraq of those who opposed his oppressive regime Saddam also targeted other minority communities that included Assyrians, Shabaks, Iraqi Turkmen, Yassidis and Mandeans. Many villages that belonged to these ethnic groups were destroyed. The Shia Marsh Arabs, who inhabited the Tigris-Euphrates marshlands in the south and east of Iraq along the Iranian border, were also ethnically cleansed and often suffered gas bomb attacks at the hands of his brutal henchmen.

At the Ministry of Defence in London, and the Pentagon in Washington DC, contingency planning staffs were fully engaged analysing the implication of this act of aggression and putting in place war plans should the need arise to oust the dictator from the peaceful lands of Kuwait. At the United Nations in New York, frenzied negotiations started and continued through the latter half of 1990 as one UN Resolution after another was proposed and rejected by some. As the months progressed, war looked more and more inevitable.

Brüggen too began to focus itself away from the usual TACEVAL routine and consider the implications and training requirements for its Tornado crews were war to come. I, along with OC Operations Wing, was summoned to see the station commander, Rocky Goodall. He came straight to the point. What would be required to prepare the Wing for a war in the Middle East and a scenario that we had never trained for? I had been mulling this prospect over and over in my head since Saddam had invaded and put forward my 'back of a fag packet' thoughts to the two senior officers who were relying on my knowledge and expertise to assist them. At the end of our meeting, and with both of them convinced that we could not sit around and wait for instructions from on high, I left the CO's office tasked with selecting the best twelve crews from across the Wing who would form the first deployed contingent of aircrew, with their Tornados, to start the assault against Iraq and Saddam's invaders. Once selected, I was to devise a training programme for the particular theatre of operations and train those twelve crews such that they were fully prepared, when the call came.

It was not an easy task, but it was not a difficult task either. It was a task well within my remit and one that I was very capable of completing successfully. I knew all the crews on the station well and I knew their strong and their weak points. Crews who had earlier in the year completed Red Flag would almost self-select themselves and others would naturally fall into place because of their experience on type and role. I selected twelve pilots and eleven navigators. With my wife's blessing I slipped my own name down as the twelfth navigator and headed to the CO's office to present my list. A quick glance and it was approved immediately and so I set about drawing up a training programme and, once approved, gathered my flock around me in the Ops Wing HQ briefing room to go through the details of the plan with them.

Likely FOBs had already been identified in Saudi Arabia and Bahrain. Dhahran was 25nms closer to the Iraqi Border than Bahrain, but even at that it was still some 600nms to Baghdad and with a full load of nothing at all except wing tanks the Tornado would be hard pressed to get there and back at high level without dropping in somewhere to refuel on route. With people shooting at you, whilst carrying a full load of JP233, the necessity for both Skyshadow and BOZ Pods and the need for a low-level dash phase into the target there was no alternative, but to conduct AAR inbound to and, in all likelihood, outbound from the target.

The snag for Tornado GR1 crews based in Germany was that our Cold War targets were just a little more than 300nms from Brüggen, half the distance, and we had never had any need to practise AAR. Thus a full training programme that would convert my team into masters of in-flight refuelling was one of the first tasks that had to be achieved. Dedicated courses were set up at the Air Refuelling School at RAF Marham and subsequently dedicated tankers were made available over the North Sea to allow me to convert each of the crews. I was assisted in my task by the fact that some of my selected crews had tanked from the Tornado on previous tours in the UK. Once they had requalified, they became my go-to men as instructors, often flying three or four times a day just to achieve the task in the shortest order.

Weaponry skills had to be honed. Unable to fly with JP233 in peacetime we flew sorties with eight inert 1000lb bombs strapped underneath to simulate and experience aircraft handling with two JP233, each of which weighed 2335kgs. We needed to develop and practise tactics for the kind of terrain that we would be flying over and we had to ensure that everybody was well aware of the implications of flying over sand dunes at ULL. Different lighting conditions can create definition and depth perception problems. Just as in mountainous terrain where an aircraft can clip the unseen ridge in front of him whilst he focuses on the far ridge beyond that he is intent on climbing over, the same applied at ULL with one sand dune merging with the one behind it. Many an experienced RAF pilot had learned this to his cost whilst trying to fly as low as possible in a Hunter or Jaguar whilst serving with the Sultan of Oman's Air Force. I needed to make sure that my team members were alert to this real hazard.

In October 1990 I was hit with a bombshell! Geoff Coop, who was now my Boss, but a good friend from my Buccaneer days, called me along to his office and hit me with the news fair and square and straight between the eyes. I was posted. I was posted to MOD and my flying tour as STAN(W) was about to come to its end. It was going to happen before the end of the year and, probably, before my twelve crews deployed to the Middle East. I protested! They cannot post me! I am going to war! It wasn't that I had a burning desire to go to war, of course. However, having trained for twenty-one years to do just that I did not want to miss out on putting my training into practice and proving to myself that I could actually do it. I had missed out, along with the rest of the Buccaneer Force, when the Turks had invaded Cyprus in 1974. I had had to defend Western Europe during the Cold War when the Argentinians had invaded the Falklands[18] in 1982. I was writing the CWEM when Buccaneers took part in Operation Pulsator[19] in 1983. So I was determined not to miss out on this show, but I did.

Geoff very considerately allowed me to bang on about how I was one of twelve trained men, was responsible for their training and couldn't be replaced no matter what the circumstances and needs of the RAF might actually be.

---

18. Operation Corporate. Buccaneers were not even considered as they didn't have the engine oil capacity for a lengthy sortie of over eight hours, and would have required far more Victor Tankers to fly from Ascension Island to Port Stanley than the Vulcans did.
19. Deployed to RAF Akrotiri for Operation Pulsator and overflew Beirut, Lebanon at very low level on 11 Sep 1983 and 13 September 1983 in support of the British contingent to the Multi-National Force (MNF) in Beirut.

Finished, he looked me in the eye with shared disappointment and told me that I had to go to MOD because Nigel Huckins, the wing commander I was going to work for, had already left for Bahrain to start contingency planning there! My shoulders dropped as he told me that I would start in my new post as MOD(AFD)TO2a(RAF)[20] in January and would leave Germany in mid-December. Certainly the job was right up my street. I had proved my aptitude for project work in the past as author of the CWEM and now in the post of STANEVAL(Weapons). I had had glowing annual reports throughout my tour in Ops Wing and was credited with having *'displayed his organisational talents to the full in preparing crews for Operation Granby'* as the mission to evict Saddam from Kuwait was now known in British circles. Disappointed at not going to war, I was actually quite chuffed with the way I had turned my career around.

There was a silver lining. With my new Boss already detached to the Middle East, I would be the only man in the office and would, therefore, have full responsibility for the day-to-day policies of the whole of the RAF's Operational Training tasks. As a result I would be entitled to claim Substitution Pay after twenty-eight days in post and that would continue until Nigel Huckins returned from the war.

I withdrew myself from the twelve and substituted another navigator. He was mighty grateful for the accolade of being chosen if not too sure about the prospect of going to war. Meanwhile, I carried on with ensuring that the training programme continued and that the task was being met. At the same time, with the focus for the Wing now being preparation for a war in which I would play no part, I started preparing for our family move back to the UK.

My career had developed in a manner that I had not expected. I loved my flying, but I knew that without combat experience the chance of another flying tour was remote. Nevertheless and undaunted I filled out the front cover of my 'on posting' F1369 Officer's Confidential Report, with my preferences for my next appointment after my time in Adastral House, in Holborn, came to an end. In order they were: Sqn Cdr/Wg Cdr Ops Tornado GR1; Exchange Tour Canada/USA; and British Defence Liaison Staff, Washington DC. Well one can dream, can't one!

Certainly a staff tour as a squadron leader had to be my next best move and the training job was a good one where, if I applied myself, I could shine, especially fulfilling the wing commander's role in his absence. Moreover, Air

---

20. Ministry of Defence (Air Force Department) Training Operational 2a (Royal Air Force).

Commodore Dicky Duckett, who was SASO HQ RAFG at the time, was moving to Adastral and would again be my Third Reporting Officer. In my final report from Brüggen he wrote:

> *'I have met with Herriot on a number of occasions and agree this report sums him up well. I am happy to endorse it and look forward to having him on my staff in my next appointment! Overall, he appears to be a late developer, and he will need to do AST[21] quite soon if we are to capitalise on his abilities.'*

I was happy. The career that had stagnated towards the end of my Buccaneer days now seemed to be more positive. My First Reporting Officer had specially recommended me for AST in my annual report in 1990 and now, with the same recommendation, it was being fully supported all the way up the line. I would have to get a move on though, there was an upper age limit of forty-two for students joining the Advanced Staff Course and I would already be forty-one when I started at MOD in January. Things were getting tight, but they were not insurmountable.

Having had to give priority to those who were bound for war I flew my last sorties in a Tornado GR1 with a 31 Squadron pilot on 17 October 1990. It could not have been a more fitting farewell as the sortie was as lead of a three-ship formation from Brüggen to RAF Leuchars in Scotland with a bundle of ULL in the Western Highlands thrown in! After lunch, we returned to Brüggen after a UK low-level and some 2 v 1 at medium level before we landed back at Brüggen in the dark. The last entry in my logbook for that tour included twenty minutes of night flying!

With Christopher and Sarah home from Stamford for the Christmas break, we packed up our belongings, cleaned all four storeys of the house and left for the UK and to spend a few days with my in-laws who by now had repositioned themselves in Cleethorpes, Lincolnshire. On the overnight ferry to Hull, Christopher took me aside and asked me a question only a son can share with his father.

'Dad, when we get back to England can we get a man's dog?' He was clearly tired of having lapdogs around the house and wanted something a bit more substantial.

I had to agree with him!

---

21. Advanced Staff Training.

Chapter Six

City Slicker

W e had been allocated an OMQ in Bushey Heath near Watford and, after a few days with the children's maternal grandparents, we reloaded the car and headed off to the A1 and our new life as city slickers. The quarter was a step down from our luxury four-storey pad at Brüggen! With the demand for housing amongst the three Services working in Central London being at a premium, we were lucky to be allocated a house at all from the outset of my tour. It was adequate for our needs, however, and with its three bedrooms there was room for us all and our new found acquisition, a man's dog.

I had done some research into a 'man's dog' whilst we had been in Lincolnshire and had found a woman, near RAF Wittering, who bred Labradors. As we passed Stamford, a quick diversion off the A1 took us to Manaroy Kennels, at the appointed hour, to meet the lady in question. It soon became apparent that we had wasted her time. She had no golden or black Labradors and did not anticipate a litter of either within the timescale that we wanted. She did, however, have a litter of chocolate Labradors if we were interested to see them. We had particularly wanted a blonde and had never even heard of chocolate before, but we decided that it was worth a look despite that fact. Fatal! Who can walk away from a kennel full of bundles of fun without actually agreeing to buy one? Not me, for sure, and not anybody who was with me that day! I should have learned from two previous experiences when we had 'just gone to see' some Cavalier King Charles Spaniels, but I had not. With their deep chocolate coats and their appealing eyes, the puppies were stunningly handsome. Their mother too was a handsome and placid bitch who had clearly done a good and caring job of rearing them since they had been born on 15 October. The puppies all pushed forward to the front of the box and, stretching on their hind legs, sought favour from the eight hands that thrust forward to stroke them.

All bar one. One puppy refused all our advances and sat towards the rear of the box with its back facing us, whilst it gave us a disdainful look over its left shoulder. We laughed at its attitude and, without further ado, agreed that that was the one for us – a dog with attitude would fit into the Herriot household easily! The kennel owner explained that all the puppies were already registered with the Kennel Club and each had been anointed with an appropriate name. All her dogs' names included the name of the kennel and, because of her location right next door to RAF Wittering, which operated Harriers at the time, had been named after breeds of harrier. Our dog had been christened Manaroy Marsh Harrier, but Christopher decided to give him the name Angus, a strong Scottish name which appealed to him. Angus was not ready to leave his mother, so I drove back to Wittering two weeks later and brought him home to Bushey Heath.

He was a true Labrador! Very soon he began to trash the skirting boards in the kitchen if we left him alone there and at night. He peed everywhere and required a heck of a lot of exercise. We overcame the peeing by corralling him into corners with a large fireguard and I tired him out by taking him for a walk at 0530 each morning, before I jumped in the shower and then headed to the city. In the evenings I would take him out again into local woodland before dinner in the hope that I could tire him out before bedtime. It was successful to an extent, but he did not get too much exercise during the day because my wife had difficulty controlling him, which was unfortunate.

My journey to Adastral House each morning required a long and slow tube journey from Stanmore to Bond Street, on the Jubilee Line, followed by a short hop eastbound on the Central Line to Holborn. It was a mightily depressing journey in the winter as at each and every overground stop, of which there were many before the train went subterranean, an icy blast or a flurry of snow would precede the mass of humanity as they boarded. It seemed to take forever to get to and from work and the only highlight of my days in London was the occasional venture to a local public house for a pint or two at lunchtime. The days were long, but the work was interesting.

The department was commanded by a 2-star RAF officer who had a 1-star officer reporting directly to him. Dicky Duckett was responsible for all flying training in the RAF. In the absence of my wing commander in Dhahran, my immediate superior was Group Captain Martin Molloy, who was anointed with the title Deputy Director Training Operational(RAF). I had an office to myself and, in Nigel Huckins' absence, reported directly to DDTO(RAF). I also held the position of 'Aircraft Authority'[1] for all the FJ aircraft currently

---

1. At the time all military aircraft had a nominated desk officer within the MOD who was the 'authority' for all aspects of that aircraft type's operation.

in service, which included a number of single seat types such as the Hawk, Hunter, Harrier and Jaguar. Quite a coup for the first ever navigator to fill this pilot-centric post.

My remit was large and included, amongst other tasks, being the Training Authority for each of the Fast Jet OCUs in the RAF; Jaguar, Harrier, Phantom and the Buccaneer. Significantly for a navigator, I was also the Training Authority for all aspects of flying training on the Hawk T1 at RAF Valley and the Hunters at RAF Brawdy and RAF Chivenor. I was also tasked with being secretary to the Tri-national Tornado Steering Group, but, in the wing commander's absence, also had to fill the role of chairman of the group, which included officers from the equivalent departments in the Luftwaffe and the Italian Air Force.

During my arrival interview with Martin Molloy he pointed out the most pressing item in my in-tray. He emphasised that I needed to focus on it immediately and directly as it was high on the Air Force Board's list of matters of special interest! Nothing like being thrust in at the deep end then! The first draft of this staff project, known as 'Mirror Image', had already been circulated by my Boss before his departure and comments on that draft were coming in. They needed to be scrutinised and, if appropriate, incorporated into the second draft by me, which I would then circulate once more for further comment. 'Mirror Image' was, in effect, a money saving exercise that would streamline FJ flying training at Valley, Brawdy and Chivenor. In essence, the advanced flying training syllabus on the Hawk T1, and the weapons/tactics training carried out at the two Tactical Weapons Units were to be combined. Brawdy was to be closed whilst Valley and Chivenor would conduct a mirrored training syllabus. By so doing, Advanced Flying Training for pilots destined for fast jet aircraft would be smoothed and savings could be made in infrastructure, flying hours, airframes and manpower. The benefits perceived by the AFB were closer harmony between pure flying and tactical flying and earlier exposure of the students to the tactical atmosphere. Moreover, the 'Mirror Image' system would make it easier to monitor and provide better standardization. Of course, there were disadvantages. Not least of these, was convincing the dyed in the wool instructor pilots at the bases on the training front line. But, more importantly, with about twenty-five fewer training hours, students would have a slightly lower standard of airmanship and less opportunity to lead tactical formations in the latter stages of the syllabus than they had had previously.

From my own perspective it presented me with a conundrum as the 'author' of the staff paper. Having come from a pure operational background, my own view mirrored, no pun intended, that of the instructors at the front line. The status quo of AFT followed by TWU had worked immensely well for a significant number of years and had produced young pilots with levels of airmanship and a tactical awareness that could not be bettered. I had seen with my own eyes the excellent product that the TWUs had produced when I had flown with fresh-faced pilots on 237 OCU and I could not for the life of me see how reducing the flying hours and sharing the syllabi would improve on the high standard set.

It was, of course, my first real lesson in being a staff officer. One's own opinions did not matter and, if the AFB said it was going to happen, then the only solution was to write the paper to match their preconceived conclusions! Defending the paper across the wider RAF was extremely difficult, but defend it I did. The paper was eventually approved at a routine Air Force Board Meeting in Whitehall and 'Mirror Image' was implemented in 1992. Just three years later, after yet another Treasury enforced Spending Review, RAF Chivenor closed on 1 October 1995 and all advanced and tactical flying training in the RAF was settled at RAF Valley. The need for a 'Mirror Image' was no longer!

Work in support of the OCUs was minimal and required me, routinely, to only 'rubber stamp' proposed amendments to their syllabi. Work in support of the TTSG, however, took up a considerable amount of my time and regular visits to TTTE at Cottesmore were quite the norm. My first scheduled meeting with TTTE staff was on 17 January 1991. I drove north on the evening of the sixteenth to stay in the officers' mess, before a morning of discussions that would help form the agenda for the first TTSG meeting at which I would act as both chairman and secretary. As I headed north on the A1, at the forefront of my mind was the fact that the UN Mandate for Saddam Hussein to leave Kuwait had expired just twenty-four hours earlier. There was sombreness in the officers' mess bar that night at Cottesmore and, when it closed, we all left for bed wondering what, if any, action might have taken place by the time we awoke. The BBC television news left us in no doubt!

Thirty minutes before midnight, hundreds of aircraft had launched from their bases across Saudi Arabia, and the littoral states of the Persian Gulf, to conduct a succession of air attacks against targets in Iraq. H-Hour[2] had been declared as 0300 hrs. Amongst these raiders were some of my best friends from Brüggen flying in their GR1 Tornados. People like Jerry Gegg and Jerry Witts, both with 31 Squadron, were amongst the twelve crews that I had selected to be part of the first wave of aircrew deployed. Also amongst the first attackers were John Peters and John Nichol, from XV Squadron at Laarbruch, both of whom I had got to know on my last trip to Red Flag only a year previously. Both had been too inexperienced then to fly on the exercise, but clearly had now made the monumental leap from 'also rans' to 'war ready'. Unfortunately for the pair of them, their aircraft was hit by a SAM near the target and, having ejected, they were missing behind enemy lines.[3] It was all very surreal as we gathered in the dining room for breakfast that morning. I felt quite uncomfortable at the morning's news headlines. Here I was about to sit down with fellow airmen to discuss the policy matters that affected this large international operational training unit, whilst fellows I had only very recently been sharing a beer with in Germany were risking their lives for the people of Kuwait! Everything that we were about to do that day just seemed so trivial and inconsequential in comparison.

The first of my TTSG meetings in 1991 was held in Florence. As secretary it was my task to arrange the travel plans for the RAF contingent from MOD, HQSTC and Cottesmore that routinely attended. The meetings were also attended by a wing commander from the Tornado 'Engineering Authority'[4] at HQSTC who insisted on organising his own travel plans. So I left him to his own devices and sorted out the tickets for the rest of the team. He was not too impressed when he boarded the British Airways aircraft at Heathrow to see me, and my party, happily munching on peanuts and downing our first G&T sat in Club Class, whilst he struggled through the cabin to find his cramped seat in Economy. He was even less pleased when we arrived at Pisa Airport to discover that his bags were last off the plane and had been dropped in a deep puddle that had recently formed during a very hostile thunderstorm. He didn't speak any Italian, but he let the baggage handlers

---

2. The time of day at which an attack, landing, or other military operation is scheduled to begin.
3. They were eventually taken as POWs and, after some seriously harsh interrogation and ill-treatment at the hands of Saddam's psychopathic interrogators, were repatriated at the end of hostilities.
4. At the time all military aircraft had a nominated desk officer within the MOD structure who was the 'authority' for all aspects of that aircraft type's engineering.

in the arrivals hall have both barrels of his displeasure, before he then turned his irate attention on the poor young ItAF lieutenant, who had been ordered to the airport to escort us to our hotel. It was bad form by him and, with his black mood continuing well into the evening, it did not augur well for our meeting the next day.

I had been left a note by Nigel Huckins that encouraged me to write the minutes of the meeting before I left the UK and then, as Chairman, steer the meeting in the direction that would match the already scribed minutes! It was great advice. It had been decided when the TTSG was set up that, from the outset and as native English speakers, the Chairman and Secretary should always be TO2(RAF) and TO2a(RAF). As both Chairman and Secretary for the meeting in Florence it would certainly ease my workload if I took his advice to heart. Consequently, I had written the minutes in my office in London to match what had been agreed at our agenda discussions at Cottesmore in the middle of January. There was no dissent at the meeting, which allowed plenty of time for me to wrap it up and then explore the sights of Florence and the many museums and art galleries there. Particularly, I wanted to meet Michelangelo's David in the Accademia.

Florence is and was a vibrant and beautiful city and I loved every minute of the two days that I was there. I not only managed to meet David, but also squeezed through the crowds in the Uffizi Galleries too and sat by the Arno River supping yet another Italian beer. It was all over and complete too soon, but I vowed to return to this so-called birthplace of the Renaissance one day. It is without doubt one of the most beautiful cities on the planet.

With both the children away at boarding school, my wife had plenty of time on her hands in Bushey Heath and looked around for activities to fill her day. With Nigel Huckins having been a flight commander on 17 Squadron she knew his wife, Sara, well. They used to meet at either house or for lunch and we were routine guests at their OMQ in Uxbridge for lunch or supper, as likewise they were at ours. Angus, our errant Labrador, was a bit of a handful and it was not always a good idea to leave him at home on his own for fear that he would trash the place in our absence. Our problems in that regard were solved when we invested in a large kennel, the size of a small garden shed, which came with its own enclosed sunbathing area! We erected it behind the garage in the back garden and introduced our dog to it. He loved it and he was very happy to be left in it whilst we were out and, eventually, so accustomed was he to it that he slept in it overnight too. Even in the winter, encased like a hamster in its straw, he would emerge in the morning surrounded by a warm mist of happiness from a great night's sleep. What the kennel gave us in peace of mind with regard to the preservation of the décor in the married quarter, was supplemented by the freedom that it gave my wife whilst I was either away from home or working in London. Rather too much freedom as it turned out! She had an affair! I tried to patch things up, bought a house in Stamford so that she could be closer to our children and we tried to rebuild, but it did not work.

Whilst my marriage and family life had taken a dive my career had definitely not. One July morning, Nigel Huckins, now back from the Middle East, informed me that the air commodore wished to see me at 1000hrs. Wondering why, I trooped along to his outer office, made my number with his PA and waited to be ushered into the inner sanctum. Sat behind his desk he greeted me with a broad smile and handed me a letter in an envelope stamped top and bottom 'Personal and In Confidence'. I read the opening sentence which informed me that I had been selected provisionally to attend No. 84 Advanced Staff Course that started on 17 February 1992.

I had done it. I had sneaked up on the inside rail and crossed the finishing line before my forty-third birthday! After almost thirteen years as a flight lieutenant, but only four so far as a squadron leader, I had beaten the odds and opened the door to the higher ranks of the RAF. There was a catch in this letter of offer, however. With an Optional Retirement Date of 26 May 1993, agreed when I was last promoted, I could not attend the course unless I signed and returned the 'Statement of Intention' that would commit me to further service on the Active List to amortize the training course. It was a no brainer. Back the form went by return of post. As the end of the year approached it became self-evident that my marriage was over and I left the family home and moved early to a quarter at RAF Bracknell in preparation for ASC.

By now I was running the TO2 office again on my own. Nigel Huckins had arrived back from the Gulf in April and had taken over the reins again. I stepped down to my own desk but, by November, he had been posted and not yet replaced, so back into the role of TO2(RAF) I went and back came the Substitution Pay for the last three months of my fourteen month tour in Adastral House. My commute now was from Bracknell to Waterloo daily. The RAF was very understanding, accommodating and supportive in assisting me with my fluctuating circumstances in 1991. The administrative personnel at RAF Uxbridge bent over backwards to assist me with my changing arrangements. Moreover, my chain of command supported me royally and, although the separation put me under a great deal of strain, I was commended for not allowing it to distract me from my duties.

I left Adastral House for the last time on 14 February 1992. As was usual in London, I was 'dined out' in a pub at lunchtime and, along with a few mates, went on a pub crawl afterwards. As the numbers began to dwindle as people drifted off home, I went for one last pint with Paul Beard, who held the post of TF2a(RAF) – the flying training desk equivalent to my operational training one – before he bundled me into a cab and pointed me at Waterloo Station.

'Where to, mate?'

'Casper's Telephone Exchange!' I blurted out and before I knew it the taxi was heading away from its planned southerly track and pointing west along Oxford Street. I have no idea where the request for 'Casper's Telephone Exchange' came from within my beer addled brain. However, I do remember that someone had once told me that it was a great place to be in London on a Friday night. Sitting in the back of that taxi, on that Friday night, having had a 'beer full of belly', as my old mate Barrie Chown had once drunkenly described his status, I must have clearly been looking for a great place to be. Deposited outside in the dark I meandered drunkenly towards the entrance of the bar and was ushered through the door by a large, but very unassuming doorman. I had no doubt that unassertive as he was upon my entry, that would not be the case for anybody who did not behave themselves once inside. The bar was situated downstairs in the cellar of a large building off Hanover Square. Opened in 1988, it was modelled on the German cabaret phone bars of the 1930s. At the foot of the stairs I was met by a smiling maître d' who, upon my indication that I was on my own, ushered me towards a table against a dark wall towards the back of the room. As I waited for my G&T to arrive I cast my weary eyes around the capacious bar with its table loads of giggling women or raucous men. They were all clearly 'city slickers' and, given the large numbers of cocktails and champagne bottles passing from waiter to guest, I had no doubt that they all had plenty of disposable income! Animated conversations were taking place on telephones that were set at each table. Flitting eyes jumped from table to table as each woman, or man, tried to identify just who in the room was on the end of the line and flirting with them. I suppose, if sighted, they would also consider whether the conversation was worth continuing!

I sat nursing my G&T and watched the developing romances with interest, but in total silence – my telephone never rang. I ordered another G&T and continued to wait in hope – nothing! Eventually disillusioned, I called over a waiter, settled my bill and prepared to leave. As he returned my coat I looked at the table to make sure that I had left nothing behind and realised just why I had been sat there in vain – there was no phone! The very astute and welcoming maître d' must have realised that I was already too drunk to participate in the fun and games, and had allocated me the only table in the place without a means of communicating with any of the beautiful women in the bar! Ah well, as they say in France, '*c'est la vie!*' Arriving back at Bracknell, two hours later than intended, I was met by the very excited face of my new best friend who was beaming at me from his kennel now relocated in the garden at 3 Birch Close.

In the bag, in those fourteen months in Adastral House, were two ACRs, each of which supported the earlier view from Brüggen that I was worthy of a high recommendation for promotion. All three were of the opinion that I would, with my strong organisational skills, apparently, make a sound Personal Staff Officer! What me! PSO material! Whatever had happened to the young lad who, at the end of his first tour, was not suitable for even ADC duties!

Chapter Seven

Three Singles to Edmonton Please!

Number 84 Advanced Staff Course commenced on 17 February 1992 and was scheduled to last just over ten months. It was planned to conclude on 4 December and, for me, the almost ten months would include one more task above that prescribed in the syllabus! I would have to spend some time with my solicitor in Stamford sorting out my divorce.

The aim of the ASC was to prepare selected RAF and civilian officers for senior positions by developing their analytical, decision-making and communication skills through the study of military, defence, political and international affairs. By the time of my arrival as a student, Bracknell had been the home of the RAF Staff College since 1945. It had a reputation across the officer corps of the RAF as a necessary evil that had to be engaged with at various points in one's career. Indeed, I had spent a month at Bracknell on the BSC in 1990. I had enjoyed that course immensely and particularly so as, from the outset, our syndicate agreed and issued a mandate amongst ourselves that we all had to be in the bar at 2100hrs no matter how well we were prepared for the next day's tasks! The ASC, I imagined, would be very much the same, but just over a longer period of time.

I had also frequented Bracknell fairly regularly much earlier in my career, as I struggled to commit to the ISS course. Far too often, I had been summoned to the place to undergo remedial training, be sanctioned for my failure to produce robust solutions or argue against why I was being removed from the course yet again! So I had mixed feelings about the place, but had heard wonderful tales of 'a year off' and 'fantastic visits' to various parts of the UK, Europe and the USA. Visits which were all deemed to be part of the learning process that would groom us for stardom in our chosen careers. At the age of forty-three I was not sure about being groomed for stardom, but I did figure that success on the course would help to push me a bit further up the ladder.

The first morning coffee break was held in a large lounge area that was draped with an amazing collection of flags of various nations. It produced a cavalcade of colourful uniforms, many of which I had never seen before. As well as a few 'cross-fertilisation' students from the Royal Navy and the

British Army, there were students from Australia, Bahrain, Canada, Chile, Egypt, France, Germany, India, Jordan, Malaysia, Nigeria, Norway, Oman, Pakistan, Qatar, Singapore, South Korea, Spain, Switzerland, Turkey, the United Arab Emirates and the United States of America. There was even a Saudi Arabian prince! We were definitely a very eclectic bunch and we were all ready to play a full part in the proceedings.

The college was commanded by Air Vice-Marshal Bob Peters who, it was rumoured, possessed an extremely light touch. His two sidekicks were Air Commodore Dick Gould and Group Captain Dave Baugh. Gould and Baugh had spent rather too long together on Shackletons and Nimrods in their previous RAF careers and had brought the 'kipper fleet'[1] attitude with them to Bracknell – they seemed to be rarely out of the bar! I knew I would fit right in!

With Bob Peters, Dick Gould and Dave Baugh at the helm I found the course to be of immense value, hard work, but, most of all, highly entertaining! As a born again bachelor I had no ties at home other than when I had a commitment to Christopher and Sarah either at exeat weekends, school activities in Stamford, or their regular holidays. Indeed, the only course activity that I missed, because of a visit to my solicitor, was a day at Royal Ascot, which was programmed into the syllabus. In true RAF tradition, Wednesday afternoons were designated as sports afternoons and I quite often went with colleagues to play golf on the West Course at Wentworth, where some students had taken out privileged membership at a special cheaper rate for the Staff College.

The syllabus was well structured and, as well as the ten- or twenty-minute talks that each student had to prepare and give, there were numerous written tasks, papers to write, syndicate discussions to be led and participated in, plus table top exercises in military strategic planning. Everything was designed to broaden and educate the military mind. Days were spent either hosting or visiting our two sister staff colleges, at Greenwich for the Royal Navy, or Camberley for the British Army, to conduct bilateral planning exercises. Esteemed politicians would visit to give us a political understanding of the world in which we lived. These lectures were supplemented with the great and the good of the RAF, who put their military spin on the political message already received. Students were encouraged to ask deep and meaningful

---

1. The maritime element of the RAF.

questions during the post-lecture Q&A sessions and it soon became apparent that the same guys would stand on their feet and ask their question with no other intent than to get themselves noticed! Unless it was meaningful, I never did, but then I was never one to push myself forward in such a manner. I was more content to bide my time, listen intently and, if I thought an individual speaker was bullshitting, raise my hand to delve deeper into just why he thought his statement was both sound and satisfactory.

Each student had to produce a well-researched and well-written Service Paper, known as the 'Brooke-Popham',[2] by the end of the course. Without a satisfactory result in the 'BP', graduation was very unlikely. It focused everybody's attention right from the outset. Students were left to choose their subject, and the comprehensive library at the college allowed plenty of scope to find all the detail required for whatever one decided to be suitable. The subject had to be cleared by one's syndicate director and, subsequently, so did your scoping paper. As a fast-jet man through and through and with my mates having been fully engaged, and some captured, in a war in Iraq, I knew that there was one aspect of military operations that the MOD lacked. For years the RAF had provided yellow Search and Rescue helicopters at various locations around the British coastline. This military force had been established during the Second World War to rescue airmen downed in the English Channel or North Sea. In peacetime it had become a force for good across the United Kingdom and in some of its overseas territories. However, in 1992, there was no force designed, equipped, trained and able to conduct SAR under combat conditions. The MOD had given it thought, but never actually found the time, energy, resources or funding to actually spend the effort in writing a paper that might convince politicians, let alone anybody else, that there was a definite need for a Combat SAR capability.

During Operation Granby, British servicemen put their faith in American CSAR resources to pluck downed aircrew or trapped troops from behind enemy lines. It worked to an extent, but it was not ideal and USAF resources were such that priorities had to be made and all too often British personnel were not at the top of the list. I researched my topic in the library and visited the office in MOD that was charged with being the operational authority and policy makers for the SAR fleet of helicopters. They were extremely grateful that somebody had realised the necessity and encouraged and supported me

---

2. Named after Air Chief Marshal Sir Henry Brooke-Popham.

throughout my planning, writing and reviewing of the paper. In addition to writing our BPs we also had to present it with full supporting slide show to the assembled course, and all of the Directing Staff, in the Brooke-Popham Lecture Hall at some point during the second term.

Socially the course was excellent. Street parties, dinner engagements, hosting lunches in the officers' mess, cocktail parties, garden parties and much, much more. As a 'bachelor', I got invited out all the time as the good wives of some of the students wanted to make sure that I was eating well. I was eating well and drinking well too as it happens! I had fallen in with a fellow 'bachelor' who had been seconded to the course by the US Navy. Lloyd Bohn had spent his flying career in the USN as a navigator on P-3 Orions. He was from the USN's 'kipper fleet' and fell in with the Gould/Baugh combo well. He spoke their language and understood their tactics both in the classroom and in the Scruff's Bar! Lloyd, however, was not strictly a 'bachelor' – he had just decided to leave his wife and family in the USA whilst he undertook the course. He behaved like one, however, and we were frequently to be found in the Horse and Groom, on Bagshot Road, long after we should have been back in our respective homes studying for the next morning! It was all good innocent fun and with Gould and Baugh leading from the front we felt invulnerable – almost!

The syllabus required the whole student body to conduct three tours to military and industrial establishments in the UK, Europe and the United States of America. In turn, and for obvious reasons, they were described as the UK, Europe and US Tours. With a tour came responsibility and every tour required a number of privately hired coaches to get the mass of students to wherever they were going. Whether that was the short hop to Camberley or a longer haul to a location in Yorkshire, Motts coach company would roll up to the college at the appointed hour and we would all troop aboard our allocated coach and settle down whilst the 'Bus Mother' called out everybody's name.

Yes! You read that right! The Bus Mother! That's what the responsible student was entitled! The Bus Mother. No matter the title it was a necessary function, as a group of officers let loose without a corporal to manage them properly can be a scary sight! We each took our turn at being Bus Mother and woe betide the individual if he got any aspect of his duty wrong or screwed up totally! Woe betide anybody who was not on the bus, sat in his seat and ready to roll at the appointed hour either. The management took no prisoners and if you were late you were late. Latecomers had to catch the coach up at the next venue by whatever means possible and at their own expense! It happened once on 84 Course's European Tour! Each syndicate travelled together and each syndicate was allowed to bid for available destinations on the UK tour. The European and USA Tour destinations were prescribed.

The UK Tour included such career-enhancing excitements as the Permanent Joint Headquarters at Northwood, the School of Fighter Control at RAF Boulmer and Portsmouth Naval Dockyard. From an industrial perspective a visit to a coal mine, with the opportunity to go underground, was high on some peoples' agendas. Locations were grouped into itineraries comprising two military and one industrial destination that were geographically proximate.

Having perused the itinerary list, my syndicate took a far more pragmatic view. We opted for Cornwall via Reading and Redruth and the Great Western Railway. Our first destination was RNAS Culdrose. Of all the itineraries, Cornwall was the furthest from home; of all the itineraries, Cornwall required First Class rail travel; of all the itineraries, Cornwall allowed the most time to drink whilst travelling!

We were not sober when we got off the train. The subsequent twenty mile coach journey to the Culdrose Wardroom[3] was not sufficient time to clear our heads before we arrived! We were met by the Wardroom PMC who welcomed us heartily. The train had been delayed so we were too late for the planned pre-dinner drinks, but he invited us to quickly deposit our bags in our rooms and head for the dining room where the tables were set for a rather more formal setting than we had anticipated! A quick 'aircrew shower'[4] and we were ready for the next phase of our adventure in the far west of England. Our hosts, who had all been to pre-dinner drinks, were quite surprised that their guests were more pissed than they were!

The next morning, whilst nursing mild hangovers, we endured a tour of the station and listened, as intently as we were able, to the briefings being given by over-enthusiastic, or so it seemed to our dulled brains, Royal Naval personnel. Thankfully, I had not volunteered to go flying in a Sea King! Visit over we jumped back on the coach and headed east for our next venue at the Royal Marine Commando Training Centre at Lympstone. A quieter night was had by all before a very relaxed visit the following morning to watch

---

3. Naval officers' mess.
4. A quick spray of deodorant.

young trainee marines going through their paces. The last port of call on our Western excursion was to a rubber manufacturer in Melksham, a town more famous for its Wadworth beer than its rubber, but by then we had had enough alcohol to last us a lifetime.

The European Tour took in the usual haunts of NATO HQ in Brussels and SHAPE at Mons, before we headed further east to meet up with the Army and Navy Staff Courses at Sennelager in Germany for a firepower demonstration. The journey was long and tedious by coach, but with characteristic aircrew initiative I encouraged our syndicate to host a champagne breakfast on board our coach for all of the thirty or so travellers on the morning of our departure from Bracknell. We purchased all the necessary ingredients and provided such delights as smoked salmon and caviar canapés all of which were washed down by ample quantities of the NAAFI's best champagne! We were in a very happy mood by the time the coach boarded the ferry at Dover! The visits were all great value and they enhanced my knowledge of the way NATO works, which I found most useful later in my career. At Sennelager Training Area the Army put on a great demonstration of their military firepower, but the weather was foul. Unfortunately, the weather precluded the RAF Harriers from releasing their live ordnance on their designated target, but they flew through the range on time even if they never managed to get below the thick cloud.

Back at Bracknell, our mid-course leave period was fast approaching at the beginning of July. For the first time in my RAF career, I knew I had a guaranteed fortnight off that would not be cancelled, so I had a plan to take Christopher and Sarah to Canada to stay with my very good friends, the Gaults, who lived in Alberta. Also, for the first time in my RAF career, I put my faith in the RAF Indulgence Scheme that would, if seats were available, get us across the Atlantic and into Alberta for next to nothing. The problem I had was convincing two mid-teens that getting a call twenty-four hours before our planned departure that would confirm our seats was a sensible method of going about arranging a holiday! Chris was quite laid back about the whole affair, Sarah was less so! True to their word, however, the telephone from the RAF Brize Norton Movements Cell came and, twenty-four hours later, we were sat on a Royal Air Force Tristar heading west across the Atlantic bound for Calgary, which was the first stop on its round robin tour of North America, dropping off and picking up passengers and freight as it went.

It was about 0300hrs, body clock time, when we rolled into Calgary International Airport Arrivals Hall. I was completely banjaxed! I collected the large suitcases and holdalls that my two offspring had insisted were essential for their fortnight in Canada, scooped them up from their slumbered state and dragged them through immigration! We must have looked bewildered as I suddenly woke from my trance to hear the words, 'Can I help you, sir, you look lost?' I looked towards the kindly face that I assumed had uttered these words, and remembered that Mike Gault had told us to catch the air bus to Edmonton and he would collect us when we got there.

'Can you point me at the air bus to Edmonton,' I mumbled, and was just alert enough to thank him when he directed me towards Gate 17. Odd, I thought, as I encouraged my two zombie-like offspring forward. I had not anticipated being given a gate to get on a bus for a one hundred and sixty mile road trip! But hey, these Canadians speak a different language so I decided to just go with the flow. At Gate 17, I asked another kindly face if I was at the right place for the air bus to Edmonton and was assured so. Now seriously tired, I listened as he pointed me towards a ticket desk behind me.

'Three singles to Edmonton please.' I asked the portly lady behind the glass window and was somewhat surprised when she requested two hundred and fifty Canadian dollars for the privilege. That was not far short of one hundred and twenty-five pounds in Her Majesty's money and more than I had bargained for in my holiday budget for four hours on a bus. I duly paid and walked with my two kids through the body scanner at Gate 17.

Hang on a minute! We just walked through a body scanner to get on a coach! Wait a minute! What have I just done!

'Excuse me, sir,' I asked of the first kindly face I met through security, 'Am I just about to get on an aeroplane?'

'Sure are, sir,' he drawled back at me, 'Boeing Seven Thirty-Seven, sir. The next scheduled "Air Bus" to Edmonton International Airport!'

Bugger! I had just paid through the nose, unnecessarily, for three seats on a forty-minute hop north. I must admit that at one point in this fiasco the thought that it must be a bloody luxurious coach had crossed my mind, but... you only live once, so what the heck! I would not get caught out like that again! I vowed quietly to myself that it would be a four-hour bus ride back to Calgary when the day came!

We spent two fantastic weeks in Drayton Valley with Mike and Siobhan who were incredible hosts. All the children enjoyed time in the pool and days out at Jasper, in The Rockies, a picnic lunch by Lake Louise, BBQs galore, visits to the West Edmonton Mall and experiencing its 'Drop of Doom', in its indoor theme park, and canoeing on the Pembina River. However, all too soon it was time to pack our bags, ready for the phone call informing us that we had seats on a returning Tristar. I had been ever so slightly frantic that the call would never come and constantly needed reassurance from the RAF Movements Officer at Calgary that 'we've never left anybody behind, sir' was an actual fact that I could rely on!

The call did come and we did get on the aircraft back to the UK, but that in itself was another true Herriot saga! A few days before our due departure, whilst I was working out timings to catch the coach to Calgary, Mike came home from work and told me that one of his children's teachers at school had offered to fly us from Drayton Valley airstrip to Calgary International. The chap was building up his Private Pilot's Licence hours and a three-hour round trip to Calgary would certainly assist. He was happy to pay for the fuel if I would be good enough to pay for the hire of the aircraft. I was hesitant! In fact, I was extremely disinclined. Having spent all my flying career surviving with professionals, I was averse to putting my life, and the lives of my two children, in the hands of a recently qualified amateur! The kids, however, thought it a great idea and, after a considerable amount of persuasion, I relented. The cost to hire a Cessna 172 was, and you guessed it, two hundred and fifty Canadian dollars!

Early on the appointed day, the whole cast assembled at the small airstrip just north of Drayton Valley. Mike, Siobhan and their five kids, Anna, Monica, my goddaughter Caroline and her twin brother David and baby Ian, plus the three of us and the pilot. I looked at the Cessna and then turned my attention to our pile of cases! You know that expression 'three into two doesn't go'! Well that's what I thought as I looked at the seat in the back. Two strapping teenagers and one very small bench seat! We stuffed as many of the cases as we could into the hold at the rear and slammed the door shut, leaning forcibly against it until the last snap fastener was secure. There was one large blue holdall left on the tarmac! I looked inside again and came up with the only solution possible.

With Chris and Sarah strapped tightly in the rear, I plonked the holdall on their lap, strapped myself into the right-hand front seat and closed the door flap under the high wing. I looked across at the fresh-faced young pilot beside me and pondered what my soon to be ex-wife would say if all this went horribly wrong! With the Gaults waving us fondly off, we taxied out for take-off. There was no ATC service. This was pure see and be seen flying!

My last thought as we taxied on to the runway was, 'I wonder if he has done any Centre of Gravity calculations'!

It was a beautifully clear Albertan summer's day as we lifted off Runway 14 and turned south for Calgary. In the climb our young pilot turned to me and, in an inquiring tone, asked me if Mike had been telling him the truth when he had told him that I was a Tornado navigator. I answered in the affirmative and, with that, he handed me a large topographical chart upon which he had scratched a line that would take us directly to Calgary International. Oh well! Navigating was my bread and butter and it would occupy the next hour as we trundled south at 2,000 feet and 120 knots. It was easy. With the visibility being curvature of the earth that day, all I had to do was keep The Rockies on our right and the vast Albertan wheat fields to our left and the city of Calgary would eventually pitch up on the nose after just over an hour. It was time for idle conversation.

'Ever flown into Calgary International before?' I asked our intrepid aviator.

'No never!' he replied candidly. Now that sent an alarm bell ringing somewhere in my head. I didn't dare look at either of the children.

'Ah. OK,' I replied, 'Do you have an en-route supplement or a Terminal Approach Chart, perhaps?' I was now slightly apprehensive. I had only ever seen Calgary from the passenger window of a wide-body jet, but I anticipated that it probably was quite a busy place with quite a lot of aircraft movements and maybe more than one runway! I expected also that, unlike our departure airfield, we would probably have to talk to somebody on the ground before we landed! Following his instruction, I rummaged around in his 'pilot sack' and pulled out the necessary TAP for the airport. Yep! Three runways! Two parallel ones, bearing roughly north/south, and a much shorter one that ran approximately north-west/south-east. I studied the chart closely and worked out where the various reporting points were. It was a start and we were now better prepared than we had been five minutes before.

As the skyscrapers of Downtown Calgary began to come into focus, I suggested to my man that now would be a good time to give Calgary Approach a call on their VHF channel. His radio transmission was met with an immediate and very professional response. I responded and informed the Approach Controller that we were approaching the Control Zone from the north at 2,000 feet for a visual approach with 'Information Mike'.[5] He

_____

5. Large international and military airports provide a broadcast service to arriving aircraft that gives aircrew all the information that they need to prepare for an approach and landing. It is alphabetically denoted to indicate the latest updates.

responded by asking me to report overhead the OTMAG reporting point at 1,500 ft. We had just passed it so, as we maintained our southerly track, I advised him accordingly as we continued our descent to the requested height. As we passed north-west of the airfield, the Approach Controller asked that we confirm that we were visual with the airport and told us to change to the Tower frequency and to expedite our landing on Runway 26.

I checked in with the local controller who cleared us to fly a left-hand downwind leg to Runway 35 Left at 1,000 feet, but to confirm that we understood that we would be landing on Runway 26. I checked that my boy pilot had understood what was required and responded accordingly. It was all going exceedingly well, despite his inexperience and my unfamiliarity with my surroundings. Quite suddenly, the man on the ground asked us to expedite our landing. The Cessna was already flat out at 140 knots and we were doing our best to get the thing on the ground as quickly as possible anyway. Again, 'Expedite your landing!' But this time the call came with a qualifying statement. 'I have a Boeing 747 on Finals to Runway 35 Left!' And then that was followed with an exasperated, 'Are you visual the 747?' We had just turned onto east to head for long finals for Runway 26 in order to set ourselves up for landing and were firmly sat at 140 knots cutting across the Approach to the left hand of the two northerly runways. I looked right and saw what can only be described as a huge behemoth of an aircraft bearing down on us! I tapped our unwary pilot on his shoulder, pointed to my right and grabbed the instrument console as he instantly squeezed the throttle further forward and pushed the column violently downwards to drop the nose and take us clear of the Jumbo's flightpath. We landed uneventfully, if somewhat disorganised, taxied into a light aircraft parking area and shut down. With our bags loaded into a large airfield wagon, we waved goodbye to the pilot and headed off to the International Terminal, while he refuelled and headed outbound back to Drayton Valley.

Our Tristar, we discovered, was jam packed full of troops being returned to Hannover following a battlefield exercise on the Suffield Training Area. There was not a spare seat on-board and the indulgees, of which we were three of many, had not yet been allocated seats! We all sat in the departure gate whilst negotiations took place behind our backs. What, I wondered, of the Movements Officer's famous quote now! Was this night of all nights going to break his record of 'we've never left anybody behind, sir'? We waited and we waited and then the decision was announced! The captain of the Tristar had decided to offload fuel rather than leave any indulgee passengers behind. It would mean that we would be late departing and it would mean that he would have to land at Keflavik, in Iceland, in the wee small hours to refuel, but at least the Movements Officer's claim was intact for a while longer. We were not unduly perturbed by the detour, we were just glad to be on our way home and not stranded in Canada. It was a great two-week holiday. The Transatlantic legs had cost me, in total, only thirty pounds each way. Thanks to my somnolent lethargy and my devotion, and eventual capitulation, to my two kids the biggest hole in my pocket had been the five hundred dollar return fare from Calgary to Edmonton!

My divorce was proceeding well and with little friction, other than both our solicitors' attempts to ensure otherwise and prolong the process for their own personal gain! My wife had given 'Care and Control' of our two children to me and had agreed that the best way forward was for the children to remain at Stamford for their schooling. I was guaranteed to be allocated a married quarter and she acknowledged that she could only provide a roof over their heads for short bursts during the school holidays, when she would take them to her parents' house. With everything seemingly settled, I was able to concentrate on Term Two of the ASC whilst the final divorce papers were assembled and exchanged and prepared for court by our two advocates.

Term Two featured more integration with our Army and Navy equivalents. Jointery[6] was the military term for what we now embarked on and regular Joint Warfare exercises were conducted to test and compare theories. The ultimate aim of these desk top exercises was to better understand the minds of our ground-loving or seafaring brothers in arms such that, together in war, we would be able to produce coherent plans that took into account the needs and services of each. For the second term, I was fortunate to have an army lieutenant colonel as my syndicate DS. David James was an infantryman from the Royal Regiment of Fusiliers and a more down to earth soldier I do not think I have ever met. He was a perfect fit in the RAF Staff College. The lieutenant colonel I met on an exercise at Camberley was, however, a completely different kettle of fish!

This Grenadier Guardsman adopted a completely different attitude to David James and took the lead when his syndicate hosted my syndicate, at

---

6. Joint warfare is a military doctrine which places priority on the integration of the various Service branches of a state's armed forces into one unified command.

Camberley, for a morning's paper exercise. The task was a relatively simple one. The joint syndicate had to come up with an agreed tactical plan for a situation that required the RAF to provide CAS for troops in contact with the enemy. Close Air Support was bread and butter to me, and since I was the only FJ man in the room, it was natural for me to assume the lead. The plan worked by my team and agreed by our Army chums was a good one, which at the end of the exercise I briefed to the two syndicates and our DS. The Guardsman was not happy. He did not like the plan and he did not like the manner in which the RAF was planning to support the troops in contact. I disagreed with him. Having done CAS in both the Buccaneer and the Tornado on many an occasion I knew the principles, I knew the theory and I knew the practice. I also knew the capabilities and limitations of the aircraft given to us to execute the plan. As a QWI I knew the weapons effects and delivery parameters better than anybody else in the room. The 'Colonel'[7] thought he knew better and told me so. I disagreed, but I was polite and did not once forget that he was one rank higher than me.

The following afternoon David James summoned me into his office at Bracknell.

'David,' he said in a questioning tone, 'do you realise that you upset the Colonel yesterday?'

'Did I? If I did I am sorry, but I only disagreed with him because his solution for the CAS plan would not have worked. I was polite throughout and always called him Sir when appropriate.'

'I know,' he responded, 'but what you do not realise is that the Army is not like the Air Force. In the Army the jump from junior officer to senior officer is between major and lieutenant colonel, whereas in the RAF it's between flight lieutenant and squadron leader.'

I knew that, but I let him go on.

'In the Army regimental system, nobody disagrees with a senior officer and Colonel Tom did not appreciate you disagreeing with him yesterday!'

'Really! So if a senior Army officer says black when it's actually white, everybody below him has to agree it's black!'

'Yes, in a nutshell, that about sums it up!'

---

7. The Army has a habit of addressing all lieutenant colonels as colonels and address them thence by their first name. It can throw confusion into a mufti-attired group who are then unable to differentiate between a half colonel and a full colonel. A feeble attempt to inflate their status and very public school boyish, in my opinion!

I was absolutely floored by that revelation. If you think about it for no longer than thirty seconds, it pretty much sums up the reason why so many young men lost their lives 'going over the top' in World War One. Orders issued by a crusty old brigadier, sat comfortably in a French chateau, who refused point blank to listen to a major who was trying to tell him that the ordered assault on an unassailable enemy position was futile. And what for? Just to advance one hundred yards to take a patch of tree-denuded mud in No Man's Land and make the brigadier feel better for the day! I kid you not!

The final exercise of the ASC was entitled Exercise Clueless! This was the course review that took place in the Brooke-Popham theatre immediately after the graduation dining-out night. It was scheduled for 3 December 1992 and it needed a couple of like-minded souls to pull it all together. Trish Heaton and I stepped up to the plate and began the process of finding willing thespians to participate, script writers to assist with comedy sketches, acts that could sing, dance, juggle, or do a multitude of other skills, scene shifters, lighting experts, scene makers, a stage manager and last, but not least, a director. In September we composed a suitably entertaining and compelling letter to our fellow students and were quite surprised when we were inundated with volunteers!

There were still four months of the course to complete, however, and that included a tri-Service dinner in the Painted Hall[8] of the Royal Naval College at Greenwich and the tour of the USA. On the afternoon of Friday, 24 July, vehicles from Mr Mott's impressive omnibus fleet arrived to convey the entire student body and all the DS, from commandant down, across London to Greenwich. The same action took place at Camberley, but theirs were military coaches rather than the luxury coaches provided for the RAF. Also unlike the RAF, their coaches drove them directly around the M25 to east London, whereas ours deposited us at Lambeth Pier on the Thames where two river buses had been chartered to convey us sedately downstream. The seven or so mile journey took just about an hour and, by the time we arrived at Greenwich Pier, we had already completed and enjoyed our pre-pre-dinner drinks! Our Navy hosts met us and after a quick pee break in the 'heads'[9]

---

8. Recognised as the greatest piece of decorative painting in England and described as 'the Sistine Chapel of the UK'. Designed by Sir Christopher Wren and Nicholas Hawksmoor, it was originally intended as a dining hall for the naval pensioners who lived at the Royal Hospital for Seamen. The walls and ceiling were painted by Sir James Thornhill in two major phases between 1708 and 1727.

9. The 'head' aboard a Navy ship is the bathroom. The term comes from the days of sailing ships when the place for the crew to relieve themselves was all the way forward on either side of the bowsprit, the integral part of the hull to which the figurehead was fastened; the ship's head.

we headed for the official preprandial drinks. The setting for the dinner was just amazing. The vast vaulted ceiling, with Thornhill's symbolism of subjects as diverse as the monarchy, religion, maritime power, navigation and trade, was just eye-wateringly beautiful. The great and the good of all three Armed Services were sat at the top table, including Field Marshal Sir Richard Vincent, Chief of the Defence Staff, whose son was a student on the Camberley course at the time, and Richard Mottram,[10] one of the highest ranking civil servants within the MOD. It was a cracking evening, which ended with a resounding singsong of sea shanties led by a Royal Marine Band who had played incidental music throughout. After dinner we assembled in the bar for a few more beers before the coaches arrived to take us back to Bracknell. Memorable! Quite memorable!

The RAF VC10 touched down at Dulles Airport just outside Washington DC and disgorged its happy, if somewhat tired, band of students and staff from 84 ASC. For once we were sober, as the RAF does not serve alcohol on board its flights! Eventually through USA immigration, coaches transported us east towards Alexandria where we were booked into the Embassy Suites in Crystal City, which was a stone's throw from the Pentagon where our next planned visit would take us the following morning. That evening, after the obligatory Embassy Suites Happy Hour, we headed out to find somewhere to eat. There were about eight of us in our group, so keeping a firm hold on them all was a tad difficult as we wandered past Chinese, Indian and Thai restaurants looking for the perfect place to feast. Lloyd Bohn, who knew the area well, had been put in charge. We passed restaurant after restaurant before we eventually turned onto 23rd Street and stopped outside number 422; the Crystal City Restaurant. Now the speciality at the Crystal City Restaurant was, and still is today Google tells me, not its food, but its girls! This was a strip joint that served pretty reasonable steaks too but, and I have to admit, it was difficult to concentrate on the food with all that naked flesh around. However, it was not as indecent as it might appear, as this was America after all! In few states in America are the girls permitted by law to go the 'whole hog'. No, this was Alexandria in Virginia and here the girls

---

10. Later Sir Richard Mottram, but at the time he was Deputy Secretary in the MOD with responsibilities for UK defence policy and strategy, and defence relations with other countries at the time of the end of the Cold War. He was the architect of the 'Options for Change' Defence Review.

were not permitted to remove their bikini bottoms and had to have 'patches' covering their nipples. Anyway, having given Lloyd the lead the only thing we could do was follow him through the door and seek a table for eight! As it happened, we were rather too early in the evening for the Crystal City's highlight acts and so, having eaten our steaks and watched the immoderate entertainment, we paid up and left hoping to find solace in a better bar closer to the hotel. Having supped our full and put, we hoped, our jet lag to bed we wandered back to the hotel at about 0200hrs! As we approached the Suites it became apparent that some form of drama had unfolded in our absence. All the hotel guests were stood outside, mostly in pyjamas and dressing gowns, having responded to a fire alarm that had gone off some minutes beforehand. Eyeing up the spectacle before us, we sauntered past, ignoring calls from our mates to join them, and headed next door to another hotel where we enjoyed a few more beers on their roof terrace garden whilst the Alexandria Fire Department's officers cleared the building next door of any signs of fire. There were none, it had been a false alarm!

After a day of Pentagon briefings, we headed south-east to the USMC base at Quantico and thence to a hotel in the Hamptons, ready for visits to HQ SACLANT and NAS *Oceana* where our tour ended at Happy Hour! It was all extremely worthwhile. Our course had moved on from jointery to Combined Operations[11] and by receiving briefings from the SACLANT staff we not only understood more about NATO, but also appreciated the imperatives of putting together a combined/joint operations plan. As well as having to endure a mass of lectures on the tour we had the delight of a guided tour around the USS *Polk*, a ballistic missile-carrying nuclear submarine, and being briefed in the cabin of a Grumman E-2D Hawkeye[12] on its roles and missions. So it wasn't all about drinking and partying, it had a lot to do with learning as well. After a few beers at the Oceana Happy Hour we climbed on board yet another RAF VC10 for an overnight flight back to Brize Norton.

By the time we reassembled at Bracknell our end of course postings had been announced. I was just pleased to have got through the course. Having watched the much younger 'thrusters' on the course, I was well aware that my career would have a limitation on just how far I might climb. I was already forty-three and imagined now that group captain or maybe air commodore

---

11. An operation conducted by forces of two or more Allied nations acting together for the accomplishment of a single mission.
12. An American all-weather, carrier-capable tactical airborne early warning aircraft.

would be my maximum. But I would have to stick at it, get promoted quickly and, and this was a very big and, get either a squadron commander or OC Operations Wing slot before too long. I got none of that out of Staff College! I was posted to the Central Tactics and Trials Organisation at Boscombe Down, in January 1993, to lead a small team in a study to revise QWI training across all the FJ fleets.

But first there was a Brooke-Popham essay to complete, a Review to organise, a Dining-In Night to enjoy and a quarter to pack, clean and hand back ready for the next course that followed in our wake. There was also a divorce to finalise.

As the end of the course approached, we once again travelled by Motts coaches to Camberley for what was probably the most eye-opening part of the syllabus. All three Services combined, in what was quaintly and colloquially described at Camberley as the 'Great Red Bedroom'[13] for three days of lectures under the banner 'The Realities of War'. It was enthralling stuff. Officers and other ranks from all four Services were rolled onto the stage to relate their first-hand accounts of being in battle. Some like Jerry Witts, who commanded 31 Squadron in Operation Granby, and Rupert Clark, a Tornado pilot on XV Squadron who was held captive as a POW by Saddam Hussein's henchmen, were both well known to me and gave riveting accounts that held the whole audience spellbound. Indeed so too did most of the briefers no matter their Service. But the two whom I found the most engrossing were, first, Police Constable Trevor Lock who, along with twenty-five others, was held hostage during the Iranian Embassy Siege[14] in 1980. A close second was a passenger, Michael Thexton, who was sat at the back of Pan Am Flight 73 when it was hijacked on the ground by four armed men of the Abu Nidal Organisation on 5 September 1986 whilst on stopover at Jinnah International Airport in Karachi. Having failed to hide the fact that he was a British citizen, he was held at gunpoint and sat at the open forward passenger door of the Boeing 747, legs dangling, throughout the siege. The 'war' session brought home to its audience just how real our chosen profession was.

---

13. It was actually called the Allanbrooke Room and was the equivalent of the Brooke-Popham at Bracknell. However, because of its décor, its bright red seating and its ability to send you to sleep it was affectionately called the Big Red Bedroom.
14. Coincidentally, the Commandant of the Army Staff College in 1992 was Major General Michael Rose who, as a SAS lieutenant colonel in 1980, commanded 22 SAS, which was the unit that undertook the assault against the terrorists that broke the siege.

At my final meeting with the chaps in the SAR office in MOD my Brooke-Popham Essay got a very strong thumbs up and so, with a few titivations and a last check to ensure that it was 'Service Writing sound', I submitted it the day before the deadline. It was well-received by those who marked it and without further ado, and the last challenge completed, I began to relax. Rehearsals for Clueless went well and, on the final week of the course, we rehearsed each night before a full dress rehearsal on Wednesday 2 December. After dinner on the following night we all assembled in the Brooke-Popham theatre where Trish and I compered 84 Course in a take-off of the BAFTA[15] Awards; we called it the Brack-hell Academy Final Trivia Awards. The sketches were cleverly scripted and we did a good job of 'extracting the Michael' from most of the staff and some of the more industrious students too. Some of the wives did a sterling job as chanteuse and the efforts of those who worked hard behind the scenes were very much appreciated. Between each act either Trish Heaton or I would announce the three contenders in each category of award and invite a distinguished guest, which included the recently appointed Chief of the Air Staff, Sir Michael Graydon, and the Commandant of the Staff College, Air Vice-Marshal Bob Peters, up on to the stage to open the golden envelope and announce the winner. Clueless was a resounding success and, in some cases, the sketches were even enhanced by the obvious effects of the preprandial drinks supplemented by the gallons of wine and port consumed over dinner! With the last exercise of the course completed to a standing ovation we repaired to the bar and drank into the very early hours of the morning.

The following morning, all nursing sore heads, we bade farewell to each other and our new foreign friends, who had planes to catch to take them to the various corners of the Globe from whence they had all come. It had been a great course and I had made some really good friends on it. I also learned quite a lot about myself and my Service as well as having a better understanding of my two sister Services, but I have to admit that, even to this day, I have still not been able to fathom out the Army and its rather odd ways.

With the march-out from 3 Birch Close completed on the Monday morning, I drove through the gates of Bracknell and headed for the M3 and to my new base at Boscombe Down. Dave Baugh had written a strong end

---

15. A televised annual awards ceremony on behalf of the British Academy of Film and Television Arts.

of course report that lauded my commitment and determination, praised me for my written and oral communication skills and for the support that I had given to the weaker members of the course, especially those from overseas. My decree nisi came through the very next day and exactly twelve months to the day since I had left Stamford. With that now behind me I felt that I could definitely move on with my life and career.

Chapter Eight

Short Stop Boscombe

In 1992 Boscombe Down was renamed as the Aircraft and Armament Evaluation Establishment (A&AEE) and its primary task, on behalf of MOD, was and remains the test and evaluation of in-service aircraft and airborne equipment. When I arrived in early January 1993, A&AEE was also the home of two lodger units, both of which were involved in the practical and theoretical side of testing and trialling. The first was the Empire Test Pilots School and the second was the unit I was to join, CTTO. A&AEE had a sizeable population, many of whom were civil servant scientists and support personnel. Significantly, however, there was a large cadre of officers from all three Services on the unit. So large was the unit that it was commanded by an RAF Air Commodore, who was a test pilot in his own right. So large was the unit in January 1993 that there were no available married quarters on the unit for a squadron leader just arrived from ASC. Thankfully, however, I had managed to negotiate the acquisition of a hiring[1] in the village of Shrewton, which was some eight miles west of Boscombe. Twin Elms was perfect for my two growing kids, my Labrador and me. There were a couple of pubs in the village and the neighbours all seemed very friendly. With Angus ensconced in his, now erected for the fourth time, large kennel in the back garden I headed off for my first day at my new employment. It was 10 December and at the end of the following week I would head north to collect Chris and Sarah from Stamford for the Christmas holidays.

CTTO was commanded by an Air Commodore whose domain was split into two groups, offensive and defensive. The task I had been given was to undertake a review of all offensive fast jet QWI training and so I fell firmly under the offensive umbrella. My post was supernumerary[2] and, because of the task in hand, I reported directly to Gp Capt Offensive Ops/EW; a chap by the name of Richard Howard.

---

1. A house rented by the MOD when there are insufficient family homes available from MQ stock.
2. Not on the established strength of the unit but created as a supplementary post until a specific task has been completed.

I found my allocated office and Bruce Chapple, a friendly face from the Buccaneer world, who had been tasked to work with me in undertaking the study. I did not find any group captain, however, until I bumped into one in the corridor on my way back from the coffee bar. He introduced himself thus:

'Are you Dave Herriot?'

'Yes, sir, I am.'

'Ah, welcome. Dick Howard.'

'Pleased to…'

'When are your children coming home from boarding school?'

'Next week, sir, I was hoping to take a day off to…'

'No! When are they home next summer?'

Remember, this conversation was taking place in a corridor which I was beginning now to think was an odd place to be holding a welcome interview.

'Not sure, Sir, mid to late June, I imagine.'

'Late June, eh! Excellent! You can run the summer ball!'

And with that he turned on his heel and resumed his passage along the corridor. I do not remember ever having a formal interview with the man, although he must have talked to me at some stage about what my task involved. But maybe not!

The task was not a simple one and any interference by a navigator into OCUs that operated single seat aircraft would have to be handled very carefully. It was fortunate that I had the rumbustious Bruce Chapple as my sidekick. Bruce was a pilot of some distinction. He had a wealth of experience on the Canberra and Buccaneer and had just come from being the Unit Test Pilot at RAF St Athan. He was well known throughout the RAF but, more importantly, he was highly respected. He was a loud and gregarious character, who took no prisoners. He also had a wicked sense of humour. We were both squadron leaders and although I was notionally in charge, I knew that I would have to 'know my place' when the time was appropriate to do so! I knew we would get on like a house on fire.

Lessons learned from Operation Granby had proven that QWIs, well trained and successful as instructors on OCUs and on academic air-to-surface range work, were not operationally minded when they were asked to put their training into practice in war. In short, the training for peace had left them sorely embarrassed when it came to putting their knowledge to the test under operational conditions. We scoped the task and put together a plan for approval by Dick Howard. The basic outline was that we would undertake research, write a report, recommend changes to the training package and implement a package of training across all the OCUs.

With our scoping exercise complete and approved, we headed out on the road to visit each of the FJ mud-moving OCUs in turn to discuss their QWI training syllabus and pose a few testing questions to assess their depth of knowledge. Some were keen to assist whilst others were a bit cagier as they felt a spotlight was being shone on them personally. Once reassured, however, that it was just an exercise to allow us to conduct a statistical analysis, things progressed quite smoothly. Unsurprisingly, answers to the quiz questions varied dependent upon an individual's experience. Some of the experienced QWIs, however, were clearly stuck in a peacetime bubble and could not answer many, if any, of the more operationally-slanted scenarios. Not one person was able to do one of the questions that involved attacking a target, which was on the side of a deep fjord, where the ridgeline above the target impeded the necessary dive angle to achieve a successful hit. It was a particularly awkward problem, and perhaps unrealistic too, but we had posed the question to ascertain not whether they could work it out, but to assess if they even knew which documents to consult in order to begin solving the problem! It was clear from that exercise alone that something had to be done to educate our QWIs better in the ways of warfighting.

Our next exercise was to visit other air forces in order to discover how they went about training their weapons instructors. First on the itinerary was Sweden. Why Sweden? It seemed like a good idea to visit a country that was outside NATO and Sweden fitted that bill. It also just so happened that, out of all the countries on our list, the Swedish Air Force Viggen base near Stockholm was available on the date requested through their embassy in London. Further visits were planned to the USAF Fighter Weapons School at Nellis AFB and the USN's 'Top Gun' school[3] at NAS Miramar, near San Diego.

The visit to Sweden was highly successful. The Swedes were extremely open about their operations and how they trained their weapons instructors. They surrendered themselves willingly to our weapons mini-quiz and proved, quickly, that their knowledge was, in part, equal to or above that of our own QWIs. They explained that, as an independent air force operating

---

3. Strike Fighter Tactics Instructor programme.

outside any alliance, they had had to learn from scratch, but that that in itself had ensured a thoroughness that would be the envy of many a western air force. Bruce and I took copious contemporaneous notes, enjoyed a guided tour of a Viggen in a freezing HAS and drove ourselves back to Stockholm for a 'tourist' weekend, before we flew back to Heathrow on the Sunday.

Stockholm in March is bitterly cold, routinely, with temperatures lurking around zero during daylight hours and five degrees colder after dark; 1994 was no exception. However, wrapped up in parkas to keep out the mind-numbing chill, the city is no different to many a western capital city. It was bustling by day and vibrant by night and offered many a hostelry packed with people only too willing to exchange a 'skol' with bar-hopping Brits. The Royal Palace has an impressive, if functional given the weather conditions, façade. However, the highlight of my stay in Stockholm, other than the exceedingly attractive receptionist in the Hotel Diplomat, was the Vasa Museum. Located on the island of Djurgården, the museum displays the only almost fully intact seventeenth century ship that has ever been salvaged. Constructed just over one hundred years after the *Mary Rose*, the 64-gun warship *Vasa* sank on her maiden voyage in 1628. Richly decorated as a symbol of the king's ambitions for Sweden, and himself, she was one of the most powerfully armed vessels in the world. However, the *Vasa* was perilously unstable with too much weight in the upper hull. Nevertheless, she was ordered to sea, but foundered after sailing just fourteen hundred yards, on 10 August 1628, after encountering a wind no stronger than a breeze. She should be in the Guinness Book of Records for the largest warship to sail the shortest distance! All that aside, the restoration in the Vasa Museum has to be seen to be believed.

Upon our return from Sweden, we started to put together an outline of our findings to date. At the same time, having formed a committee of experts, I set about organising the officers' mess summer ball. I had had considerable success organising events, including one summer ball, at Laarbruch in the early years of my career and so I knew what was required. However, it was good to have a coterie of young and eager junior officers available to do much of the spade work. I soon discovered that organising a summer ball at Boscombe was no small feat! Indeed, with its large number of serving officers on the base and a significant number of civilians who all seemed to have been adorned with officer status, it was one of the biggest summer balls in the RAF. It required the hiring of two marquees for a kick off just to accommodate the numbers wishing to dine. Various menus and food bars had to be considered and agreed upon. Gallons of alcohol had to be costed and ordered by the bar officer. A theme had to be decided upon and a team organised to decorate the mess in the week running up to the ball. Having my team around me helped immensely and I was confident that each would respond to my bidding as the weeks progressed and the fine detail was hammered out in committee. A price per head was set and I sat back and monitored progress, whilst Bruce and I got on with our primary task. Then it dawned on me! I needed a partner to take to the ball!

It was a relatively lonely existence in Twin Elms. The village did have three pubs, but it was a close-knit community and, as a lone newcomer, I found it a little difficult to break the ice. One of the mess barmaids encouraged me to drink in her local, The George, and join the village cricket team, but I was well out of practice on the crease and the regulars in the pub were curious to know what this forty-four year old divorcee was doing chatting to their Susan! I was dropped after my first duck by the cricket team and Susan and I realised that there was no future in any form of relationship. However, I was saved from the loneliness of life in Shrewton whenever the children came home from school and took solace, after work, with long walks over the local pasture with Angus, who was always glad to see me after a long day cooped up in his kennel.

Before we could venture further afield to continue our QWI analysis I was summoned to the air commodore's office one day in mid-June. Without any hesitation and with delight in his eye he informed me that I had been selected for promotion to the rank of Acting Wing Commander. I was also posted back to London into a prestigious job within the department of the Assistant Chief of the Defence Staff Operational Requirements(Air). The posting was to take effect in early August.

I was absolutely delighted at the prospect of greater responsibility and the chance to work in Whitehall. It was pretty clear from the air commodore's final remarks that there was little point in me spending too much time on the project and that I should hand it all over to Bruce, who could run with it until my successor arrived, and concentrate on the final planning for the summer ball. I also had to begin to organise my move up to London and book some leave with Chris and Sarah.

With plans all set for the summer ball it looked very much as if I was going to have to attend on my own until a neighbour, who had been a junior pilot on 31 Squadron at Brüggen, suggested that a friend of his wife's might make a suitable blind date for the evening. With no other options available I accepted his kind offer. I had never been out with a hospital matron before so the summer ball would be a first.

Two days after I had agreed to escort Philippa to the ball, I received a call from Jacqui James, the wife of one of the pilots on the unit, with whom I had been friends on 17 Squadron at Brüggen. Jacqui asked if I might be interested in escorting her friend, Jo O'Shea, to the ball as she was attending, but did not have a partner. Jo was the widow of a fellow navigator from my days on 17 Squadron.

Damn, blast and double damn! If only her call had come a few days earlier. I remembered Jo well from our time in Germany, but had not seen her since she had left Brüggen in 1988 after the terrible Tornado accident that had killed her husband, John. I remembered her as an attractive and delightful woman who would have been a far more suitable partner for the evening than somebody that I had never met before. I apologised to Jacqui and explained the circumstance of the blind date. Unperturbed she invited me, and my 'partner', for pre-drinks in her garden before the summer ball.

The evening got off to a great start with the pre-drinks, but I had to leave that thrash early to ensure that everything was going smoothly at the mess. Philippa was pleasant company and she seemed to be enjoying her first encounter with the military in a formal setting. However, after a while it was evident that her night shifts were getting the better of her and, by midnight, she needed to get to her bed. I drove her back home before I had had too much more to drink and then returned to the officers' mess to continue the festivities and ensure that all our plans were working, that the party lasted long into the night, and that people enjoyed themselves to the full.

It was while I was meandering between the bar and the ante-room that I bumped into Jo in the corridor. She looked stunning in a long black, low-cut dress that displayed handsomely her bountiful décolletage. We chatted for a long time asking about how things had been since we had last met and what we each were up to now, and so on and so forth. As we parted she said that if I was ever up in Nottingham I should give her a call and we could meet for dinner or the theatre or some such. I walked with a lighter step back to the bar and hoped against hope that she had not noticed just how much I had been staring at her ample cleavage rather than her eyes.

The summer ball was an outstanding success and was apparently, from reports, enjoyed by all. It does not take much to amuse a group of RAF officers, let me assure you, so I seek no kudos here. A surfeit of beer, excellent company, a well-stocked fish bar, a grand buffet and a few ice sculptures, plus a modicum of contemporary and loud music, and all supplemented by formal attire will usually suffice. The 1993 Boscombe Down Summer Ball had all of the above.

I woke up in my car at about 0730 the following morning. Thank God I had had the good sense not to drive at whatever ungodly hour I had left the party. I certainly knew I had not had much sleep and I felt bloody awful! The hangover from hell had not yet kicked in! The following week, I received high praise from all corners of A&AEE, from the commandant down, for my efforts in organising the ball and managing my team. It had been a very successful evening and even the mess staff had enjoyed it. At the wash-up afterwards, however, there was some suggestion that I had screwed up the VAT calculations, but I left the task of resolving that to the station accounts staff and went on leave with Chris and Sarah to a holiday cottage on the shore of Loch Earn in the Highlands. I was done with CTTO after just six months in post and already looking forward, once again, to London Life!

We had a great holiday, just the three of us. It was helped greatly by having our two dogs Angus, the Chocolate Labrador, and Beauty, my ex-wife's Cavalier King Charles Spaniel, as well as Christopher's canoe with us! The kids spent a great deal of time windsurfing and canoeing on the loch and learned to waterski too at the Lochearnhead Watersports Centre. Days were busy and active. One particularly energetic day we climbed Ben Lawers and, for a relaxing evening, took in an Alan Ayckbourn play at the Pitlochry Festival Theatre. We all very much enjoyed our seven days in Scotland and despite just one rebellious moment when Sarah determined that she would not wear a helmet for a twenty-three mile bike ride around the loch, it was a great family bonding session. Sarah, who was eventually persuaded to wear her helmet, was rewarded with an additional ten-mile detour to Balquidder to pay our MacGregor[4] respects at Rob Roy's grave in the churchyard there.

When I got back to Shrewton there was a message on my answer phone from Jo. I listened to it a couple of times just to make sure that I had heard it correctly – she had two tickets for the theatre in Nottingham and wondered whether I would like to go with her. Most certainly I would!

---

4. On 3 April 1603 James VI (First of England) issued an edict that banned the use of the name MacGregor under pain of death. MacGregors were compelled to adopt other surnames, such as Drummond, Murray, Graham, Grier, Stewart, Grant, and even Campbell. One of these adopted names was Whyte, the surname of my maternal great-grandfather.

Chapter Nine

Arms Dealing – Legally!

I started in Whitehall on 11 August 1993 and instantly found myself in a busy environment. ACDS OR(Air), Air Vice-Marshal Ian McFadyen, had a broad remit that covered all aspects relating to the air-delivered operational requirements of all three Services that were, by their very nature, predominantly RAF. Everything from air-delivered maritime operations through all aspects of air defence and air-to-surface weaponry fell on his desk. He had a huge remit that included Eurofighter 2000[1] and a sizeable staff to cover it all. Two air commodores supported him and a multitude of deputy directors, at group captain level, ran various sections within the MOD's Main Building in Whitehall. I worked directly for Dusty Miller who in turn reported to DOR(Air)1, Air Commodore Bill Tyack, who was a quietly spoken Irishman and an erstwhile 'kipper fleet' man. I knew Dusty well. He had been OC 17 Squadron at Brüggen during the latter period of my time as STANEVAL(Weapons) and we got on well together. There were five major projects on the books in my office all of which I was responsible for. Thankfully, the RAF had provided me with three young and very capable squadron leaders to share the load and between us we managed the task admirably.

The role of an OR(Air) staff officer was to primarily prepare the operational requirement staff papers for approved projects within the MOD from concept to conclusion. Not only prepare them, but staff them through the department and then more widely through the applicable desks within the appropriate Service HQs and MOD departments. If necessary, the other two Services might also have to have been consulted, and comment sought, in order to ensure both a full picture response and clarity for onward submission. In the latter stages of a project's life, when final funding needed to be guaranteed to get the contract in place, papers were staffed through the offices of those within MOD who had fiscal responsibility, ultimately to gain approval from the Equipment Approvals Committee (EAC). The EAC,

---

1. Later to become known as Typhoon in RAF service.

which consisted of very powerful high ranking civil servants and military officers, had ultimate sanction over whether a project represented good value for money or not. Quite rightly so! Moreover, throughout its gestation, a project would go before the EAC a number of times, particularly during the annual spending round, when three things might happen to it. It could get through unscathed. It could get through, but have a large chunk, in millions of pounds sterling, carved out of its budget for that year, thereby imposing yet more delays to its In-Service Date. Or, it could suffer an inglorious death and be carved out of the programme completely because it was either unaffordable or, in the eyes of the EAC, was no longer required. Staff officers in each of the three OR environments[2] would quiver at the prospect of years of work being thrown down the drain for what was, in their eyes at least, a valuable and necessary piece of equipment.

A Staff Target (ST), formed from a perceived need in a young staff officer's eye, started out its life as a service paper written at desk level and supported up the line until the need was acknowledged by the EAC and became a Staff Requirement (SR). STs did not feature in a funding line – they were, after all, just targets. SRs, on the other hand, were funded notionally year-on-year and within each year, it would be hoped, sufficient funds might be made available to progress the requirement by means of a technical demonstrator.

My post was titled Operational Requirements 51(Air) and my three squadron leaders were identified by the suffixes a, b and c. By the time I arrived in post the last ST(A) on the desk of OR51(Air) had just been cancelled. ST(A)1244 had been for the development of an air-delivered nuclear weapon to replace the WE177 that I had become so familiar with during my flying tours on the Buccaneer and Tornado. However, with the new peace accord between west and east and the government's decision to invest purely in a submarine-launched nuclear deterrent, the need for an air-delivered tactical nuke was no longer part of the defence plan. I was glad that ST(A)1244 had gone. I didn't quite fancy all the necessary trials, tribulations and security measures that such a programme would have imposed. I had enough on my plate without that.

I had three live SR(A)s to contend with plus two Urgent Operational Requirements. SR(A)1236 was for a Conventionally Armed Stand Off Missile, SR(A)1238 for an Advanced Air-Launched Anti-Armour Weapon

---

2. Sea, Land and Air.

and SR(A)1242 was needed to replace stock of Laser Guided Bombs that had been expended during Operation Granby. The LGB requirement was acute and my team was already working closely with Texas Instruments to replenish the Paveway 2 stock as quickly as possible. At the same time we had to investigate options for an enhanced weapon using GPS to supplement the laser homing system and, possibly, extend the release range of the weapon to make it fly. The other two requirements had been in the pipeline for a considerable length of time. Indeed, upon his arrival in post, and having read through the staff bundle that I gave him, Phil Osborn, remarked of SR(A)1236 'this bloody project's had a longer career in the RAF than me'! He was not far off the mark. The requirement for CASOM had been gestating for twenty-three years and year-on-year it had fallen foul of the EAC and each of the spending reviews. However, post the war in Iraq, there was a new energy in the MOD for a better inventory of air-delivered weaponry and so, for CASOM, the planets were aligned.

The case for AAAW was less robust. The peace dividend had militated against a requirement for a new weapon that could be used against vast columns of WP tanks. Additionally, with the British Army working a requirement for an attack helicopter, there was a conflict of interest between the two Services! SR(A)1238 needed considerable development and work if it was to succeed in my time in OR (Air). It too had had a troubled past but, with a favourable wind and tenacious defence of it in the equipment programme, I felt confident that we would succeed.

The two UORs were smaller in scale, but nevertheless equally important. Project Passover was a programme to develop a system that would assist Special Forces operating behind enemy lines – so you will not hear detailed mention of it further within these pages! The other UOR was to provide the in-service BL755[3] weapons with a medium-level release capability. BL755 had been developed by Hunting Engineering Limited and had been purchased in large quantities by the MOD for its air-to-mud FJ aircraft. BL755 Mark 1 was designed to be delivered from low-level against an area of enemy armoured vehicles. It was mechanically initiated by a clockwork timer that could be set before flight to ensure that the one hundred and forty-seven bomblets, held within each bomb casing, were deployed over the target area in a pattern necessary to achieve the required P_k. Each of the

---

3. Cluster Bomb.

bomblets was fitted with a coronet at its rear which sprang free on release and provided stability in flight and a pre-determined striking angle when it hit the ground. The pattern of the bomblet strikes was random, dependent upon the clockwork timer setting. It was designed as an area weapon to be used against an area target. The clever bit was the explosive mechanism. Each bomblet was fitted with a shaped charge warhead specifically designed to penetrate the armour of a Soviet tank of early 1970s vintage. The external sides of the warhead were etched in a small cubed pattern that would, on detonation, shatter into approximately two thousand two hundred anti-personnel fragments that would be cast across a radius of thirty to forty metres. With advances in Soviet armour, some BL755 bomblets had been modified to enhance their striking angle by the fitting of a small parachute instead of the coronet. These were designated BL755 Mark 2. Experience in the Falklands War of 1982, and in Operation Granby, had proved that there was a definite need to have a capability to release such a weapon from medium altitude rather than low-level. With a clockwork timer defining the moment of bomblet ejection, however, release from medium level would have resulted in far too great a dispersion pattern and too steep a striking angle for the weapon to be effective if no modification took place. The UOR thus defined a requirement to fit a radar proximity sensor to the bomb tail that would recognise the appropriate height above ground to engage the clockwork timer such that the bomb body could open and the bomblets ejected. A number of Mark 1 bombs were to be modified and were designated as Mark 1a or RBL755. This, the simplest of the projects on my desk, passed all scrutiny measures and, with funding available, a contract was placed with HEL in 1995 to enhance the stock weapons required. By 16 May 1999 a total of four hundred and twenty-three RBL755 bombs had been dropped by the RAF in support of Operation Allied Force in Kosovo. In February 2007, the UK Ministry of Defence committed to removing BL755 and RBL755 weapons from service by the following year. At the time, the total inventory of BL/RBL755 comprised three thousand six hundred and fifty dispensers, which represented a need to dispose of over half a million submunitions.

Once again I discovered that there was a dearth of families' accommodation in London and so my early days in Whitehall started with a drive from Shrewton to Andover and a train journey to Waterloo. It made the days quite long, but I heeded the advice of a friend who, hearing of my posting to London, told me that the best thing to do was to set your time of arrival in the morning as a routine, which would then be accepted as your norm. I did and it was. My work day commenced at 0840 and concluded, usually, at 1700 on the dot. I rarely left the office at lunchtime and usually worked through.

Jo had tickets for the Theatre Royal in Nottingham to see a comedy entitled '*Fur Coat and No Knickers*'.[4] Unfortunately, it was a mid-week performance, which made it particularly difficult for me to get out of the office and spend a night away. More importantly, I had two dogs holed up in Twin Elms in Shrewton that could not be left unattended for longer than a day whilst I was in London! I was keen to meet up with Jo again and so made an arrangement, with her blessing, to travel north on the afternoon of the day in question with the dogs, stay overnight and depart the following morning for a meeting with Alan Flewitt at the UK offices of Texas Instruments, in Northampton. I needed to meet with Alan anyway to discuss our Paveway replenishment and, with his accommodation, the plan worked. We spent a very pleasant evening together and I departed the following morning with the understanding that we 'must do it again sometime'. The journey to Northampton was a much brighter one after an evening at the theatre with Jo.

Not long after my arrival in Whitehall, the department held a dinner in a restaurant in London to dine out a number of officers. I thought it an ideal opportunity to reciprocate Jo's hospitality at the theatre and so rang her to ask if she would care to be my guest for the evening. I was delighted when Jo willingly accepted my invitation. I booked two rooms in the RAF Club and met Jo off the train from Nottingham on the Friday night. The evening was a great success and she did not flinch when I slid my hand over hers in the taxi on our way to the venue. Back at the RAF Club she politely informed me that she had already 'consumed all the coffee' in her room and that she looked forward to seeing me in time for breakfast.

Jo's husband John had been killed in a Tornado accident in May 1988 and since then she had brought up her two daughters single-handedly. Her parents had kindly helped out by babysitting Helen and Hannah at her home in West Bridgford, whilst she spent the weekend with me. It was a thoroughly enjoyable weekend. The evening in London had gone especially well and on the cab journey back to the RAF Club I had felt a sure and certain comfort in Jo's company. After breakfast, I settled the bill for both the rooms and we

---

4. A Comedy by Mike Harding; the title is an English expression for people who are superficially elegant and beautiful but actually common.

headed out to Waterloo to catch the next train to Andover and a weekend in Shrewton. With time to wait at Waterloo we entertained each other by people watching! A game I had often played whilst waiting in stations previously, trying to guess occupations, where people had been, what they had been up to and where they were going! Jo was good at it and confessed to having played the game previously on her own and with others.

'Accountant!' said I.

'No, solicitor!' was her response.

'Shopping trip!'

'Yep, shopping trip, I agree!'

Headmistress. Soldier on leave. Badly hungover student. Football supporter. They all got the once over from each of us in turn as we sat in the station concourse waiting for our train to be declared fit for purpose!

'Going home for the weekend after a week working in London!'

'No! Rushing home to his wife after an illicit night with his secretary!' said she.

Wow, I thought as I squeezed her hand! I think I am going to enjoy this lady's company.

Our Saturday and Sunday in Wiltshire were great fun and it was very clear to me that we were going to get on extremely well together. Of course, it was early days in our relationship and there were many paths to be trodden and bridges to be crossed along the way, but, for the first time in many years, I felt that the warmth I was showing towards another human was being responded to. When the time came for Jo to depart for Nottingham on the Sunday afternoon I did not want her to leave me. Her planned route home involved a long and tedious train journey into London, followed by a further long and tedious train journey north from St Pancras. She would have had a considerable amount of 'holding' time on route and nobody to share her people watching skills with! I decided that I could reduce her travel pain whilst, at the same time, I could spend more time with her if I were to drive her home myself. She insisted that she was quite happy to take the train as she had previously planned. I, however, was equally insistent that it would be absolutely no trouble for me to drive her home and that I could not tolerate the thought of her stuck on a train for hours on end. Eventually she relented and I got to spend three more hours in her company; I also got to meet her parents, but not yet her children.

The following week we spent hours on the phone to each other. I have no idea what we discussed, but I do know that neither of us was prepared to be the first to close the conversation. We were like a couple of teenagers who had never been in love before. We started to meet regularly at weekends and I soon found myself spending my weekends in West Bridgford and overstaying until the early hours of Monday mornings, when I would head back to Shrewton, jump in the shower and then catch my train up to London. The weeks seemed longer and longer as we grew closer and closer. Eventually I was allocated a three-bedroomed quarter in Lees Gardens in Maidenhead, which greatly reduced the length of my Monday morning journey south from Nottingham. It also eased my daily commute into the city. I yearned for the weekdays in London to pass quickly so that I could get back on the road to Nottingham for our much anticipated weekends together. The long nightly telephone calls continued and eventually I was introduced to Helen and Hannah at a quite posh Indian Restaurant in Nottingham city centre. I do not remember much about the meal, but I do recall that Jo's six-year-old daughter, Hannah, was ebullient whilst Helen, at eight, was quite shy and considerably more reserved.

My office was all too often 'invaded' by company representatives. These chaps were almost invariably retired senior RAF officers who, with ready access to the building, were foot-padding as business development managers for their individual companies. As well as my man from Texas Instruments, I routinely welcomed visitors from BAe (Dynamics), Boeing, GEC-Marconi, HEL, Hughes, Lockheed, Martin Marietta, Matra, McDonnell Douglas, Rafael, Raytheon, Rockwell and, very occasionally, the Swedish company Bofors. Each of these companies was a probable bidder in any one of our projects although some, like Hughes, who manufactured the Tomahawk cruise missile, were particularly interested in CASOM. Whilst I did not always have time to talk to these people, I always welcomed them and made space in my day for them to tell me all that they wanted to tell me about their product. Of course, their real purpose in making the office call was to try and glean from me as much detail as possible about each of my projects and how each was progressing within the overall equipment programme. They were astute individuals and very good at their job, but there was also benefit in accommodating them as it usually resulted in a free lunch! Of the fourteen companies, eleven were going to be serious contenders for SR(A)1236 when our 'Invitation to Tender' was issued, which we hoped could be released by

1995 at the latest. Of these, six[5] were in the USA. Accordingly, CASOM project staff from the Ministry of Defence (Procurement Executive) made regular trips across the Atlantic to research possible technical solutions and, annually, I would go with them.

These journeys across the USA took something in the order of seventeen days to complete and, including the two transatlantic legs, could involve up to twenty flights! My first served the purpose of introducing me to the key players in the USA who were involved or had an interest in our projects. From MOD(PE)'s point of view, it was their annual opportunity to send their big armaments cheese stateside to touch palms with the great and the good of the US Armaments companies and the key movers and shakers in the Pentagon. In September and October 1993 I travelled on his tailcoat and, subsequently, was invited back each year to accompany Director General Armament (DG Arm) on each of his subsequent autumnal pilgrimages to the USA. These visits were to all intents and purposes a hearts and minds tour. Each of the companies in the States needed to be updated annually on the latest stage of our various projects and, to give it purpose and gravitas, it was important that they spoke with the most senior man in MOD(PE) responsible for their eventual procurement. At the same time, it provided an opportunity for the companies to update the UK representatives on their systems. There was nothing 'gravitas', however, about John Mabberley, a two-star civil servant with a wicked sense of humour and a keen eye for detail. DG Arm was a delightful character and I very much enjoyed his company and that of his sidekick and able foil, Air Commodore Richard Fletcher, who filled the post of Director of Air Armament and was there to provide the technical specification input. I was in support to ensure that neither of these two engineers lost sight of the actual operational requirement.

It was always a comprehensive and exhausting itinerary that took us from the Eastern Seaboard of the USA to California via some of the most thrillingly named places from the cowboy stories of my youth. The main players in the CASOM programme were always included: Orlando to meet with Martin Marietta;[6] Atlanta for Rockwell;[7] St Louis for McDonnell

---

5. Hughes, Lockheed, Martin Marietta, McDonnell Douglas, Rockwell and Texas Instruments.
6. AGM-142A Popeye, manufactured in conjunction with the Israeli armament company Rafael.
7. AGM-130.

Tornado just airborne for Op Shader armed with Brimstone. (*Crown Copyright*)

Change of Command. Taking over from Gp Capt Ray Horwood. RAFDet Gioia del Colle, Italy, 25 April 1997. (*Crown/RAFDet Gioia del Colle*)

Author in No. 6 Dress Uniform, Gioia del Colle, Italy. (*Jo Herriot*)

Welcoming CDS, Sir Charles Guthrie. Operation Deliberate Guard, Gioia del Colle, Italy. (*Crown RAFDet Gioia del Colle*)

CDS and DCDS (Commitments) are briefed in the RAF Reconnaissance and Intelligence Centre (RIC). Sir Charles Guthrie, Flt Lt Nick Prytherch, Author, Sir John Day. Operation Deliberate Guard, Gioia del Colle, Italy. (*Crown/RAFDet Gioia del Colle*)

War is Hell! The morning after the night before's madness with CDS and his entourage. Operation Deliberate Guard, Gioia del Colle, Italy. (*Crown/ RAFDet Gioia del Colle*)

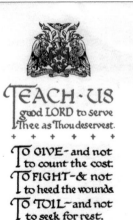

Three months into our four month deployment, NATO Former Republic of Yugoslavia medals awarded – Sqn Ldr Graham Lovell (Det Eng O), Author (Det Cdr), Sqn Ldr David Williams (Chief of Staff), Fg Off Lee Bryden (Det Admin O). Operation Deliberate Guard, Gioia del Colle, Italy. (*Crown/RAFDet Gioia del Colle*)

RAF College Cranwell. College Prayer. (*Author's Collection*)

Hard at work in Whittle Hall, RAF College Cranwell. Wing Commander Cadets, Department o' Initial Officer Training. (*Jo Herriot*)

'Carriage of imitation fissile material'. Exercise Cobalt Blue, DIOT Field Leadership Camp. (*Author*)

The leader briefs his team on the task ahead. DIOT Field Leadership Camp. (*Author*)

'Building a chariot from parts that were located at various grid references along the way'. Chariot almost completed. Exercise Ultimate Challenge, DIOT Field Leadership Camp. (*Author*)

Ready for yet another Guest Night in College Hall. Department of Initial Officer Training, RAF College Cranwell. (*Author*)

Skiing at Ancelle in the Haute-Alpes, courtesy of the French Air Force École de l'Air. (*Author*)

Meeting OC Cadet Wing, Officer Training School, RAAF Point Cook, Melbourne, Victoria, Australia 1999. (*Royal Australian Air Force*)

Flt Lt Chris Lay RAF, supervising his flight of RAAF officer cadets. RAAF East Sale, Victoria, Australia – 1999. (*Author*)

50th Birthday Champagne Breakfast (organised by my irrepressible wife!). Sqn Ldr Paul Beard, Je Herriot, Author, AVM Bill Rimmer. College Hall Officers' Mess, RAFC Cranwell, 26 May 1999 (*Crown/RAF Cranwell*)

My mother and her family, assembled for my 50th birthday party. RAFC Cranwell, 30 May 1999. (*Author*)

Acting/Director Department of Initial Officer Training, with my wife. 180 Initial Officer Training Course Graduation Parade. RAFC Cranwell, 25 November 1999. (*Crown/RAF Cranwell*)

HMS *Illustrious* and HMS *Ocean* leading the Saif Sarrea armada in the Mediterranean – 20 September 2001. (*Crown/HMS Illustrious*)

The Joint Force Commander and his senior executives awaiting dinner in the Admiral's Wardroom. I am on the admiral's left. HMS *Illustrious*, somewhere in the Red Sea, September 2001. (*Crown HMS Illustrious*)

Feeling the desert heat. Exercise Saif Sarrea 2, Oman, October 2001. (*Author*)

Change of Command. Taking over from Wg Cdr Tony Bown. Air Warfare Centre, RAF Cranwell, November 2001. (*Crown / RAF Cranwell*)

In Ye Grapes public house, Shepherd Market, London with my two children Sarah and Christopher. Summer 2003. (*Author*)

Author and his wife. RAF Cranwell Officers' Mess Summer Ball. Daedalus Officers' Mess, RAF Cranwell, June 2005. (*Author's Collection*)

Proof, if ever it was needed, that aircrew never grow up! Author leading his Buccaneer mates on charge around the party, whilst still seated, at Nick Berryman's 60th Birthday Bash, November 200 (*Author's Collection*)

ecoming a magistrate, with my wife as a witness. Swearing-in Day, Nottingham Magistrates' Court, 7 October 2006. (*Author's Collection*)

Serving up the Sea Bass'. Italian Cookery Course, Casa Panfili, Perugia, Umbria, Italy, 18 March 2007. (*Author's Collection*)

Buccaneers over Table Mountain (one of each: FAA; SAAF; and RAF). Presentation to Phill Weyers (great-grandson of Jan Smuts), National President South African Air Force Association, b the Buccaneer Aircrew Association. Swartkop Air Base, Gauteng, South Africa, 8 November 200 (*South African Air Force*)

Still conducting the choir/drunks 35 years on. Buccaneer Aircrew Association 50th Anniversar Reunion. Skukuza, Kruger National Park, South Africa, 12 November 2008. (*Author*)

My last ever flight in a 'military' fast-jet, Buccaneer S2B, ZU–NIP (aka XW986). Thunder City, Cape Town, South Africa, 14 November 2008. (*Author*)

Handing over the reins to the next generation. Jo, Helen and the author. My elder step-daughter's commissioning graduation, RAF College Cranwell, 13 August 2009. (*Author*)

Award of 'Master Air Navigator' by the Honorary Company of Air Pilots. Guildhall, London, 2 October 2017. (*HCAP*)

Two of the best two-seat, fast-jet, strike/attack aircraft ever built. (*Crown/MOD*)

Douglas;[8] Dallas for Texas Instruments;[9] Tucson for Hughes;[10] and Los Angeles for Lockheed.[11] But the itinerary would also always include various sub-contractors to discuss warhead options and companies who could provide the necessary guidance systems required to get both CASOM and AAAW to their targets successfully. Occasionally I found myself in a meeting where I had no vested interest in the company's project, but DG Arm had and so the itinerary rolled along relentlessly. Boston for Raytheon one year to discuss their Advanced Medium-Range Air-to-Air Missile, more commonly referred to as AMRAAM. General Dynamics in Burlington, Vermont, to discuss the Royal Navy's 'Goalkeeper' requirement for a Gatling gun for new frigates, the next. More than once would be a visit to Eglin AFB to discuss the possibility of securing the use of their vast range complex for CASOM development trials.

It was always an astoundingly varied and interesting itinerary. I learned a lot and I met some very interesting characters along the way. It was hectic, however. At every destination we were met by the company's UK business development manager who had travelled ahead and was on hand to ease our passage. Once he had introduced us to attendant local representatives of the company, he drove us to our hotel, gave us five minutes to change before then driving us to a fine restaurant for the obligatory company-funded dinner. There was not a moment to draw breath or contemplate jetlag. Every morning, after a fitful night's sleep and a hearty American breakfast, and with our bags packed and loaded, it was off to the company for briefings, lunch and a factory tour before being whisked back to the airport and on to the next leg of our journey. We always spent a number of days, and usually the weekend, in Washington DC, where we held meetings with Pentagon staffs, particularly those from the USAF and USN who respectively led the project teams looking at the procurement of the Joint Direct Attack Munition and the Joint Stand Off Weapon, commonly known as JDAM and JSOW. Interestingly from a UK standpoint, despite the fact that both these programmes were considered to be 'Joint' neither US Service had much interest in the other's project. Each was determined to seek the procurement

---

8. AGM-84A Harpoon (the company were planning to propose an Extended Range version entitled Harpoon ER).
9. AGM-154 Joint Stand Off Weapon and Paveway 2/3.
10. AGM-109 Air-launched Tomahawk Cruise Missile.
11. AGM-158 Joint Air-to-Surface Standoff Missile.

of 'their' JDAM or 'their' JSOW at the expense of the other and neither had any intention at that stage of amalgamating their needs. I may have been standing in an office in the Pentagon, but the thought did strike me that their inter-Service politics were no different from ours!

In Washington I found myself, once again, accommodated in the Embassy Suites in Crystal City, but with time now to explore all the Smithsonian Museums on the National Mall. It was always a fascinating weekend and I walked the length and breadth of the 'Mall' several times in my tour in Whitehall taking in all of the museums, the White House, Capitol Hill, Union Station and the memorial monuments to Lincoln, Washington and Jefferson. I wore out the leather on my shoes tramping around Washington, but the two most sobering sites were always the Holocaust Museum and the Vietnam War Memorial. Both of these were places to pause, contemplate and draw breath. Not unnaturally I spent much of my time in the National Aerospace Museum, which is a must-see place to visit for anybody with an interest in aviation.

On my first visit with John Mabberley to the USA I had been intrigued to see that on Friday, 8 October the itinerary was planned to take us to Albuquerque in New Mexico. Over a quiet beer in Washington, D Air Arm had explained to me that DG Arm had spent a very enjoyable tour working on exchange at the Los Alamos National Laboratory[12] some hundred miles north of Albuquerque. Routinely, if the itinerary permitted, he always planned it so that he could go back again for 'old time's sake'. The itinerary permitted it in 1993 and so off we went to New Mexico for the night.

We picked up a rental vehicle at Albuquerque airport and headed for our adobe-clad hotel in town. Bags dumped in our rooms the two engineers decided it would be a good idea to take me up Sunrise Mountain, which rose out of the desert to the east of the town, to see the sunset. The view across Albuquerque to the west was stunning as the sun, dipping behind the far mountain range, glinted on the adobe buildings. We sat in the mountain top bar to watch the whole show whilst we enjoyed a very cooling beer. From our lofty perch overlooking the city, I could well see why the famous Albuquerque balloon festival attracted so many visitors from across the Globe. Unfortunately the 1993 event had been held the week prior to our arrival, so we missed it.

---

12. America's Nuclear Weapons Engineering Laboratory.

After breakfast the following morning, we climbed back into the rental car and headed for Los Alamos. The town is no different to any mid-western town in the USA apart from the fact that most of the personalised number plates I saw had some reference to its role as the nuclear weapon capital of the USA. It took us over two hours to drive the approximate one hundred miles north from Albuquerque and after a short stop to take lunch we headed back to Albuquerque airport and our onward journey to Phoenix. The most interesting aspect of my one and only visit to Los Alamos was nothing to do with their nuclear programmes. From a professional aviator's viewpoint I was more intrigued by the horrendous cliff-edge that formed the approach end to the airport's westerly runway!

Phoenix was but a transient stop as our real destination on the Saturday evening was Tucson so that we would be in place, come Monday, for our scheduled meeting with the Hughes Corporation. After a good dinner and an early night we woke on the Sunday morning, ate breakfast and jumped into another rental car for a day in the desert. This time we were off to Tombstone, another of John Mabberley's favourite haunts. The town still had all the trappings of its once notorious cowboy past. The OK Corral, famous for its gunfight, still stood where it had been on 26 October 1881. So too stood the Bird Cage Theatre that operated from 1881 to 1889 as a combined theatre, saloon, gambling parlour and brothel! Even the saloon bars still had swinging doors that allowed those evicted to leave unharmed! And on the edge of town was the renowned Boot Hill Cemetery where lie the deceased cowboys from the OK Corral gunfight. The headstones in the cemetery are a sight to behold. Most of them are wooden; most of them are original; and most of them with a simple inscription thereon. Such epitaphs as: 'Will Deloge Killed playing cards, 1883'; 'Billy Clanton, Tom McLaury, Frank McLaury, Murdered on the streets of Tombstone 1881';[13] and 'Dan Kelly, Hanged 1884' are, but three examples. But there were some with a touch of humour in them too and you have to commend the poets who came up with these:

> 'Here Lies George Johnson
> Hanged by mistake 1882
> He was right, we was wrong
> But we strung him up and now he's gone!'

---

13. During the gunfight at the OK Corral (unstated).

And my favourite:

> 'Here Lies Lester Moore
> Four slugs from a 44
> No Les
> No More'

On the way back to our hotel, we took the scenic route via Sahuarita in Arizona so that we could visit the Titan Missile Museum and take a tour of the silos and the control room. Quite a fascinating experience for somebody who had spent their entire flying career in the nuclear weapon releasing business!

Winding up our tour in Los Angeles we were hosted to pre-dinner drinks whilst cruising off Newport Beach on a large schooner that was owned by Lockheed for just such pleasures! It was but one example, of many that I had experienced, of what life in the legal arms dealing business was like. With business over the following day, and with time to kill, we took in a visit to the Queen Mary, berthed in Long Island where it served as a tourist attraction. Unfortunately we failed to see Howard Hughes' Spruce Goose aircraft as, sat inside its protective dome, it was closed for renovation.

At the end of our 1995 tour to the USA I ended up visiting the Boeing factory in Seattle on my own to discuss a small millimetric wave transceiver that Boeing was proposing as a seeker for SR(A)1238. With every visit to Boeing's Seattle plant, one has to participate in the 'grand factory tour'. Whilst being guided in a golf buggy around this vast hangar[14] I espied a set of aircraft seats set in an engine nacelle high above the ground. Two sets of three airline seats with a gap, typical of an aircraft aisle, separating them, and all housed within a nacelle! They must have been anticipating my question. Everybody who goes on the tour must ask this question. Why else would they be there other than to force the question that the Boeing guide clearly delighted in answering? I asked the question and was flabbergasted at the guide's answer. The six seats abreast inside the nacelle were used to indicate that the diameter of a Boeing 757 fuselage was the same as the diameter of a Boeing 777's engine nacelle! Crazy dimensions – the Boeing 777 must be

---

14. At 13,385,378 m³, Boeing's Everett Factory, on Paine Field, Seattle, is the largest building in the world, by volume.

huge, I thought, but then nobody had ever considered building a double-decker airliner[15] in those days!

Over lunch my host, a chap by the excellent name of D'Arcy Zimmerman, asked me if I was flying First Class back to London that evening. I put him right! Then, the MOD had drawn in its purse strings and only allowed an individual to fly across the Atlantic in Club Class if he was going straight to a meeting upon his arrival. I was going home to Maidenhead. I was being flown back in Economy! There was a long solitary queue in the Departure Hall at Seattle-Tacoma International that evening and the queue was heading for the check-in desks for the overnight BA flight to Heathrow. I took my place at the end of it and despondently shuffled my suitcase along with me as we snaked slowly towards the desks. I was in no hurry; D'Arcy had got me to the terminal in plenty of time so I knew I would not miss the flight.

'David Herriot? I'm looking for Mr David Herriot!' a distant voice in my ears. As the person calling out my name came closer I stepped out of line and owned up.

'Mr Herriot? Could I see your passport please, sir!' I obliged. 'Would you come with me, sir?' I was politely asked as she collected my suitcase and moved me out of the line of people who were now all looking at me agog and wondering just what I might have done and what was about to befall me!

'Sir,' the polite young American woman addressed me, 'D'Arcy Zimmerman has rung us and asked us to upgrade you. You will be flying back Club Class to London this evening.' Well done D'Arcy! You see it's not who you know that counts. It's the people who know the people that you don't know who matter! As I slipped into the very front passenger seat by the window on the port side of the Boeing 767, I fastened my seatbelt and thanked the young lady who had just brought me my first Gin and Tonic. D'Arcy Zimmerman, I owe you one!

I had always enjoyed my time in the States previously, but I had never ever experienced anything quite like those armament tours to the States. It gave me an incredible insight into the culture of the land, its people and the variations from the east coast right through the mid-west to the sunshine and wealth of California. I liked America and the prospect of the annual autumn trip 'Across the Pond' always made the days tied to a desk in London seem that much more worthwhile. Our visit in 1993 finished up in San José and the

---

15. Airbus A380.

ten hour overnight flight from San Francisco back to London got me home somewhat jaded, but the prospect of reuniting with Jo at the weekend was enough to brighten my mood as the taxi dropped me off outside my quarter in Maidenhead.

On Saturday, 16 October 1993, Jo and I dined at our favourite restaurant, 'Perkins' in Plumtree. I had arranged a quiet corner table towards the back of the restaurant and, across the table, we chatted long and lovingly about what we both had been up to for the previous three weeks. As we had now become to expect, the meal was perfect and as we relaxed over our coffee I leant across the table, took Jo's hand in mine and asked her quietly, and without any fanfare, if she would marry me. A week later we were making plans for our wedding! Our delight, however, turned to shock just four days later when Jo's father died suddenly at home. As soon as I received her call, I raced north to Nottingham and together we went home to Thorne to comfort her mother and brothers who, like Jo, were in complete shock. Ted Higham was just 61-years-old and I had only ever met him once! Indeed, Jo had not yet got around to telling him that she was going to remarry.

The staffing process continued apace for all five projects and routinely meetings were held with the MOD(PE) project manager in MOD's St Giles Court building and at the Defence Research Agency at Farnborough in Hampshire with the warhead experts there. As well as having responsibility for all tri-Service air-to-surface weapons projects, I was also accountable for the direction and coordination of elements of the Applied Research Programme and was the UK's point of focus for international collaboration through NATO and other armament groups. The former added to my desk load whilst the latter took me regularly to NATO HQ in Brussels for biannual meetings of the NATO Air Forces Armament Group that dealt specifically with 'mud moving'! I was also tasked as First Reporting Officer for the civil servants who provided clerical support within Dusty Miller's directorate. Day-to-day it was a busy schedule, but it was never as busy as those who worked within the Operational Divisions of the MOD. At least I could fix a routine and usually maintain it at the pace required to meet the deadlines set either by me, my Boss or the EAC. Rarely did I have an in-tray much higher than six inches and rarely did I receive 'Red Flagged' files that needed an immediate response. Chaps who worked two floors above me and closer to the ministers on the sixth floor all had skyscraper in-trays packed with files that required their immediate attention. I was grateful for small mercies!

Jo and I set the date of our wedding as Christmas Eve 1993. We felt there was little point in delaying it as the miles being travelled on the M40 each weekend were beginning to take their toll both physically and financially. Moreover, there was plenty of room available in my quarter in Maidenhead and Jo wanted to settle her two girls down in their new family as quickly as possible. From my perspective too it was an ideal day to get married – I would never ever forget the date! Because I was divorced we were obliged to solemnise our wedding in the West Bridgford Registry Office with our four children around us along with my Mum and Dad, Jo's Mum and a few family and friends who had made the effort to support us on Christmas Eve. Naturally, a quiet wedding reception was held at Perkins before we bundled the children into our two cars and headed south to Maidenhead where we arrived not long before Santa and Rudolf. Some people thought us mad, but we thought it to be the perfect day to unite two families. On 12 February the following year our marriage was blessed by Padre Gerry Moore in the CSFC Church[16] at RAF College Cranwell and, on Valentine's Day, we headed for Heathrow in a snowstorm to spend our honeymoon in Rome.

There was definitely something of the international jet set life working in OR(Air). As well as my annual autumn pilgrimage stateside, along with the MOD(PE) project team and my desk officer for SR(A)1236, I took the opportunity to visit Rafael in Israel to discuss their proposal that they hoped would match our requirement. The company had, under licence from Martin Marietta, been manufacturing the Popeye missile for some years which they had successfully sold back to, and had been in-service with, the USAF as Have Nap. With the enhancement of a turbojet engine and folding wings to give it extended range and stability, Popeye was a good contender for CASOM. Our visit to Israel was helped immensely by my being friends with the then air attaché, Simon Erskine Crum, a fellow from the Buccaneer world. Simon did an outstanding job of ensuring both our safety and our entertainment whilst we were in and around Tel Aviv. He also accompanied us on our visit to the Rafael factory near Galilee and gave us a guided tour of some of the ancient relics of the Middle East. Unfortunately, demonstrations in Jerusalem precluded a visit there.

---

16. The RAF denominate religion into three groups: Church of England; Roman Catholic; and Church of Scotland and Free Churches (CSFC) or odds and sods as they are colloquially referred to!

In 1995, Bill Tyack led a team to Riyadh in Saudi Arabia to provide briefings on some of the ongoing projects within his MOD department. Our opposite numbers in the Saudi MOD were particularly keen to learn more about Eurofighter and CASOM and so I went along, as part of the briefing team, to give them an unclassified update on all our weapons programmes. From as early as the mid-1960s, the UK had been trading arms for oil with friendly countries in the Middle East and particularly with the Saudis. Sales of Lightning fighters and Strikemaster light bombers were contracted between the British Aircraft Corporation and the Royal Saudi Air Force in 1966, but in the late 70s the USA got their foot in the door with a contract for F-15s to replace the Lightnings. So when Tornado came along Margaret Thatcher, the then Prime Minister, lobbied hard on behalf of British industry and on 26 September 1985 the defence ministers of the UK and Saudi Arabia signed a Memorandum of Understanding (MoU) in London for the purchase of forty-eight Tornado bombers, twenty-four Tornado interceptors, thirty Hawk training aircraft and a range of weapons, radar and spares, as well as a pilot-training programme. A further tranche of Tornado bombers was ordered in July 1988. The MoU was known as the Al-Yamamah Project and in 1995 it was still going strong. We were undertaking our Riyadh briefings under the terms of the MoU. The MoU insisted that flights inbound to Riyadh were undertaken on board the Saudi Arabian national carrier, Saudia, but that flights outbound to London could be taken with British Airways. I think the real truth of the matter was that inbound on Saudia passengers arrived sober, whereas outbound one needed a drink to get over the Saudi culture shock!

So there I was sat with my colleagues in the front row of the upper deck of a Saudia 747 on a Friday evening in early May, drinking their Club Class carrot juice and preparing for my alcohol-free overnight flight to Riyadh. Suddenly, there was an almighty crashing sound and the aircraft lurched ten feet to its right; well it felt as if it had. Nobody said a word, but everybody stopped supping for just a moment. No conflagration ensued and the stewardesses went about their business as if nothing untoward had happened at all. They were trained to remain relaxed in a crisis. Either that or they were oblivious to what had just happened! We continued to sup our foul orange liquid whilst all the while musing that a G&T might have been a better tipple given the circumstances we now found ourselves pondering. Eventually the flight deck door opened and a seemingly bemused aircraft captain sauntered past and headed downstairs. He was back within five minutes and immediately on the cabin intercom.

There was an intense gale blowing outside and, before we had boarded, Jo had rung me to tell me that a garden fence had blown down and that she had been in touch with Uxbridge to get somebody out to repair it. She is a very capable woman and so I knew that it was more an info call rather than a plea for help.

Bing Bong! 'Ladies and gentlemen, this is your captain speaking. I am afraid that a very large container has been blown across the apron and it has struck the number three engine. I'm afraid this aircraft will not be going to Riyadh tonight. If you would like to remain in your seats, the cabin crew will organise an orderly exit from the plane where you can meet with service support personnel' etc. etc. etc…

This presented a problem for Bill Tyack and our team. We were planned to arrive in Riyadh in sufficient time to shower and get ourselves to the Saudi MOD on the Saturday morning, the start of their working week, to brief our opposite numbers. Without a flight on the Friday night we were scuppered. The service support personnel were apologetic and informed us that hotel rooms at Heathrow were being arranged and that flights would be organised the following morning to get us to Riyadh. Helpful, but not helpful given our deadline. After thirty or so minutes contemplating 'what next', I noticed three letters on the top right-hand corner of my boarding card. Three letters that came courtesy of Al Yamamah, I suspected. The three crucial letters, V, I and P, might just open a few doors for us, if I were to point them out to the staff still loitering at the gate and rebuffing questions from still anxious passengers.

I hadn't opened my mouth before I was hit with 'We are doing our best, Sir, please be patient.' I sidled a bit closer and as tactfully as I could I pointed to the top right corner of my boarding card! Things started happening before I had got to the end of my 'I wonder if this might carry any…'

Before we knew it we had been escorted from the gate back into the Arrivals Hall and straight up to the Check-In Desk for the overnight flight with Gulf Air to Bahrain. There we were issued with Club Class boarding cards, meal vouchers and an invitation to spend the five hours until boarding at 2200hrs in the American Airlines Admirals' Lounge. Well! It was 5pm! It was Friday!

It was Happy Hour in every RAF officers' mess in the land! The Admirals' Lounge seemed an excellent place to while away five hours and, what's more, the booze was free! As the Gulf Air jet taxied to Runway 27 at Heathrow just after 10pm I settled into my first on-board G&T, looked around at my now very mellow travelling companions and pondered what might have been had the container stayed put and the Saudia flight left on time!

The OR(Air) team rolled off the Boeing 767 in Bahrain into the early morning sun and the blazing heat of a Persian Gulf Saturday. After a quick shower in the terminal, we all climbed as soberly as we could up the steps of a Saudia 737 that then whisked us west to Riyadh, where we arrived just in time for our appointment in the Saudi MOD building at 1000hrs.

The briefing to the Saudi MOD staff went well, in general, with lots of good questions being asked about Eurofighter and its capabilities and performance. Unfortunately for me, my CASOM pitch was last on the agenda and I felt sure, as I took to my feet, that the audience felt that they were now there out of sufferance. The senior man present was a Saudi one-star officer who, I discovered subsequently, spent most of his time watching cartoons on a television screen below his desk during my presentation. However, despite his lower rank, the man in overall charge, who sat right by the entrance door to prevent early departures one presumes, was a RSAF major who was a prince of the House of Saud. He had been watching and listening to the whole proceedings and had, from my observation, been more interested in the attentiveness of the audience than the subject matter at hand.

I did not particularly enjoy the experience of my first and last visit to Saudi Arabia. The limitations on daily life imposed by the House of Saud on the population, visitors and contract workers alike are, in my opinion, outrageous and an infringement on modern day society and the population's – particularly the women – human rights. My visit there in 1995 convinced me that no matter what my career prospects might be, upon my retirement from the RAF, I would not be going to work in Saudi Arabia. I was only too glad to climb onboard the British Airways 747 out of Jeddah at the end of the visit and head back to Heathrow.

Following a last minute call to support air operations in Operation Granby in 1991 and having served in the Royal Air Force as a 'stop gap' measure for twenty-five years, the Buccaneer was eventually laid to rest on 31 March 1994. To commemorate its remarkable military career with both the RN and the RAF, as well as twenty-six years with the SAAF, the 'mother of all parties' was organised over the final weekend at Lossiemouth. John Fraser, whom I had first met at Laarbruch in the early 1980s, was tasked with its organisation. He was, like my elder siblings, a Tain lad. 'Fras' had done a marvellous job of organising sponsorship for the event, which included, amongst other things, an impressive open day with an equally impressive air display,[17] a hangar party, a dinner night in the officers' mess and a church service. A full three-day event! As many people who could get there made it to Lossie for the weekend and, just as the advertising beforehand had stated, it was a fitting closure to an outstanding era for all those who flew and serviced the mighty Buccaneer throughout its thirty-six years of faithful service in the air. Much beer had been drunk throughout those years, some good friends and highly competent aviators had not returned and from its many operational excursions across the Globe either in the hands of FAA, RAF or SAAF crews many war stories had been told.

As I nursed a very serious hangover on the flight back south, I considered the thought with Jo that it was important that we did not let the spirit of the Buccaneer Force die just because the aircraft had come to the end of its useful life. Her response was typical.

'Well do something about it then!'

Back in my office in MOD I began to put some feelers out and before very long it became quite apparent that there was a strong swell of opinion that supported my view. Why wouldn't there have been? The people who flew the Buccaneer were a privileged few. We considered ourselves to be members of an exclusive club. We all loved the aircraft like we loved our first girlfriend. So in early 1995, with the support of Air Commodore Graham Pitchfork who volunteered to be chairman, I set about recruiting members to the Buccaneer Aircrew Association. Sir Michael Knight, who had been my station commander at Laarbruch on my first tour and who was then a retired air chief marshal, accepted the role of president and Vice Admiral Sir Ted Anson, who had been the RN's first Buccaneer squadron commander and had done test flying with Blackburns in the aircraft's earliest days, took the reins as vice-president.

We offered life membership for the princely sum of £100 and annual membership for the much reduced figure of £10 per annum. Our plan was

---

17. Buccaneers 'wiring' Lossiemouth at extremely low heights and maximum speed, actually!

to use the life members' contributions to purchase a Buccaneer from the scrap metal dealer who had bought all the airframes from the MOD. I was astounded when, by return, over two hundred and twenty aircrew took out life membership and some one hundred and fifty opted in as annual members. Our airframe, XX901, cost us just £6,000 and so, with nearly £25,000 in the bank, we secured not only the aircraft, but also its movement to the Yorkshire Air Museum where it remains to this day on public display! One of the peripheral advantages of being in a weapons related job in MOD at the time was that I was able to touch up my contacts for display weapons to stand alongside XX901 at YAM. HEL provided me with four BL755, whilst BAe (Dynamics) gave the association a MARTEL TV missile and a Sea Eagle. Texas Instruments donated a dummy Paveway 2. MOD itself provided the BAA with two 28lb practice bombs and two SNEB pods with two 68mm rockets. But my *coup de grâce* was the securing of a WE177 nuke training round from my contact at the RAFASUPU. All these weapons are held on inventory and are on permanent display at YAM alongside XX901.

With the aircraft and its move to Yorkshire complete we still had sufficient funds to sustain the association over its projected lifetime, subsidise a biennial dinner and refurbish the aircraft as and when it was required. With our annual income we decided to publish a biannual sixteen-page glossy newsletter where members could submit and read articles that allow them to relive the war stories we used to regale each other with in the bar. In 2019, even with some seventy members who have departed to the great hangar in the sky, the BAA membership stands at just under five hundred.

We took two conscious decisions. The first was that we would never attempt to regenerate the aircraft as a flying machine and the second was that we would maintain its 'sand pink' camouflage from Operation Granby rather than risk an unseemly battle between retired air marshals who might seek to use their 'seniority' to have the aircraft decked out in 'my squadron's' markings! For many years before the BAA was formed we had always been an egalitarian bunch of drinkers at our annual Bucc Blitz and whilst we deferred to our knights of the realm, rank held no place at our social gatherings; it seemed sensible, therefore, to ensure that the decorating of XX901 followed that simple, but sensible rule! As the BAA's founding member I took on the role of association secretary and, in 2019, have held the position for twenty-four years!

With my now customary dedication to seeing a task through to its end, I arranged with my desk officer at Innsworth that I would remain in OR(Air) for an extra year to see the projects through to conclusion. The contract for SR(A)1242 had been signed off in Dallas with Texas Instruments to replenish our Paveway stock, Project Passover was complete and some of the stock of BL755 was in the process of being upgraded to RBL755. Both SR(A)1236 and SR(A)1238 had received EAC approval to issue 'Invitations to Tender' and so, having spent three years fighting for their very existence, I did not wish to leave the department at this most crucial time.

We received seven bids for SR(A)1236 and a smaller number for SR(A)1238. AAAW was the Cinderella project compared to CASOM, which had attracted much more interest from industry and was deemed in HMG circles to be the more necessary requirement. At one point over the previous three years I had had to fight to retain SR(A)1238's whole funding to avoid the Treasury taking it back into core to build a new hospital in East London. Twenty years on MBDA's [18] Brimstone missile, formerly referred to in MOD as SR(A)1238, is winning high praise in both the House of Commons and the UK press for its outstanding success and its effective pinpoint accuracy against the Islamic terrorist organisation 'Daesh' in both Syria and Iraq. I am so glad that my tenacity and the efforts of my team in OR51(Air) secured Brimstone as the worthy winner of that down-selection.

With a requirement for nine hundred missiles at a budgeted unit cost of £1M each the CASOM contract was worth £900M to the winner. It was, therefore, a much more lucrative project than AAAW from a company perspective and bids came from across the Globe. From the USA, Hughes offered an air-launched variant of Tomahawk, Texas Instruments a long-range variant of JSOW and McDonnell Douglas proposed Harpoon ER. Rafael in Israel offered Popeye whilst BAe Dynamics and GEC-Marconi together offered a poor contender that went by the name of Pegasus.[19] However, racing through on the rails ran a dark horse from Germany, KEPD-360, manufactured by Daimler Benz/Bofors. Taurus, as their missile was called, fitted the SR(A)1236 requirement almost completely and was

---

18. At the time of contract award, Brimstone was being offered by GEC-Marconi based in Stanmore in Middlesex. However, shortly afterwards, the company was absorbed into British Aerospace Dynamics and has subsequently morphed into MBDA.
19. Not to be confused with the air-launched rocket developed by Orbital ATK capable of carrying small payloads of up to 443 kilograms (977lb) into low Earth orbit.

affordable. Others either did not match the SR(A) as well, were incomplete or not advanced sufficiently to meet the required 'In Service Date' (ISD).

Just before the winner was announced BAe Dynamics submitted a 'Best and Final Offer'. Not only did they submit a BAFO, but within it they announced that they were amalgamating their bid with Matra, forming a new company called Matra British Aerospace Dynamics and basing their bid predominantly on the Matra Apache/SCALP missile. The receipt of that BAFO forced the MOD to invite BAFO's from all the original bidders, delayed the project significantly if not considerably and resulted in nobody being able to compete with the Anglo/French missile.[20] And thus Storm Shadow was born! I use the term 'born' very loosely here as, at the time of contract signing in 1996 no metal had been bashed and Storm Shadow was very much a 'paper' missile with real concern that it would never make its ISD. Thanks, however, to Saddam Hussein's invasion of Kuwait in 1990 and thus a precipitous drive to give RAF Tornado's an alternative weapon to JP233, Storm Shadow made it into service in late 2001 and was first used in anger during the 2003 invasion of Iraq.

My four years in MOD came to an end in early 1997. I had thoroughly enjoyed my time as a staff officer at the heart of the MOD. I had even enjoyed my commute from Maidenhead to London every day, albeit the sweaty tube journey from Paddington to Embankment was beginning to pall by the time it was coming to an end. I had thoroughly enjoyed my first three years of marriage to Jo although it had not always been easy bringing together two sets of children who had been rocked by quite different traumas in their young lives. Jealousies abounded and they were not always well settled by two adults keen to protect their own offspring. Jo and I had been able to mix business with pleasure and I had, at our expense, even managed to get her out to Dallas for a long weekend when I was dealing with Texas Instruments and again to San Diego for a few days before Christmas at the end of one of my lengthy tours to the USA. I had acted as deputy for the group captain, had managed the civilian staff in our department, taken a 'roadshow' around all the RAF's mud-moving units to brief them on our projects and gain feedback from operational aircrew that assisted with the development of our

---

20. There was some suspicion within MOD that somebody within the Department of Trade and Industry had sneaked necessary information to Matra/BAeD in order that a 'British' company secured the contract but nothing was ever investigated or proved to the best of my knowledge.

staff requirements and I had, according to my ex-brother-in-law who was my second reporting officer:

… run the busiest and highest profile office in OR (Air); succeeded with first-class results; and kept my team working well and pulling together.

Apparently in his words:

I didn't seek limelight gratuitously and was managerial, supportive and inspirational!

Chapter Ten

Deliberate Guard

All-in-all I was extremely satisfied with my first tour as a wing commander, and what turned out to be, my last tour in the MOD-box! After thirteen years treading water as a flight lieutenant, I had managed to reverse a downward trend in the next rank and, after four years as a three-ringer, was heading back upwards in my chosen career. I needed, however, a flying tour to continue the progress and at almost forty-eight years of age that was looking less and less likely. Accordingly, I negotiated with my desk officer for a posting to the Department of Initial Officer Training (DIOT) at the RAF College Cranwell as Wing Commander Cadets. I had tried to get there as a flight lieutenant whilst on 12 Squadron and, not surprisingly given my misdemeanours early in my career, had been given a 'Not Recommended' by my then squadron commander. Now was my chance, if I was not going to fly again why not try the next best thing as a commanding officer and deal with people. Cas Capewell, whom I had known from Buccaneers and had attended ASC with, was now my desk officer at RAF Innsworth. He needed to argue my case against the background of my historical youthful transgression. The air commodore who made the final decision in this game of poker was also a Buccaneer man. He had known me last some twenty years prior and held the highest card!

Cas sweetened the pill for his Boss by recounting my 'changed character' on the ASC and my clear and sincere ambition since becoming a senior officer. The fact that I volunteered for an Out of Area appointment immediately, and prior to any subsequent posting, persuaded the One-Star to give me the chance. I was posted to DIOT on 1 October 1997, but only after I had accepted a four-month deployment to the air staff at Incirlik in Turkey, in support of air operations policing the skies of Iraq.

In March we moved from Maidenhead to a married quarter at 4 Plantation Road, Cranwell and settled in whilst I began preparing for a summer in the sun. I had explained to Jo that it would not be possible for her to visit me in Turkey and so arranged for her, her mother and her two daughters, Helen and Hannah, to spend a fortnight in a rather upmarket villa on the north-eastern corner of Cyprus. Just after I had booked and paid for this extravaganza, I was informed that I would not be heading to Turkey, but to one of my old stomping grounds at Gioia del Colle in Italy. There, throughout the summer of 1997, I was to fill the post of RAF Detachment Commander responsible for the running of a Non-Formed Unit deployed to support air operations on NATO's Operation Deliberate Guard.

I arrived at Bari Airport via Rome in late April 1997 and was met by an MT driver who ferried me back to Gioia. The post of RAF DetCo up to that point had been held by a group captain but, upon my arrival, had been downgraded to that of a wing commander. The handover from Ray Horwood was swift and, after a quick introduction to the Italian Base Commander, I was left in charge of some two hundred personnel, which included aircrew and groundcrew for a flight of six Jaguar GR1A that were tasked in the CAS and recce roles over Kosovo. My officer cadre consisted of two squadron leaders, a Chief of Staff, who was my deputy, and an Engineering Officer, and a junior officer who ran the personnel staff. The squadron personnel rotated regularly, to and fro, between the three Jaguar squadrons at RAF Coltishall in Norfolk. However, my Non-Formed Unit personnel were there for four months as a minimum. As well as the three other commissioned officers, there was a weather man from the Royal Auxiliary Air Force's Mobile Meteorology Unit and twenty plus airmen of different ranks to man the bomb dump and service the communications, catering, security, supply and administrative needs of the unit. There was even a NAAFI manager who managed himself and his small shop and an army postman who ran the British Forces Post Office that received and dispatched 'blueys'[1] for the unit's personnel.

The aircrew lived in the Hotel Svevo, whilst all the troops were accommodated in hotels within easy reach of the airbase; some delightfully positioned on the Adriatic shore with all the usual 'holiday attractions'! My officers lived in self-catering flats close to the hotel and within easy walking distance of the town centre; I was allocated my own two-bedroom flat in the same complex. A flat, I must add, that was eminently capable of providing a holiday in the sun for my wife and family and one that would have, had I known early enough, saved me £1500 on their holiday in Cyprus; but hey – *c'est la vie*! If rumour is to be believed, such was the wealth that our presence

---

1. A 'bluey' is similar to an airmail letter but is issued free and sent post-free. They are especially made for sending to and from the Armed Forces; termed 'a bluey' because of the colour of the lightweight paper used.

brought to the local community, that the local Mafia had issued a protection order on behalf of all the RAF personnel at Gioia! Certainly, there was never any trouble in town that involved my personnel and we were always warmly welcomed whenever we ventured ashore to dine or enjoy the festivals with the townsfolk.

The work schedule was moderate as the squadrons managed their own affairs and relied on me, and my staff, to ensure that all their needs were catered for. There were awkward moments on both sides when communication broke down and demands were not met but, in general, it was a smooth passage. Despite the fact that there was concealed envy by some of my troops, there was little friction between the squadron people, who served a maximum of two months in theatre, and my Support Unit personnel who were away from home for twice as long.

Amongst my other tasks during Operation Deliberate Guard, was to prepare for the unit's annual participation in the Remembrance Day Service at Bari War Cemetery. Although I would be long departed from Gioia by November, a recce had to be conducted, local delegates spoken with and an Administration Order written. I was fortunate that I had a personal assistant to man my office, type and answer the telephone when I was out and about and an interpreter to help negotiate with the locals. One of the most pleasant tasks for the Gioia DetCo was to take tea with an elderly Italian lady who had owned the first ever yoghurt factory in Italy. To my eternal shame, I can no longer remember her name and I suspect by now she is long dead, but the afternoon spent in her company was a most wonderful experience. As a young girl she had been living in Bari when Allied Forces took the town during the fall of Italy in 1944. As elements of the British forces swept north up the Adriatic coast in an outflanking manoeuvre that avoided the main battles at Monte Cassino and Anzio she met her future husband, a young British officer, who after the war returned to Italy to marry and take her home to Liverpool. There she had lived on the banks of the Mersey for many years until she and her husband decided to return to Italy to set up their own yoghurt producing business. After his death, she had continued to manage the company and, in retirement, had issued an ever-lasting invitation to the RAF DetCo to join her once during his tour to take tea and listen to the story of her wonderful life and her passion for all things British.

As well as having my own apartment, I was issued with a rather large Lancia as my personal staff car to allow me to fulfil my obligations in the local community. Although a driver was allocated to me for official journeys, I chose to dispense with his services and drive myself to and from meetings usually. I also used it routinely at weekends to visit the Auchan supermarket on route to Bari; to drive to Monopoli, on the Adriatic coast, to buy gargantuan T-Bone steaks at an American Base Exchange there; or to get to the air base's private beach at Chiatona to sunbathe by the Gulf of Taranto. Bari was within easy striking distance, but was a bit of a dive in the evenings and so not particularly suitable for a night out. Indeed, one of my most difficult periods in command at Gioia followed a troops' night out in Bari when three individuals, that included the army postman, were stabbed following an altercation outside a Bari night club. Hospitalised, but not in a life-threatening condition, I became a regular visitor at their bedsides in Bari Hospital where, under the Italian medical system, patients relied on family and friends to sustain them during what seemed to be a 'medical assistance only' environment!

On two occasions, Jo spent a week with me in Gioia and on the second occasion brought Helen and Hannah with her, both of whom very much enjoyed relaxing on the beach at Chiatona. On Jo's first visit to Gioia we were invited as honoured guests of the Base Commander to attend the official opening of the beach! I had been using it almost every weekend since I had arrived, but it did not formally open until June when the Italians decided it was warm enough to be summer! For me, June was the month when it became too bloody hot to sit anywhere other than under a parasol, but I guess the locals knew best! The official 'opening' was a comical affair. As it was to be an official and formal function, I took the decision to use my driver to get us to and from the beach, which was close to thirty miles south of the air base – not too far from the Riva dei Tessali Golf Hotel that I had visited with Steve Cockram ten years previously when we had been stuck at Gioia with a sick Tornado. We dressed in what we thought was appropriate British attire for a 'beach party' but, bearing in mind my position and the formality of the occasion, we left our flip-flops and beach towels behind! Chinos and an open-necked shirt seemed to me to be the order of the day. We arrived early! So early that we had to hide out of sight until we were sure that the majority of people had arrived. Not with any desire for a 'grand entrance', you understand, but more because we were unsure of how things might pan out and our Italian was no better than an ability to put an inflection on the end of our words and maybe, if we remembered, the occasional 'i' or 'a' sound too! We were met on our arrival by a very humble, welcoming and fawning young maggiore[2] who kissed Jo's hand and took mine into his soft and clammy grip for a less than convincing shake. Ushered to a table we sat amongst a group of people who had not one word of English; we were now struggling. We struggled even more when no drink was presented and no food was forthcoming. We sat and stared at each other whilst I racked my brain to come up with something I might have learned in my ill-spent days as a junior officer in Decimomannu. '*Quattro Birra*', somehow did not seem appropriate under the circumstances and nor did '*Che diavolo è il ritardo!*'[3] had I known it at the time! As we smiled and attempted to engage, it soon became apparent that nothing could happen until the Base commander arrived – not even a beer could be issued let alone be drunk. Some forty-five minutes later the party got under way – with a religious service. A priest emerged from the crowd in his full regalia, walked forward to the Colonello and kissed his hand before he extracted him from his seat at the front and walked him smartly forward to the water's edge where, with his thurible[4] wafting potent incense, he blessed the surf! He then blessed the sand, the chairs, the tables and the parasols before blessing the assembled throng; he even blessed the pedalos! Upon completion, and to the accompaniment of much applause, the Base commander stood to the fore and declared the Chiatona Beach open! The event lasted no more than a further thirty minutes and, as soon as the Colonello took his leave, the bar closed and the sandwich trays disappeared.

I was not my own Boss at Gioia. I worked directly for a group captain who was based at HQ 5 ATAF at Vicenza in Northern Italy and went by the title of Commander British Forces Lodestar[5] (Italy). Routinely, I had to fly from Bari to Venice, via Rome to meet with my Boss and discuss aspects of the operation that could not be dealt with over insecure phone lines. It was a worthwhile exercise also from my perspective because, as his deputy in theatre, it allowed him to share with me issues that had manifested themselves in the other units for which he had direct responsibility. Operations such as the RAF's AWACs and Nimrod R1 operations based at Aviano and the Tristar Tanker that was flying out of Palermo, in Sicily, and providing AAR

---

2. Major.
3. What the bloody hell is the delay!
4. A metal container suspended from chains, in which incense is burned during worship services.
5. Lodestar was the name that the British had given to the operation known to NATO as Deliberate Guard.

for the Jaguars. It was also good to have a night out in Vicenza, which was far more cosmopolitan than Gioia, and build up my Alitalia Air Miles account!

One of the problems of commanding an out of area operational deployment was that the unit was always in the firing line for high level visits. I had two such visits during my time as DetCo. The first of these visits was from the Command Accountant's team at HQ Strike Command who wished to visit to seek clarification on what allowances we received for serving in Italy and how these could be reduced and, thereby, save the Command Accountant a few pence in his budget.

There were a number of remarkably good restaurants in Gioia and my staff and I frequented them routinely rather than scratch around cooking for ourselves in our flats. That said, the T-Bone steaks were usually enjoyed most when pooled together for a team barbecue on the roof of the Svevo and washed down by vast quantities of beer and local wine! And there were occasions when I chose to dine alone so that I could catch up with paperwork, work on my family history, action papers that Jo sent me associated with my task as secretary of the BAA, or catch a match from the British Lions tour to South Africa. But often we would gather for a couple of beers after work and then head into town either to the Bougainvillea restaurant or the Trattoria dai Bizantini where I was routinely welcomed as '*Signore, il grande formaggio*';[6] a title ordained by my team on an earlier visit!'

As with virtually all military postings at the time, personnel in overseas locations were entitled to Local Overseas Allowance to offset the differences in the cost of the local standard of living. Gioia del Colle was no exception and after the unit cashier had doled out wads of Italian Lire to expectant and overjoyed officers and airmen each Friday, the postmaster, with open arms, did a roaring trade as almost each and every happy recipient deposited his LOA straight into a post office savings account. I know from my own experience that it soon built up and there are a set of rather fine Le Crueset pans still in use in this household that were purchased on the strength of the UK Pound against the 1997 Italian Lira and the tax free purchasing offered by the NAAFI Manager!

Anyway, back to my tale! With the impending arrival of the Command Accountant's bean counters I knew that there was only one instruction that needed to be given if LOA was to survive at the levels that we received it in

---

6. Sir, the big cheese!

Southern Italy. I gathered all the officers together and instructed them that we would be hosting the visitors in town that night, but we were all to be well aware of their motives for coming to Gioia. There was to be no Bougainvillea or Bizantini this night! Both these restaurants were to be bypassed and our guests were to be entertained at the colloquially named 'Chicken Shack' further along the Corso Garibaldi! It was to be made clear to the accountants that this fine eatery, a fried chicken and chips emporium, was all we could afford on the 'meagre' LOA provided. Unfortunately, LOA was not increased as a result of their visit, but neither was it reduced!

The second and much more important visitor to Gioia during my tenure was the Chief of the Defence Staff, General Sir Charles Guthrie. He brought with him Air Marshal Sir John Day who was at the time Deputy Chief of the Defence Staff(Commitments) and Chief of Joint Operations. Between them they had a considerable entourage of PSOs and ADCs. No Chicken Shack for this lot then! It was all hands to the pump to organise a suitable banquet and gathering in the Svevo! They arrived just after lunch on a very hot July afternoon in an aircraft of the Queen's Flight which was parked on the main ASP at Gioia. With full Italian pomp and with honour guard and bugle band assembled, Sir Charles stepped from the aircraft to be welcomed by the Base Commander, before I stepped forward to salute and welcome him to Gioia; Sir John followed behind him. They had come from Vicenza and it was evident from their banter and relaxed pose that they had clearly been well entertained the night before. The following morning they were bound for Sarajevo. In the meantime, I had to brief them on my unit's role, the Jaguar Boss had to do likewise for his team and young Nick Prytherch, the flight lieutenant commanding the Reconnaissance and Intelligence Centre, had to show them some of the better results from Jaguar recce missions over Kosovo. The visit was an outstanding success and thanks to the efforts of all of the NFU staff who had worked overtime to ensure that the place was in tip top readiness we departed base in my car for the Hotel Svevo, where rooms were booked for all the visitors, and a Dining-in Night.

By Christ, these people were clearly attuned to drinking! They were on a bit of a round-robin of the European conflict zones and had had more practice than us in the previous few days! The hotel had put on a marvellous spread and although the two knights of the realm were safely tucked up by 0200hrs the 'tail end Charlies' were still going strong come 0400hrs! CDS's PSO, Captain Charles Style RN, was the absolute ring leader and, some years later, I was to have the delight of reminding him of his delinquent night in Gioia when he and I had been drinking until the very early hours on the back of a fine dinner in the Hotel Svevo! Their aircraft departed at 0800hrs prompt with all passengers fully accounted for! I spent that morning relaxing in a large leather armchair on the veranda outside the back of my office whilst inspecting the inside of my eyelids! I was hidden from general view as no footpaths or roads passed my location! Unfortunately, I forgot about the fire escape from the RIC that exposed me to those of its staff when they popped out for a smoke! The subsequent photograph and ransom note that arrived on my desk later within a brown OHMS envelope was testament to the fact that the previous evening's largesse had taken its toll on me! War is hell!

The signal, directed to CBFL(I) in Vicenza, from CDS's office that followed after their departure wrote very favourably about the warm welcome, hospitality and professionalism of my team – no mention was made of the early hours drinking session! The next signal I received, that announced my next group of visitors, was somewhat more serious and was marked IMMEDIATE. This was an 'eat after reading' signal and advised me that I was about to be inundated by personnel participating in Operation Alleviate. Now look! There's no point in diving onto Google – you won't find it. Well not in a military context anyway! However, the signal gave us less than twenty-four hours to prepare. It directed me to organise accommodation on base for a number of Support Helicopter personnel, their crews and aircraft and to ready and secure a hangar area where a significant number of Special Forces personnel would bed down until they either went into action or were stood down. No other information was forthcoming, but it was clear from all the communications received that Alleviate took priority over all other activity currently being undertaken by the British at Gioia! The Earth did not stop revolving, but my team and I went into overdrive to prepare for the arrival of the clandestine force.

They came, they planned, they ate and slept on base and they recovered to the UK without taking action! Whatever had boiled up in Albania had simmered down without the need for UK Special Forces involvement! It was for me, and my team, an eye-opener and proved to me once again that when the pressure is on, the training, expertise and will of the average serviceman will come to the fore and succeed.

All too soon my four months in the sun were coming to an end. My successor was inbound and I had, after twenty-eight years in the RAF, earned my first campaign medal. Earned? Well OK! After three months on operations on the periphery of a war zone and in direct support of operations one had 'earned' one's medal. For those flying regularly over hostile terrain or engaging with the enemy in country the rules were more accommodating, but nevertheless I was entitled to wear it just like the rest of my team who had completed three-quarters of their tour at Gioia del Colle. With my boxes, which were packed with Le Crueset pans, cases of wine from the local vineyard and all my military equipment that I could not fit in my suitcase, already airborne in the weekly resupply C-130 and on their way back to the UK, I welcomed Ashley Stevenson to Gioia del Colle and headed off to Bari to catch my Alitalia flights home.

I had some disembarkation leave to take before I reported to Whittle Hall at Cranwell and was looking forward to spending time with my family. When I got home, I was delighted to discover that Jo had booked a quiet, romantic weekend together in Queen Victoria's very own suite in the Royal York Hotel.

Chapter Eleven

I'm Spartacus

In December 1915, when the Royal Naval Air Service split from the Royal Flying Corps, a young Navy lieutenant was sent north in his biplane to find and establish a location that would fill the Navy's need for an independent flying training school. Landing just east of the Lincoln Edge[1] and west of the village of Cranwell he planted his White Ensign on a patch of grass that seemed, to him at any rate, to be a suitable landing strip fit for naval purpose! Happy with his selection, the RN opened their Central Depot and Training Establishment at Cranwell in April 1916 and operated successfully there for two years until the formation of the RAF on 1 April 1918 when the airfield fell into light blue hands. When the Great War ended in November that year, Sir Hugh Trenchard[2] determined that the RAF must remain an independent service rather than be subsumed back into either, or both, of the Army and the Navy. The establishment of an air academy, which would provide basic flying training, provide intellectual education and give a sense of purpose to the future leaders of his Service was therefore at the top of his list of priorities. Trenchard selected Cranwell as the most suitable location for the RAF College because, in his words:

> *'Marooned in the wilderness, cut off from pastimes they could not organise for themselves, the cadets would find life cheaper, healthier and more wholesome.'*

He was not wrong. Cranwell is peculiar for a village of its size in that it does not have a public house. The College history tells us that, in an effort to retain control of the cadets and remove temptation in the local village, a ban was imposed on there ever being a pub in Cranwell. To this day, no pub has ever opened its doors to the public.

---

1. The Lincoln Edge, or Lincoln Cliff as it is also known, is a limestone escarpment that runs roughly north-south through Lincolnshire.
2. Chief of the Air Staff and Founder of the RAF.

The large and imposing neo-classical College Hall, which incorporates design aspects of Christopher Wren's Royal Hospital at Chelsea, was completed in 1933 and was granted Grade 2 listed status in 1987. It forms an impressive backdrop for any casual motorist looking north from Cranwell Avenue, the public road that separates the College from the operational flying side of the RAF station. I was very much looking forward to becoming part of its establishment and a cog in the process of the training and education of the future officer corps of the RAF.

I took over from Chris Adams as Wing Commander Cadets on 1 October 1997 and found very quickly that there was a serious morale problem amongst my staff! At that time the Initial Officer Training Course lasted twenty-four weeks and was split into three parts. The first four weeks formed the basis upon which the other two phases could build. It was a militarisation phase, for want of a better expression, and included typical training in military skills – drill; weapon drill and maintenance; personal hygiene; managing your kit; and physical training. All things that are common across all three Services were covered and all of which converted Joe Public into a military being, or tried to. The other two phases focused on Leadership and Officer Development in that order. Failure to become a military being in the first phase would result in a four-week back course or rejection and, similarly, failure at the subsequent mid-course break point or pre-graduation would have similar disastrous results.

The morale issue had been created by a senior hierarchy that deemed that 'a bum on a seat was better than no bum at all'. The problem that that presented was that my directing staff officers were disgruntled because, despite their hard work, written reports and verbal debriefs, candidates that they had recommended for suspension from training were being allowed to continue by the executive officers at the time and endorsed by the commandant.

I commanded four training squadrons at DIOT. Each squadron was commanded by a squadron leader and staffed by flight lieutenants. These junior officers filled the role of flight commanders or training advisers dependent upon whether they were on one of the three mainstream training squadrons or worked for my deputy, Squadron Leader Cadets, with the remit of setting the standards required of my staff and preparing and booking all field activities. At one point in my time at DIOT I had sixty annual reports to write for my junior officers. It was a sizeable wing and low morale was a danger that could become an issue; especially if it was detected by the student body.

After just a few weeks in post, I assembled the staff of Cadet Wing in a lecture room and laid my proposal on the line to them. I let them know from the outset that I trusted them implicitly. I made it clear that I understood their frustration and I told them that I would do everything within my power to resolve the situation to both their satisfaction and to mine. However, I did point out that some of their reports that I had read were incoherent, grammatically poor and had glaring holes in their argument or made unsubstantiated recommendations. In short, I promised them that if they tightened up their reports I would back them to the hilt. I further promised that after each case was discussed and agreed at either the mid-course or the pre-graduation Matrix Meeting, I would promote those who deserved promoting or reject those that either needed further training or were to be shown the door. I also confided in them that it was my view that the RAF was a club and that only those people who deserved membership should ever be permitted to join our club! I put it as simply as this. If you would not choose to stand in the corner of the bar sharing a beer with an individual then he or she probably did not deserve membership of our exclusive club. However, the paperwork supporting their exclusion would have to be tight and, of course, could not use that analogy as a reason for his or her dismissal!

I was confident that if they backed me and I backed them and their reports were improved and endorsed to the hierarchy by me, then we would have no further problems. Following my first Matrix Meeting, which was a mid-course review, I presented six candidates to the commandant for suspension from training and six candidates returned their RAF uniforms and caught the next train out of Grantham station. Morale improved instantly!

I also made it clear at that meeting that I suspected that the reason the staff were at DIOT was because they had, like me, wished to come back to their alma mater for a fulfilling tour. I also stressed that I was hopeful that their motive was driven by their own experience of the IOTC when they had first undergone it. I think it is fair to state, at this stage, that for all those present at that initial meeting, and who were from the ground branches of the officer cadre of the RAF, both of those statements were true. It was not necessarily the case for those whose last tour had been in a cockpit of a fast jet or on the flight deck of a 'heavy' or helicopter. Many, but definitely not all, of the aircrew present were consigned to Cranwell either because there was no cockpit available when they were posted from their last unit or they had not cut the mustard in that flying role. I was certainly not happy that that was the case, but in my initial months at Cranwell there was not a lot I could do about it!

Unfortunately, for the first year of my tour, I had to contend with a 'Yes Man' as my immediate superior! I found it incredibly difficult working for a man who could not make a decision without thinking first whether that decision would be acceptable to the man above him in the chain. He dithered over whether cadets should be put forward for review or not. He dithered over whether a particular group of cadets could participate in a particular activity. He hid in his office if he thought that he might be asked at a group discussion whether he might have a view on a particular subject. If I went to him with a problem and a sensible solution he would deliberate for days before deciding whether to go with me or not. Anyway, it was a nightmare for the first twelve months and so I decided in the end to declare UDI[3] and only trouble him with detail or seek an answer to a question when I had no alternative, but to do so.

I was fourth down the pecking order from the commandant, an air vice-marshal, and I reported directly to the group captain who was dubbed Director Department of Initial Officer Training. He in turn reported to an air commodore who was the Director of OASC. My office in Whittle Hall was next door to the group captain's, but between us in her small office sat Angie Taylor, his PA, who did a sterling job of managing us both and keeping visitors to our doors regulated. Another wing commander, Wing Commander Training, was responsible for all aspects of administration relating to the cadets, for ensuring that our training syllabi met the stringent standards set by the RAF's training professionals (he was one of their branch) and for ensuring that all aspects of graduation were prepared in a seemly manner. He was also responsible for cadets undertaking the first four weeks of the course – the militarisation phase. My task on paper was a simple one. Receive from Wg Cdr Trg all those cadets who successfully completed the initial phase of the course and, over the next eighteen weeks, turn them from 'military beings' into competent RAF officers. The mathematicians among you will

---

3. The Cabinet of Rhodesia declared a Unilateral Declaration of Independence (UDI) from Great Britain on 11 November 1965 by announcing that Rhodesia would from then on regard itself as an independent sovereign state. Since then UDI has become a commonly used term for such action in an informal setting.

be trying ever so hard to calculate where I have lost two weeks on a twenty-four week course! Well I will save you from yourselves – the last two weeks were spent preparing for and completing the graduation ceremonial parade. It did not mean, of course, that a cadet could feel able to relax after the twenty-two week point. No promises were given and all notices given after the last Review Board, on Champagne Monday,[4] carried a clear caveat that graduation was dependent upon a cadet's 'continued good progress!'

When the behaviour of one cadet was brought to my attention, I was less than pleased with his officer qualities. He had imbibed rather too heavily at Champagne Monday and decided to have a go at a flight commander, whilst also speaking to him on first name terms. I had no difficulty with the lad enjoying a good drink. I had been there myself in the past. But I did take exception to the fact that he had clearly overstepped the mark with the flight commander. He was not commissioned yet and might not be if he failed to heed again the caveat that had come with the announcement that he had passed the course. His squadron commander and I came up with the perfect punishment. Since he had been offensively drunk and had embarrassed both himself and the flight commander, we decided to publically shame him. The corridor outside my office in Whittle Hall was out of bounds to cadets unless they had a need to be there. Their need to be there was usually driven by them being summoned to my office for some serious transgression of the DIOT code or a failure in their ability to progress on the course.

Many years previously a story had circulated around the RAF about a Vulcan co-pilot who had been lounging in the squadron crewroom when the telephone rang. The conversation went something along the lines of:

'27 Sqn, Flying Officer Bloggs.'

'Bloggs, AOC here, is the squadron commander in the crewroom?'

'AOC… Fuck off!' responded Bloggs, thinking it was a set up.

Bloggs subsequently found himself at HQ 1 Group, sat inside the AOC's outer office at 0800hrs one morning. He waited and waited and waited to be summoned before the great man, but nothing happened. Eventually, at about 0910hrs, Bloggs leapt to attention as the AOC arrived for work, threw his SD hat on a peg and went into his office. Bloggs waited. Morning coffee went in and out and eventually, at 1230hrs, the AOC left his office and headed off

---

4. The day, two weeks before graduation, when cadets were informed of their success, or failure, on the course – champagne flowed that night.

for lunch. Bloggs was instructed to get some lunch in the officers' mess and return by 1315hrs, when the AOC would see him. Back again in the outer office, Bloggs waited and waited. The AOC returned from lunch at 1400hrs, gave the stood-at-attention Bloggs a disdainful look, and disappeared back behind his closed door. Afternoon tea went in and came out. Bloggs was still there at 1615hrs when the AOC came out of his office and said to Bloggs:

'You've been here a long time. Have you come to see me?'

'Yes, Sir,' replied Bloggs, 'Flying Officer Bloggs, 27 Squadron, Sir.'

'Ah! Bloggs! 27 Squadron?'

'Yes, Sir.'

'Bloggs… Fuck Off!' said the AOC and retired back behind his door. Message received and understood by Bloggs and humiliating punishment delivered.

My 'Bloggs' was called to see me, but upon his arrival Angie informed him to wait in the corridor until I was ready to receive him. Cadets who were 'stranded' in the corridor were obliged to stand at ease, but come to attention whenever a commissioned officer ventured into the corridor. Unfortunately for him, his squadron commander had organised a procession of flight commanders to circle through the corridor in a 2-minute cycle such that, for the next hour, Bloggs was seen by virtually every officer in the department and for whom he had to come to attention, continuously, and then recover to the at ease position. When he eventually came into my office, he received a mild dressing down and a word of warning about his future behaviour. He learned his lesson, left with a smile on his face as he realised what we had done and graduated with his comrades ten days later. Bloggs was not my only problem at DIOT, however. There were plenty of cadets who brought with them their personal issues, some easily manageable and others not.

Towards the back end of my tour, I was surprised to discover that I was *in loco parentis* for another cadet who had been at Cranwell for about two months. A Scot, he had graduated from his school[5] in Aberdeenshire at the age of sixteen with the necessary grades to enter DIOT. Now seventeen years of age, he had been joining in all the activities of mess life wholeheartedly; including the drinking sessions. There was little I could do, without embarrassing him, other than to monitor the situation.

---

5. Depending on their month of birth, it is possible for a child in Scotland to leave school with the Scottish equivalent of A-Levels before their seventeenth birthday.

We had our fair share of cadets from other nations in Cadet Wing, some of whom created more mayhem than they could ever solve. During my time in post, and other than the usual clutch from the air forces of Qatar, Oman, Bahrain and the United Arab Emirates, we trained cadets from the Air Wing of the Seychelles Peoples' Defence Forces, Ghana Air Force, Belize Defence Force, Guatemalan Air Force, Royal Brunei Air Force and the Hungarian Air Force. All were trained under the umbrella of 'Foreign and Commonwealth' funding and all brought different challenges for my staff. For those who did not perform to the required standard we, charged with their commissioning, could take little action without the support of their individual embassy. The embassies, for their part, were often not prepared to take action against failing students because many, particularly those from the Middle East, had royal or political connections. It was all very frustrating and equally so for those RAF cadets who viewed the situation, perhaps rightly, as a case of double standards. What could we do other than cause a diplomatic incident? It all changed one day, however, when an Omani cadet and a Qatari cadet were caught cheating in their Bandar[6] Essays. One, or the other, had taken the other's essay and substituted the word Qatar for Oman throughout, or vice versa. It very quickly became apparent that it was the Qatari who was the cheat and a quick telephone call to the Qatari Embassy by Wg Cdr Trg, thankfully his task not mine, brought a delegation from the embassy's air attaché's office to confront the young cadet. DIOT officers were not allowed to be involved and, before we knew it, the young lad was gone and on an aeroplane back to Doha. God knows what retribution befell him when he was back in his homeland. There was no more cheating, however, and all the Qatari cadets improved their performance ever after!

One RAF cadet, who hailed from Wales, had been brought up and educated in the Welsh language. He struggled with written English. He was a good lad. Keen and determined to succeed on the course, but if he couldn't communicate effectively, he was unlikely to do so. We solved the problem easily by paying for him to attend English tuition classes in Lincoln on Saturday mornings. He passed the course and joined the RAF Regiment as a Junior Officer. I hope his troops appreciated the effort that we went to so that they could understand him and read his orders!

---

6. During the course, each cadet had to write an essay about an air power topic of his choice. The best essay of the academic year won its author a trip to the Middle East as an official guest of Prince Bandar bin Saud al Saud, who had himself been a Cranwell cadet and after whom the essay is named.

I use the generic term 'cadet' to describe those under training at DIOT. However, in truth there were three categories of cadet and two designations of rank/position. The term Officer Cadet (OC) referred to those who had joined the IOTC either straight from school or from the ranks of the RAF. Student Officers (SOs), conversely, held a degree and were usually fresh from university or, if an ex-ranker, had achieved a qualifying degree at the Royal Military College of Science at Shrivenham in Wiltshire. SOs were granted greater seniority on graduation and with that came an entry salary greater than those in the other two categories. Whilst SOs and ex-rankers brought with them life experience they also brought attitude, which was often their downfall in the intense training environment at Cranwell. OCs, on the other hand, who had come straight from their mothers' apron strings, were the easiest to train and educate and, whilst they may have struggled initially, often turned out to be the better product by the end of the course.

The process at DIOT in the late 90s was such that at any one time there could be up to one hundred and eighty cadets on one of two courses progressing through the Cadet Wing syllabus. As one course approached graduation another would be completing Field Leadership Camp (FLC) and undergoing its progress Review Board. Following the successful passage of FLC, cadets would attend a Training Dining-In Night in College Hall whilst those about to graduate would, some seven days later, participate in their graduation Dining-In Night in the same venue. But this time they would be wearing their Mess Dress for the first time rather than the interim mess kit that they had worn for the practice event. Thus, as Wg Cdr Cdts, I attended two Dining-In Nights every eight weeks! Indeed, a tour in DIOT was a social whirl and not at all like anything I had experienced, even on a flying tour.

Each function was formal in the sense that it was held in a formal training setting. When the cadets arrived from their basic phase, a 'Meet and Greet' was held for them in which they were assessed by their flight commander on how they integrated with each other and adapted when senior officers were present. As well as the two Dining-In Nights, each squadron also held a dinner night at the end of FLC, at which I was routinely present having travelled to one of the three training areas[7] that we used for this critical leadership training exercise. The final term started with a cocktail party

7. Stanford TA in Norfolk, Otterburn TA in Northumberland or Sennybridge TA in Powys, Wales.

that introduced cadets to the format of the RAF's annual Battle of Britain Receptions and, to close the course, a graduation ball was held in College Hall that was organised by the cadets. Routinely, selected staff officers were invited by the commandant to attend 'Lodge Drinks'[8] with groups of pre-graduation cadets. Add to that the normal social whirl of an RAF station and it was quite an event in the calendar when Jo and I could sit quietly and have a night at home together!

As the commanding officer of Cadet Wing at Cranwell I did not routinely have direct personal contact with the cadets. I adopted very much a 'hands off' approach and left the squadron commanders and their junior officer instructors to get on with the job. When he heard of my posting to Cranwell, my good friend and erstwhile Tornado pilot, Tim Anderson, told me that, when he had been a cadet, the very words 'Wing Commander Cadets' would strike the fear of God into the hearts of the cadet body. I did not want that to be the case during my tenure. I remembered also my unfortunate encounter, in the staff officer toilets, with that former incumbent of the post who had wanted to throw me out of College Hall when I was on the Weapons Employment Course, because my hair was too long! I wanted to have a more open and friendly relationship with both my staff and students. I suspect that the squadron commanders appreciated the fact that I was not breathing down their necks, but was always there with words of advice or guidance when they requested, or needed it. Throughout my tour I had some excellent squadron leaders commanding the four squadrons in my Wing and there was rarely a time when I felt the need to 'advise'. One, Paul Beard, had been a fellow staff officer in the Department of Flying Training in 1991; he was the man who put me into the taxi that, eventually, deposited me at Caspar's Telephone Exchange. Paul took over command of D Squadron in early 1998 and, subsequently, became my deputy as Squadron Leader Cadets, with responsibility for the organization of all the ancillary activities that related to the successful running of the three active training squadrons. He was responsible for all aspects of leadership training, the booking of training areas and the management of all camp deployments from Cranwell. His squadron was also responsible for the running of all short courses within the Wing and for those cadets placed in a holding flight whilst they recovered from medical or pastoral issues that had forced their temporary withdrawal from

---

8. The commandant's residence at Cranwell was 'The Lodge'.

training. Having enjoyed his company in the bars around Holborn when we both worked in Adastral House, and spent a further two years with him as my sidekick in Whittle Hall, we have remained firm friends since and have been known to whack a few balls around our respective golf courses together in our retirement.

Occasionally, however, cadets were singled out to host me, and my wife, at social functions. Probably the most nerve-wracking for the chosen cadet was to host me at the Meet and Greet. Fresh out of the four-week basic phase, it must have been a daunting prospect when their flight commander informed them just who it was that they had to drag round the function and introduce to each of the flight leaders. I always tried to put them at their ease and Jo, who is the easiest of going people, ensured that that was so too. It was interesting to watch how the cadets in each group responded to being introduced to a senior officer. Some were clearly very nervous and some were, occasionally, overbearing or overconfident – neither of which is a good characteristic for a potential officer. I enjoyed finding out where they had all come from, what their background was and, for those with a degree, what subject they had studied at university. After a couple of these gatherings, I developed a trick that surprised some of the cadets who had a degree in Aeronautical Engineering.

'So what did you study at university, Jones?'

'Aeronautical Engineering, Sir'.

'Ah, so you must be a pilot then?'

'Wow, how did you know that, Sir?'

It was easy; all aeronautical engineers want to be pilots. Mechanical and electrical engineers are much more down to earth in their career choices! But we got all sorts. As well as those with engineering degrees, we had cadets with arts and science degrees, some with the most obscure specialisms, all of whom wanted more than anything to gain a commission in the RAF. But perhaps the strangest group of graduates were those who arrived at DIOT with medical and veterinary degrees, but who wanted to be pilots. If I had been their parents and had watched, and paid for, their progress through medical or veterinary school, I think I might just have been a little grumpy at their sudden change of career path!

The squadron commanders seemed expert at selecting suitable cadets for the role. Cadets who, in the main, had very little experience of military life and its quaint social customs always seemed to come up trumps and I never ever wrote an adverse report for a host at a Meet and Greet. The same can be said for those cadets who hosted us at the mid-course Cocktail Party – all outstanding performers. The same cannot be said for some of those not charged with hosting and who allowed the occasion and the alcohol to make them drop their guard. Whilst my hosts would, most often, receive a laudatory report following these events, others, occasionally, would receive an adverse one.

The cycle of the IOTC was such that there was always something for me to get involved in. If it wasn't a dining-in night, it would be a few nights in the field supervising a squadron's Intermediate Leadership Training (ILT) exercises. If it wasn't ILT it might be hosting cadets from the Royal Military Academy, Sandhurst, or Britannia Royal Naval College, Dartmouth, at the annual Inter-Collegiate Games. Or better still, travelling to the German Air Force Academy at Fürstenfeldbruck or hosting Dutch staff and students from the Koninklijke Militaire Academie in Breda, Holland for yet another Inter-College sporting fixture. There were top table lunches and top table dinners either hosted by the College for visiting dignitaries or by cadet syndicates to invited members of staff, me included. Participating in activities organised to introduce cadets from the USA, South Korea and Norway on a cultural exchange were routine. Skiing! Yep, skiing too! Great skiing in fact!! Great skiing in the Alps thanks to the French École de l'Air at Salon-de-Provence who willingly came to Cranwell with their cadets as part of a cultural exchange, but insisted that we used their skiing facilities at Ancelle in the Haute-Alpes on our half of the exchange! It was relentless, but it was all great fun.

In fact, that is the word that I instilled into my staff at that very early meeting when we vowed to resolve the morale issue. I wanted everybody, including the cadets, to have fun during their time at DIOT under my command. I especially wanted the cadets to leave at the end of their course with a warm feeling that the twenty-four weeks, for all its hardship and scrutiny, had been well worth the effort and had been fun. Goodness, I had certainly enjoyed myself as a junior officer. I had got myself into trouble on many an occasion and I had always come out the other side of a bollocking ready to have a bloody good laugh again, and probably at somebody else's expense! It hadn't really done me any harm and I wanted most of all to instil into my charges the fact that, although flying operations and the support of flying operations was a serious business, life in the RAF was also about having fun. I suspect that I didn't succeed with them all, but the fact that in later life I have often been accosted, with affection, by a significant number of my graduates who have told me how much they enjoyed their IOTC, I am gratified that at least many of my students did enjoy themselves at Cranwell.

I always looked forward to FLC that came for each course just before the midway point. The exercise lasted ten days and I would join each squadron for the last few days to monitor the final weekend's exercises, view Exercise Ultimate Challenge, receive a hot 'wash-up' on each student's progress, attend their camp dining-in night and enjoy a few team-bonding drinking sessions with my staff. The squadron commander would allocate me to a syndicate where, most commonly, the selected lead cadet was struggling with producing a convincing performance as a leader. It was useful to see for myself just how an individual performed before his or her case was brought before me at a Matrix Meeting. Sometimes, of course, I was sent out with the cream of the crop which was equally informative if only in the opposite sense and to provide measure to the standards set and achieved.

A typical day on FLC started before dawn and often the first exercise would be undertaken as the sun came up. Each cadet in a syndicate would have the opportunity to take the lead and would, usually, have two leads over the ten day period; weaker candidates would likely be given a third opportunity to lead and prove themselves, or not, as the case may be. Including brief and debrief each task would last up to two hours, which allowed something in the order of five or six exercises to be completed before lights out. The pace was intense for the cadets and staff alike and the latter's days were extended as each leader had to have a 'Form 3'[9] completed and debriefed as quickly as possible, and certainly before his subsequent lead. Distances covered to complete the tasks were not huge, but were sufficient to require a six kilometre per hour pace to be set as a minimum, which over a twelve-hour day was exhausting. Catering staff from the College provided field catering for breakfast and lunch, but occasionally, after supper, exercises were conducted at night to test map-reading, night awareness and safety skills. River crossings using ropes and pulleys, crossings of simulated minefields with heavyweight items and the carriage of imitation fissile material all added complexity to the

---

9. A form used throughout DIOT to report on a cadet's performance. It could be laudatory or adverse and was used for everything from social ineptitude in the officers' mess to deficiencies in leadership or, in a laudatory sense a solid performance, in hosting a senior officer or giving a ten-minute talk to a cadet audience.

leader's task and tested the best of them. Although it helped one's cause it was not necessary to complete the task to its conclusion. It was much more about whether the leader led effectively and efficiently and whether his team was prepared to follow him as a result. It was as much about followership as it was about leadership and the management of the team. The mantra was 'Task, Team, Individual' in that order. Focus on the task, lead the team and manage individual needs. Some had it naturally, some had to work at it and others were absolutely out of their depth.

I did my utmost to ensure that the cadets enjoyed their days in the field. I had been youthful and exuberant in my time and I saw no need to change just because I was a wing commander. I certainly did not see a need to change my attitude just because I was Wg Cdr Cdts! It was great to walk with them and get the inside track on what they felt about their training and their progress. I was there purely to observe, but it did not stop me putting in my pennyworth when the need arose. Most of the flight commanders were exceedingly good at what they did, but just one or two needed encouragement with their assessments, and a quiet word in their ear, after a difficult debrief, would usually suffice.

On the second last morning of FLC the cadets were roused early and directed to the parade square where instructions were issued to leaders on an early morning Escape and Evasion exercise. This was my favourite! I didn't walk with them on this task, but drove around the exercise area acting as a buffoon Camp Commandant arresting those who failed to evade effectively. It was great fun and those 'arrested' were quickly deposited in a holding area where breakfast was served and hot drinks issued. At Stanford TA it was a building within a corral, at Sennybridge a barn in a disused farm and at Otterburn we used a revetment area in the field. Porridge and a full fry-up were the order of the day and the cadets were all soon sat around guzzling into their food. They were at that stage classed as Prisoners of War and so there was to be no chatting as I and their flight commanders stood guard over them. They were sat in rows on their Bergens with their backs facing the front.

Being a good Scotsman I take my porridge with salt and milk. The caterers, being English, added copious amounts of sugar to their mix, which I cannot abide, so they very kindly and without asking produced a personal bowl for me that had nothing added to it. Unfortunately, on one occasion at Otterburn, the cadets had worked out that I had a privileged bowl – and nicked it! I searched everywhere just assuming that I had picked it up and forgotten where I had put it down.

'OK!' called out the squadron adjutant to the assembled cadets. 'Who's taken the wing commander's porridge?' Not a word, just stony silence interspersed with the odd giggle and muttering. 'Come on! Own up. Who's got it?' Nothing – silence! After about two minutes a lone voice in the middle of the one hundred and twenty called out, 'I'm Spartacus!' Then another, 'No, I'm Spartacus!' Then another, 'I'm Spartacus!' And so on and so on, 'I'm Spartacus!' Soon they were all at it! 'I'm Spartacus!' 'I'm Spartacus!' 'I'm Spartacus!'[10] The place erupted! The staff instructors were falling about the place and the students too were in hysterics – we'd lost our composure, but it didn't matter. It proved one thing to me. Morale was high and the cadets were thoroughly enjoying themselves.

What was particularly encouraging at Cranwell was that there was almost no difference in performance on the course between male and female cadets. Indeed, in many ways the females outshone their male counterparts. Some certainly had greater moral and physical courage. However, whilst there were plenty of grey men in the middle of the pack, the women tended to be either bloody good or bloody awful. Given their low percentage numbers on each course it was, I suppose, pretty difficult for females to adopt a middle ground position and stay off the staff radar. There were two occasions particularly that stick in my mind and both occurred during different 'Ultimate Challenges'.

The exercise was the culmination of FLC and took place on the very last morning after a usually cold and damp night spent under a cadet-made A-frame survival shelter in the woods. It started with a very early morning reveille and a muster parade where kit was inspected and cadets prepared for the off. Parade over and inspection complete the cadets formed up, in 'column of threes', and set off on a six kilometre route march carrying all their kit. That phase complete there began a race across the moors in syndicates building a chariot from parts that were located at various grid references along the way. Staff patrolled the route in Land Rovers picking up stragglers or administering helpful advice or First Aid, if and when required. We were all very Health and Safety conscious even if it had not formally been ordained in those days. The whole route covered something in the order of

10. For those too young to have seen the 1960 film starring Kirk Douglas in the title role – go watch it!

twenty-five kilometres and was arduous in the extreme, hence the exercise name. I was walking with the lead group of the route march on one occasion and was chatting to the flight commander who was setting a considerable pace for his team. In the lead rank were two strapping young men and a short, slightly plump, ex-primary school teacher with a shock of blonde curls atop her very smiley face. She was a delightful young lady and was bound for the Supply Branch. Like the rest of the cadets she was carrying a massive Bergen that weighed heavily on her shoulders. Surreptitiously a cadet eased forward from two ranks back and I heard him say, in quite a gallant manner:

'Would you like me to carry your pack for you?'

'No thanks', said the bubbly blonde. He eased back to his previous rank and the march continued. Two minutes later he was back.

'Are you sure you wouldn't like me to carry your pack for you?'

More forcefully this time: 'No!' He retired back into line. Two minutes later he was back, but before he could open his mouth she was on him.

'Look! If you don't fuck off back into line I'll punch your bloody lights out!' He retired and was not seen or heard of again.

That young lady completed the exercise with her Bergen, completed the course to a high standard and graduated into the Supply Branch where I would like to think she has had a most rewarding career and, as with the cadet at DIOT, earned the respect of the men and women she commanded in the RAF.

On another Ultimate Challenge I was called away from the finish line, at West Camp in Otterburn, to speak with a female cadet who seemed to be struggling and holding her syndicate back. She was about three miles from the finishing line and when I met up with the group, in my Land Rover, she was manfully assisting with the hefting of a sixty-gallon oil drum into position on the chassis of the chariot. She claimed to be fine. She did not want to take a ride back to camp. She didn't want to leave her team. She was happy to continue. And so with a couple of words of advice to her flight commander, who had already thought of all the necessary actions that he needed to be aware of, I took my leave and headed back to the finishing line. I watched her syndicate as they appeared out of the woods and loped down the hill and began to cross the river bridge with their chariot. She was trailing behind a little, but still within contact of her group and with another cadet and her flight commander in support. She crossed the finishing line last and in strong spirit, but her body collapsed when the adrenalin gave way to her elation at completion. She was whipped off to the medical centre and from there she was taken to the hospital in Hexham where an X-Ray proved that she had a hairline fracture of her pelvis. Such was the strength and determination of the females who went through DIOT when I was there. They never failed to impress and only a very few were not worthy of gaining Her Majesty's Commission by the end of the course.

The end of every FLC was celebrated with a dining-in night in whatever accommodation was available, wherever we were in the field. Normal formalities were exercised, with all present suitably attired if not in formal rig for the occasion. Food was prepared by the catering staff and wine flowed freely throughout. Mr Vice took the chair after the meal and speeches, which were then followed by an evening of entertainment as those cadets with an artistic or thespian talent presented their FLC Review. It was all thoroughly entertaining and it was a good occasion that allowed the cadets to let their hair down, even if we staff members opened ourselves up for some friendly banter and mild ridicule. If proof were ever needed that officer cadets at DIOT, in the late 90s, were of the same make-up as all those who had preceded them, then this song, written and performed by Number 2 Flight of 174 IOTC at Otterburn in 1998, provides it:

Cranwell Rhapsody
(By Kev Greensill and Dom Chan; with apologies to Freddie Mercury)

Is this the real life
Is this just fantasy
Stepped on a land mine
No escape from this IOT
Open your eyes
Look up to the skies... F3...

I'm just a new boy
I need some sympathy
Because when we say yes, they say no
Left from right... we don't know
Anywhere they post me
Doesn't really matter to me... to me...

Ma'am, just killed a man
On a mission that I led
Forgot my standards now he's dead
Ma'am my control was good
But now I've gone and thrown it all away...

Ma'am... oooh...
Didn't mean to lose my team
If they're not back again this time tomorrow
Carry on, carry on...
As if nothing really matters...

Too late, my FLR's done
Sent shivers down my spine when I signed the bottom line
Goodbye everybody, I've got to go
Got to leave you all behind... and cross the road...

Ma'am... oooh
Please not 175
I'd sometimes wish I'd never joined up at all

Guitar Break...

I see a little silhouette of a man
It's the CWO, it's the CWO will he give us restrictions
Thunderbolt and lightning he's very, very frightening to me
Run and hide (echo), run and hide (echo), run and hide
(together)... Figaro... Magnifico... oh... oh... oh... oh

I'm just on 2 Flt... nobody loves me...
He's just on 2 Flt they're Duty Flt... AGAIN!
Spare him his life and a stack of Sheet 3s!

Essays come, briefings go... will you let me go...
It's Skirving... No! He will not let you go! Let him go!
It's Skirving... He will not let you go! Let him go!
It's Skirving... He will not let you go! Let me go!

Will not let you go! Let me go! Will not let you go! Let me go! Oh... oh...
    oh... oh
(Never! Never! Never!)
No! No! No! No! No!
Oh Ma'am mia Ma'am mia Ma'am mia let me go
Beelzebub looks like Squadron Leader Wright to me!
To me! To me! To me!

Guitar Break! Shake hair!

So you give me a Sheet 3 and spit in my eye
So you give me a Sheet 3 and leave me to die
Oh baby... can't do this to me baby
Just gotta get out... just gotta get WRIGHT out of here!
Guitar Break (Ooh yeah...)
Commission really matters
Anyone can see
Commissioning really matters to me
Commissioning really matters to me...

These were cadets after my own heart!

When the cadets went off to their beds to prepare to break camp in the morning and head back to Cranwell, we staff members would retire to our staff anteroom for our 'team bonding session'. Alcohol flowed freely, mess games prevailed and lengthy and meaningful 'policy discussions' took place long into the night.

Another task that befell me in my capacity as the officer commanding was to receive, and manage, branch change requests from cadets. The system allowed for such requests, but I was always wary of supporting them as branch allocations were quota driven and the quotas did not change within a financial year. Accordingly, I was loath to raise a cadet's expectations. Nevertheless, if there appeared to be a good and valid reason, I would stick my neck out on behalf of a cadet. Close liaison with OASC was imperative to be successful and occasionally I was. Some cadets had no real reason for wanting a branch change other than the fact that they had decided that they did not want the branch that they had accepted originally. Others, destined for the Fighter Control branch, had discovered that there was a high suspension rate from the course and no longer fancied their chances of success – so wanted to cut and run rather than face suspension. They never did manage to secure a branch change whilst at Cranwell. One female cadet in particular came to me with a plea to change her branch from Flight Operations to Navigator. Her reason was medically based. Having suffered with childhood asthma, the medical board at OASC had decreed her unfit to fly. I thought this grossly unfair. My own son had been diagnosed with childhood asthma, but in his maturity had suffered not one asthmatic attack. In my office, during a formal interview, the cadet told me her story, which was almost identical to Christopher's. I discussed her situation long and hard with the Deputy Director of OASC who, eventually, saw reason and pointed her at navigator training upon completion of her officer training course. In general, however, my efforts were fruitless and cadets went to the branches allocated in their letters of offer from OASC. Some, however, were more successful after Cranwell, particularly when they applied in the next financial year when quotas had shifted.

We held two Matrix Meetings during each course, one after FLC and one pre-graduation, and at each meeting the squadron involved would present their reports on each and every cadet. With, on average, one hundred and fifty cadets on each squadron it was a tall order for me to know and remember each of them individually as they progressed through their twenty weeks on Cadet Wing. However, before each Matrix Meeting and helped by my involving myself in FLC and then Exercise Peacekeeper, their final field test, I was able to identify the strong and the weak. To assist further I used to spend the hours before the Matrix Meeting devouring cadet files such that I had an intimate knowledge of the progress of both the top and bottom of the pack. The meeting would last a full morning as each cadet's case was presented to me in the conference room in Whittle Hall. Most I agreed with, some I doubted and many I asked penetrating questions of each flight commander. If it was a pre-graduation board, prize winners would be agreed. Many a young flight commander was flabbergasted at my depth of knowledge of each cadet, but none ever realised that I rarely spoke with any knowledge about the grey men in the middle! My tactic served its purpose well, however, and no flight commander ever tried to flannel their way past me. In so doing I ensured that only those who deserved their commission were awarded their commission.

My life had improved dramatically when the 'Yes Man' group captain was posted and was succeeded by a Tornado navigator who had been Squadron Executive Officer on 17 Squadron during my STANEVAL tour. With Dick Middleton in charge DIOT was a much more pleasant place to work. Moreover, with a Boss who was proactive and not afraid to stand up and take decisions, opportunities arose for us to make changes to procedure and policy around the department. For a start, when I arrived the department held a muster parade every Monday morning where the whole cadet body, staff and students alike, paraded in front of College Hall at 0800 hours. Whilst I took charge of the parade and put the cadets through some simple drill manoeuvres, no worthwhile inspection was carried out; with the numbers involved there wasn't sufficient time to do it effectively. It was a little bit like having an open air school assembly without the hymns. It was my view that the squadrons could use the time much better and, if necessary, conduct a more meaningful inspection than could be conducted, en masse, on the vast parade square. Once a month was sufficient as far as I was concerned and without much debate at all Dick Middleton agreed.

Between us, and with the help of HQ PTC, we also introduced a better means of selecting staff to fill the role of flight commander. There were a few non-volunteers amongst the flight commander body and it soon became evident that, for them, their heart was not fully engaged in our work. I had also been disappointed with two of my staff members who had overstepped the mark. One had been witnessed using an intimidating approach towards his cadets and, despite remedial training and opportunities to be more considerate, he found it difficult to change his ways. He was moved to a post in the department that gave him less direct contact with students. Another, whilst away from home on the syllabus station visit and beyond supervision, thought it appropriate to try his luck with one of the female cadets. His advances were unsolicited and reported back to me. He had proved himself to be untrustworthy in the DIOT environment and so I sacked him. With these two challenges, as well as changes that we were making internally, it seemed sensible to introduce a boarding system for flight commander selection that matched their skills against a professional profile that Dick and I drew up. It worked and, with a new induction training programme to match, there were never any more problems with staff members. Indeed, such was the quality of my new staff members that many of them have gone on to fill some of the higher and highest echelons of the RAF.

With support from our wives, Dick and I introduced a 'Partners' Day' just after the mid-point of the course. It was held on the Friday of the syllabus Cocktail Party, which helped with the logistics for partners who would be travelling to Cranwell for that and the post-CTP thrash that followed. It was my wife Jo, along with Andrea Middleton, who had come up with the concept of a Partners' Day and it was they who hosted it. They had identified that by that stage in the course, post-FLC, cadets were in the 'officer development' phase and, before too long, would become commissioned officers. Their partners, however, had no idea what that status might mean to them nor how it would affect their lives. Few had ever experienced the working life of an RAF station let alone seen inside an officers' mess! Consequently, Jo and Andrea drew up a day's programme of events that would at least skim the surface and give them an insight into what life as an officer was like and the demands that such a career would place on a family. The visitors also received a guided tour of College Hall, which introduced them to the history of both the College and the RAF, had a buffet lunch and afterwards the respective squadron commander gave a briefing on just what their partners had been through, since they had left home some fourteen weeks prior. It was a very popular and successful event and attracted a broad cross-section that included wives, husbands, young and old alike, as well as sweethearts not long out of university.

Jo also proposed an eminently sensible addition to our course 'Day Out in London'. During the final term, it had always been the case that each IOTC spent a day in London at the RAF Museum and then at the RAF Club on Piccadilly. The first, after a briefing on the work of the museum, allowed them to have a hands-on historical tour of the RAF. A short coach journey from Hendon to Piccadilly was then followed by a tour of the club's facilities that was hosted by the Club Secretary, with the hope that many would take up membership once commissioned. That was followed by a buffet lunch and a briefing by a senior member of the Air Force Board who popped along from MOD to give a 'state of the nation' chat to the newest members of the Service. Jo, however, came up with the idea that a day out in London was wasted if it did not include a visit to St Clement Danes Church[11] on the Strand. Despite complaints from the contract coach drivers who had to deal with the traffic chaos, the visits hosted by the Dean of St Clement

---

11. The central church of the RAF.

Danes, an RAF chaplain, were an outstanding success and added further to the students' comprehension of the traditions of their new Service life.

We also reinstated the flight commander exchange programme with our sister school in Australia. The Royal Australian Air Force Officer Training School, then at RAAF Point Cook near Melbourne, ran a similar length course to ours and, upon contact, was very keen to re-establish a programme that had been running successfully some years before. By mid-1998 the exchange programme had been authorised and funded and later that year a RAAF officer arrived for six months to work with D Squadron. Upon her departure back home, we reciprocated and sent Flight Lieutenant Chris Lay, a VC10 pilot, to take up the other half of the exchange. His regular reports back to my office proved that there were many similarities to our way of working, but that there were also some significant differences too. After some four months into Chris's six-month tour in Victoria I received an invitation from the RAAF to visit the OTS to view their training programme for myself. I therefore put forward a case to do just that and, to fortify my case for T&S, I added that such a visit would allow me to undertake a pastoral visit to a member of my staff. Amazingly full financial approval was granted by the budget holder and was supported by Dick Middleton and the new Commandant, Bill Rimmer.

My visit to Melbourne lasted just ten days. After twenty-three hours courtesy of Singapore Airlines Raffles Class, I was allowed three hours by my hosts to shake off the jet lag. Then, feeling quite shabby, I was collected from outside the officers' mess and ushered into a staff car by my opposite number who drove me some one hundred and forty miles to East Sale air base where the RAAF cadets were on field exercise – the equivalent of our FLC. The first and most obvious difference from our training programme was that the RAAF cadets stood 'Stag'[12] throughout the exercise and were treated as raw recruits rather than potential officers. There was a clear difference in the relationship between staff and student too. The Australian staff officers seemed quite hard-nosed towards their students and did not at any point seem to empathise with them. It was a knock-back system and one with which I was not particularly comfortable. It reminded me very much of my time at 2 Air Navigation School some thirty years before. In the RAF in the late 60s and early 70s the training process had been quite intimidating and here, in

---

12. To be on Guard Duty.

1999 in Australia, I detected a strong whiff of that same methodology! The RAF had moved on from those days and my attitude at DIOT was to nurture those who were attempting to gain a commission, rather than knock them back at every turn and belittle them.

I also visited the Australian Defence Force Academy in Canberra where officer cadets from all three Australian Armed Forces were undertaking a three-year cadetship and degree course that included an undergraduate war studies syllabus underpinned by the University of New South Wales. As the RAF had dispensed with its three-year cadetship and university level war studies programme at Cranwell in the early 1970s, I found this aspect of my visit to Australia to be very informative and distinctly worthwhile. Whilst we did have a department within DIOT that provided Air Power lectures it was manned thinly by erstwhile officers and, within a twenty-four week course, there was insufficient time to cover much of our doctrine other than through a series of historical cameos. The removal of the cadetship system in the RAF had placed our officers at a distinct disadvantage in comparison to our fellow officers who had graduated from RMA and BRNC. I took that message back to Cranwell in the hope that something might be done to improve the doctrinal education of the RAF's future generations.

Over my one free weekend in Australia, Chris Lay had laid on a full entertainment package. He booked us into a wine tasting trip in the Yarra Valley organised by the Army and Navy Club in Melbourne and secured tickets for us to attend a hybrid Aussie Rules/Gaelic Football match between Australia and Ireland at the Melbourne Cricket Ground. In Canberra, we visited the Australian Parliament Building, the National War Memorial and its fascinating museum, and took lunch at the top of the Telstra Tower that overlooks the city and Lake Burley Griffin.

All-in-all my ten days in Australia were extremely well spent both socially and professionally and the trip was well worth the almost forty-eight hours, spent in a Boeing 747, that it took to get me there and back. What is more I was able to report back that Chris Lay was alive and well, making the most of his six months in Oz and had not quite gone native – at least not yet!

Before my arrival at DIOT there had been a 'duty of care' problem and a lack of consideration towards some cadets who had been deemed, probably wrongly, to be shirking. Positive measures had been taken in an attempt to change the culture and some staff members had been moved on as a result. There were legacy issues, however, that I had to contend with.

One was a particularly difficult case and related to a female student officer who, eventually, served more years on the strength of DIOT than I did. When I arrived in October 1997 she had been in the Medical and Special Holding Flight for a number of months. Throughout that period she had done no formal officer training whatsoever as she had damaged her Achilles tendon on only the second or third day into her training. It had been her own fault. Despite being instructed not to wear high heel shoes whilst attending Clothing Stores to be issued with her military kit, she had done so. Then, when instructed by the flight sergeant to hurry up and get back on the bus, she had run in her high heels, gone over on her ankle and ruptured her Achilles tendon.

MASH Flt was managed by a flight lieutenant selected specifically to considerately and carefully look after those who had either injured themselves or for other reasons fallen out of training and were unable to continue temporarily. Cadets with fractures, shin splints or personal issues, for example, would spend a period in MASH until such time as they were ready to continue training. It was a caring and considerate environment where the staff went out of their way to ensure that nothing exacerbated their injuries whilst they were rehabilitated. Cadets in MASH Flt with longer term injuries were even deployed to RAF stations where they could experience life on an operational RAF unit and thereby maintain their morale. The cadet with the Achilles injury fell into the long-term sick category and was, therefore, occasionally detached to other units.

It was a Friday afternoon at about 1500hrs when Dick Middleton walked into my office with what looked like a very thick report in his hand. He handed the bundle of papers over to me and asked me to produce a draft response for the commandant. The letter, which was from 'Achilles's' father and was addressed to the Prime Minister, was eighty pages long and was entitled 'Cranwell Inmates'. This was not going to be an easy draft to produce. For a start eighty pages would take some time to consume and then deliberate upon. Moreover, with top level interest in Downing Street and the need to progress the draft up through my command chain, it needed to be a considered and well written response. I started to read it, but, frankly, it was a rambling diatribe.

It transpired that he wished the Prime Minister to be aware of the conditions that officer cadets at Cranwell lived in, the degrading manner in which they were treated, the poor medical care that they received and how, particularly, his daughter's treatment was a classic example of an uncaring, medically inept and bullying organisation masquerading under the flag and colours of the Royal Air Force.[13] It was nonsense and full of glaring inaccuracies and untruths, but interestingly, he criticised and made personal attacks against everybody in 'Achilles's' chain of command; information he could have only obtained from his daughter! Everybody from the Air Member for Personnel at HQ Personnel and Training Command down to Group Captain Dick Middleton in the office next door to mine.

By the middle of the following week my approved draft was forwarded to AMP at Innsworth so that he could produce his own response for the Prime Minister. 'Achilles' was interviewed and advised that a letter had been received from her father; she claimed to know nothing of it. She was reassured, by me, that she need not fret and that once she was fit again and reinstated on the course she would be able to progress through it without further ado. To her concern that flight commanders might distrust her because of her father's involvement I reassured her that, if I heard of that happening, the flight commander concerned would not last long at DIOT. Not unsurprisingly, the next letter received from her father accused me of turning his daughter against his family. 'Achilles' was clearly playing both sides off against each other – and likely getting some personal kick out of it.

'Achilles' eventually spent just under four years on the strength of DIOT and never re-entered training. She only ever completed three days of officer training and the whole of the rest of the time was spent in MASH Flt or on the road, mostly at RAF Coltishall. Eventually the matter was closed by the Air Force Board who charged AMP with her immediate commissioning. Dick Middleton and I were incensed when we heard this directive from on high. To commission anybody after only three days of officer training ridiculed everything that we stood for as officers in the RAF and as the senior staff in DIOT. It undermined the training system of the RAF and it discredited the commissions of all those officers who had gone before and would follow after her. Whilst we were unable to countermand the order of the AFB, we stood our ground over where and how 'Achilles' would receive her commission. Dick and I were determined that she was not going to have the satisfaction of stepping up and into College Hall, to the strains of Auld

---

13. I clearly do not still have a copy of his eighty page letter but in short that sentence pretty much sums it up in its entirety.

Lang Syne, alongside those new officers who had fought tooth and nail to earn their commission over a twenty-four week course. Her commissioning scroll was sent to her in an envelope and the matter was closed as far as DIOT was concerned. She subsequently sued the MOD for damages and much to my – and everybody else involved at the time – disgust was awarded a substantial six figure sum in compensation. Thankfully, the RAF ended her commission at their first opportunity.

The 26 May 1999 was no different to any other day at DIOT apart from the fact that it was my fiftieth birthday. It was a Wednesday, but nothing much was planned other than a visitation from all my family over the following weekend. My father had passed away on his eighty-sixth birthday on 31 May 1996 and a clan gathering that weekend seemed most appropriate to celebrate my half-century and remember our patriarch. I parked my car as usual in front of Whittle Hall and sauntered through Angie's outer office and was about to throw my SD hat on the coffee table in my office when I became aware of a presence behind me.

'Keep your hat on, the Commandant wants to see you!' Turning towards Dick Middleton I enquired as to what he might want to see me for, but was met with an indifferent face and a stony silence! As we crossed the parade square in front of College Hall, I asked him again. 'Any idea what this is about?'

'No idea, he just said he wanted to see you in his office and that I was to accompany you.'

Now I had been in this situation before as a junior officer and when you are told to take your hat there is usually just one outcome! I racked my brain as we walked together towards the grand entrance to the College. Had I done anything that could have reaped the wrath of the commandant? If I had it was news to me! Had something from my past caught up with me at last? I bloody well hoped not.

As we walked up the steps and through the portico I began to hear the faint call of the Highlands. Somewhere, somebody was playing the bagpipes! As the double doors of College Hall were opened for me – which was odd, I had never before been treated with that importance despite my standing within the College hierarchy – I espied three pipers in full Highland Dress who were playing 'Highland Cathedral' it seemed, for me! As I stood there with mouth agape, round the corner came Bill Rimmer accompanied by my wife. Bill had a huge beaming smile across his face, it was rarely ever any different, as he wished me a very happy birthday.

Jo had done it again. She took me by the arm with the commandant and Dick in trail and walked me out of the Rotunda and around towards the rather grand Dining Room. Again the doors were swung open as I approached and there, standing behind their chairs, were all of my staff officers hungrily waiting for me so that they could tuck into a champagne breakfast that Jo had organised for me. She is a very resourceful and a very loving woman. Any woman who can do that sort of thing without once slipping up or giving any indication that she was up to something has to be watched! Resourceful, loving and cunning that's my wife!

Dick and I did have a problem with the over-indulgence of alcohol in the College Hall Officers' Mess. Not by us you understand, but by many of the cadets. Unlike my early years in the RAF when aircrew drank pints of beer and let their hair down in a relatively gentlemanly fashion, the cadets at Cranwell in the late 90s seemed to have brought their contemporary 'binge drinking' culture from university with them. All too often we received reports about loutish, drunken behaviour in the mess bar and, occasionally, reports of vomit being deposited under cushions in the ante-room with never a word of apology or an admission after the fact. It was becoming far too common and something needed to be said. Dick and I were not averse to drink. Indeed, quite the opposite, we both had pasts. But there was a limit and the cadets had overstepped it. The whole body of cadets were assembled in the Whittle Hall lecture hall when Dick and I took to the stage. Dick dressed them down and pointed out to them that they were there to enjoy themselves, but at the same time, they were being assessed as to their potential to hold the Queen's Commission. Binge drinking was not part of an officer and gentleman's lexicon and they needed to stop getting blind drunk every night on beer and vodka with Red Bull. The message struck home and things did improve, but never to my complete satisfaction. Like everything in life, there is always one who spoils it for the rest of us.

In truth, like in any walk of life, there were strong candidates and weak candidates in the training system. OASC had a system of scoring their candidates from 1 (weak) to 7 (strong), but they never ever told us their scores whilst the cadets were at DIOT. When cadets arrived with us, they were a blank canvas. When I suspended one particularly very weak cadet from training after FLC, OASC did confess that they routinely sent us candidates graded between 3 and 5. However, this individual had scored 1 at OASC and had been sent to us to see how he got on. He had not and, as a result, I agreed with OASC that, upon graduation, it would be a good idea for them to inform us of graduating cadets' OASC boarding grades such that we could equate them to their overall position on the course. It was a sort of rudimentary quality assessment of the system, if you like. It helped and it ensured that OASC remained honest in their future selections. Whilst some cadets were good leaders, but lacked officer qualities, others were impeccable officers, but could not lead. Few had all the qualities required, but with good training and responsible staff we were able to nurture and improve their individual weaknesses sufficient to let the majority graduate.

In the final weeks of each course, leading up to graduation, I routinely had the privilege of addressing the cadets in the Whittle Hall Lecture Hall twice. The first was in my capacity as the RAF Club's recruiting agent. My briefing took place just before lunch and after the twenty minute briefing and slideshow that I gave to the assembly, I left application forms with the course leader with a quip that the doors of Whittle Hall were sealed until he got them all filled in and back to me. It worked! My casual and friendly approach usually pulled in about ninety-five per cent. It was all to their advantage as, having completed their payment details on the application form, they then received one year's free membership upon graduation. The Club's hope, mostly realised, was that they would then forget to cancel their membership after that year and become members for life – just like I have been. My second encounter with the graduates in Whittle Hall was twenty-four hours before the graduation parade. There they had to sit through three fifteen minute sessions of 'words of wisdom' successively from me, Dick Middleton and then the commandant. I always spoke to them directly and adopted a friendly tone; after all they were just about to become officers in the RAF. I congratulated them on their efforts, encouraged them to remember the principles taught at the College and asked them to try to adhere to them. I also emphasised that although they may not find those principles practised on every RAF unit, they would never be wrong if they fell back on the Cranwell model. I urged those who had joined on a Short Service Commission to give serious thought to a full career and acknowledged that for some pilots in the group the RAF was but a mere stepping stone to a future career in the airlines. Finally I encouraged those who were keen to progress to the highest ranks of the RAF to make sure that they did not crush their fellows in their drive to succeed. My address went something like this:

'There are those amongst you who will seek to rise to the highest echelons of the Royal Air Force. May I commend to you, whilst thrusting yourself upward, that you take care of those whom you pass by on the way. Because should you then slip on any of the rungs of the ladder do not expect many people to catch you on the way down!'

That got them thinking! I then went on to say: *'Amongst this group today there is probably a future Chief of the Air Staff.'* Male chests puffed themselves up noticeably at these words, but I very quickly brought them back down to earth when I closed with: *'So to you, Ma'am, the very best of luck!'* Not one of the male cadets in the room had ever given a thought to the fact that a female might be better than them. It happened every time on every course that I gave that final talk to. I knew that many of the women were stronger candidates than the men that they sat with but, as ever in a male dominated society, male egos failed to realise that fact! If nothing else, I made them think!

What I liked most about my time at DIOT was the camaraderie and the work ethic displayed by both my staff and by those students who were determined to succeed. I was delighted to discover that the attitude of the cadets in my charge was no different to that of my fellow cadets when I had joined the RAF almost thirty years before. I was thrilled to have had a tour where I dealt primarily with people rather than bombs, weather and aircraft emergencies. It was truly what being an officer in the RAF was all about – its people. I had tried, and hopefully achieved, to set a standard of enjoyment, humour and fun throughout my tour and had even encouraged the occasional high jinks.

Not least of these was supporting a charity event where Jo and I had donated our ancient piano to allow cadet teams to race each other to smash it, pass its bits through a porthole sized orifice, before then setting fire to it – whilst we all consumed copious amounts of beer! It was an 'RAF tradition' that I had been introduced to on my first tour in the RAF. I saw no need for the cadets not to learn it at an early stage in their careers and we had no requirement for the piano because towards the end of the tour we planned to move back to our own house in West Bridgford, where the piano would not fit.

And then there was the moment when the commandant, Bill Rimmer, leant across to me at a graduation Dining-In Night to ask me if it would be appropriate to ask for any cadet with a motorbike to bring it into the

Mess! As a cadet himself in the 1970s he had participated in just such antics where a motorbike had 'appeared' and been raced up and down the one hundred and fifty yard central corridor of College Hall at Dining-In Nights. The moment seemed right for him to relive his youth and introduce the graduates to yet another 'tradition'! So, of course, I supported him; why not! I had witnessed Barrie Chown doing it on a number of occasions during my time on 12 Squadron, and other than a fool Vulcan co-pilot who had managed to break both his wrists doing so, it had not caused anybody any harm. So up stood the commandant and a motorbike duly appeared, raced round the dining room for a couple of laps before it disappeared out and along the main corridor of College Hall. Of course there was the 'I'm Spartacus' moment too!

After a slightly elongated tour where, as Dick Middleton's deputy, I had been asked to stay until he recovered from major hip surgery, I packed my office up and prepared for pastures new. Without any prospect of that longed-for flying tour as a wing commander and with only four years left to serve I had negotiated that these final years of my RAF career be spent in Lincolnshire to allow Jo and me to settle back in our home from where I could commute daily. With my desk officer's support, I managed to secure a posting to the Air Warfare Centre at RAF Waddington in July 2000. There I took the role of Staff Officer Air Power 1 tasked with writing, editing and preparing operational doctrine for the RAF, the Joint Services and NATO.

Apart from Paul Beard and Chris Lay, whose adventures in Australia provided me with a need to travel there and thus relate those events in this story, it would be inappropriate for me to identify for high praise individual members of my staff in Cadet Wing. They were, in the main, outstanding individuals and many have surpassed me in their own RAF careers. They were hard working, conscientious and physically fit individuals who all made my task at Cranwell so very easy and extremely enjoyable. They know who they are and, if they are reading this now, they have my utmost respect and thanks for a job well done on a very rewarding and satisfying tour. If we meet again, just remember that mine is a malt – a double, please!

During my time as Wg Cdr Cdts I had been commended for adopting 'Old School' principles and setting high standards for both my staff and students alike. I behaved in a manner that I believed was appropriate for an officer and a gentleman and followed the principles that my career and my parents had instilled in me. But most of all I had gone out of my way to ensure that all those who worked with me, for me and studied under my regime enjoyed their time at Cranwell.

I can safely say, without fear of contradiction, that the three years I spent as Wing Commander Cadets at the RAF College were amongst the happiest years of my RAF career and, certainly, including all six flying tours, my DIOT tour ranked amongst the highest for thorough enjoyment and personal satisfaction.

Chapter Twelve

Nobody Goes to War in a Hire Car!

After thirty-eight years, four months and twenty-five days I retired from the Royal Air Force on 26 May 2007. I had enjoyed every moment of my time in a light blue uniform and especially the eighteen years that I had spent in the cockpit of both the Buccaneer and the Tornado. I had achieved over three thousand hours in the air and got away with it. I had had some hairy moments, but I had never had to get out in a hurry with the help of Martin Baker! It had been close on occasions, but the Buccaneer and Tornado had always held firm, thanks to their robustness, the skill of my pilot, or both! I had also enjoyed all of my time flying a mahogany bomber[1] at Strike Command and in the Ministry of Defence and I had had a whale of a time as Wing Commander Cadets at DIOT, which as far as I am concerned must rate as the best job in the RAF other than flying! The worst was probably the thirteen months spent at the AWC at Waddington, which was where I arrived from Cranwell after a spot of summer leave.

I was a great believer in doctrine. I knew there was a need to provide better doctrinal education for RAF personnel; I had discovered that on my ASC at Bracknell in 1992 when I compared my strategic understanding with that of my army colleagues. But I had not anticipated just how turgid it would be to be the producer and reviewer of draft doctrine. Add to that the fact that I had become accustomed to, and enjoyed, the solitude of my own office where I could work in peace and quiet. So my arrival in the 'Doctrine Office' in the Thomson Building at Waddington came as something of a shock to me. There were some thirteen wing commanders, or equivalents,[2] in a large open plan area that also served as a through passage between the Tactics Division and the coffee bar. Thirteen senior officers, who all had an opinion, wanted to be heard and seemed to have no idea that some people liked to work quietly on their own and seek an opinion when they needed one. I was responsible primarily for doctrine that involved mud-moving and support of the army.

---

1. Desk jobs.
2. A Royal Navy commander, an Army lieutenant colonel and a USAF lieutenant colonel added to the mix of uniforms on display.

My desk buddy was a loud, obnoxious and highly opinionated navigator who held court over matters of air defence! Unfortunately, like most highly opinionated people, he had a view on every subject and there was never any other valid opinion than his! I did not enjoy my time there and I found the prolonged meetings with our army counterparts, home or away, mind-numbingly boring and tedious.

There were ups, however. My role once again gave me a position at the head of the table for the NATO Air Operations Working Group. As Head of UK Delegation to and Secretary of the AOWG, I regularly returned to NATO HQ in Brussels where I eventually stood in for Dick Middleton, who had followed me from Cranwell to be Group Captain Offensive Operations at the AWC, as Chairman of the group. The AOWG was tasked with the production and sanction of common NATO doctrine that would allow allies to conduct combined operations when the need arose without getting in each other's way. Whilst it was still 'doctrine', it was a blessed relief from the humdrum, but cacophonous atmosphere in the Thomson Building. Moreover, with few people sitting around the table with English as their first language it was sometimes fun to explain to them the quaint idiosyncrasies of our language and then watch as their minds tried to digest, with incredulity, how we could ever manage to communicate with each other! Foreign minds boggled as I explained that varying spellings allowed us to pronounce the same word, but for it to have a completely different meaning.

There was one other 'up' in my short time doing doctrine! As a member of the doctrine team and now with an Air Battle Staff Course qualification I, and my fellow doctrinaires,[3] were eligible and often required to supplement HQ staff during large exercises. In late 2001 NATO's Allied Rapid Reaction Corps was planned to participate in a large exercise in a snowy Bavaria; a number of air force SO1s[4] were required to bolster its air cell. There was little icing on the cake when the request for volunteers came with the caveat that it would be a case of living under canvas in a Southern Germany winter for four weeks. I did not volunteer. That verbal request was followed immediately by the announcement of a further need to support Exercise Saif

---

3. Thesaurus definitions: pedants, obfuscators, scholars, nit-pickers, theoreticians, sophists – sounds about right!
4. Staff Officer 1 – commander, lieutenant colonel, wing commander.

Sareea 2,[5] in Oman, some two months earlier. The caveat this time was living under canvas in the middle of the Omani desert for six weeks without air conditioning! I had been in the RAF far too long to want to volunteer for that one either! Then, with almost all the qualified SO1s in the office now committed, there came the final announcement.

'OK, chaps, we need one SO1 to spend six weeks on board HMS *Illustrious* as a member of the Red Force[6] JFACHQ[7] team during Saif Sareea 2.'

My hand shot up and with a rather nonchalant, 'I'll do that!' I was booked and on my way to an air-conditioned cabin on one of Her Majesty's aircraft carriers for six weeks in the Arabian Sea!

One week before my planned departure, we were watching the BBC News Channel on the TV in the office, which we used to keep us bang up to date with world happenings. Breaking news from New York was broadcasting scenes from the World Trade Center – an aircraft had just piled into the North Tower! It looked very much like an accident until, just seventeen minutes later, another smashed into the South Tower. It was no accident and my first words to the assembled throng now gathered around the TV screen were, 'This is World War 3, folks!'

On 16 September 2001 I travelled to join '*Lusty*'[8] via RAF Northolt and a BAe 146 of the Queen's Flight, which flew me to Cyprus, via Bari in Italy. Chris and Sarah, now twenty-four and twenty-two respectively, were living away from home and had not been present when I left. So with a cheery wave and a so long to Jo, Helen and Hannah I set off for the M1 in a hire car that had been provided by the RAF. Helen, now sixteen, was in floods of tears – she knew the implications of what might ensue after 9/11 and had worked out that my departure on 'exercise' might just be a cover story for something a bit more sinister. She was quite inconsolable. Well, inconsolable until her

---

5. Exercise Saif Sareea 2, Arabic for 'Swift Sword 2', was a major military exercise in September and October 2001 involving military forces of both the UK and Oman. It was the largest single deployment of UK forces since the 1991 Gulf War. Over 22,500 personnel, 6,500 vehicles, 21 naval vessels, 49 fixed-wing aircraft and 44 helicopters were deployed to Oman and the Arabian Sea along with 11,000 Omani military personnel.
6. In NATO terminology the Red Force defined the notional 'baddies' whilst the Blue Force described the 'goodies'.
7. Joint Force Air Component Headquarters – the United Kingdom's deployable air command and control unit.
8. HMS *Illustrious*.

younger sister, Hannah, remarked: 'Don't be daft, Helen, nobody goes to war in a hire car!' How right she was.

Along with the rest of the supplementary JFACHQ team that had gathered in Cyprus, I was flown onto *'Lusty'* in a Chinook from RAF Akrotiri but, as I descended into the bowels of the ship I met the appointed commander of the JFACHQ heading back to the flight deck and onto the helicopter. As we passed he called over his shoulder, 'Dave, I've been recalled to London to undertake contingency planning for Afghanistan. You're the senior RAF man on board – go see the admiral!'

Rear Admiral James Burnell-Nugent was a delightful man of similar years to me. He welcomed me into his cabin and informed me that, in the absence of the air commodore, I was now his appointed Joint Force Air Component Commander! Without any further ado he then invited me to join him, the ship's captain and the two Royal Marine colonels for dinner every evening whilst we were at sea and also for breakfast and lunch. Dinner was preceded by preprandial drinks at 1900hrs sharp and I was to wear 'Red Sea Rig'[9] rather than normal working dress. I had come prepared with the RAF's equivalent of Red Sea Rig, but was quite unprepared for the gastronomic delight of dining in the admiral's cabin; he was a man very much at ease with 'haute cuisine'. I did feel slightly embarrassed, however, when I realised that everybody else on the ship had to endure centralised messing whilst dressed in their combat gear, which they had to wear at all times other than when they were asleep.

I was even more delighted when I met the ship's captain. He had been PSO to CDS when Sir Charles Guthrie and Sir John Day had visited me in Gioia in 1997. Charles Style had been one of the team who had kept me up drinking until the very early hours of the morning in the Hotel Svevo! Shortly after being reintroduced to Charles, I reminded him of our first encounter in Italy. Having reacquainted ourselves with memories of that drunken evening I knew that my time at sea, in the company of Captain Style and Admiral B-N, was going to be much enjoyed. If the ship had not been painted grey and fast jet aircraft had not been roaring on and off its flight deck by day and by night it would have been the most wonderful, cheap and idyllic cruise ever in the Indian Ocean! Cunard could not have done it better.

---

9. Worn for informal evening wear on board ship; it consists of a white short-sleeved shirt, worn with rank shoulder boards, without medals and with black trousers, black shoes and a black cummerbund.

The thrust of the exercise was a build up to war where the Red Forces, assembled at sea, were eventually to conduct an amphibious assault against the Blue Forces assembled in Oman. I, along with Charles Style, who was the JFMCC,[10] and the two Royal Marine Colonels, were responsible for coordinating the admiral's war plan, in his capacity as the Red Joint Force Commander. My role, as JFACC, was to act as B-N's air advisor and lead a small team tasked with preparing the Air Tasking Order for integration into the admiral's overall daily plan. To assist me, I had an intelligence cell, an aircraft engineering cell and an operations cell, all of whom I could rely upon to produce a workable ATO with the air assets available to me. My FJ force was made up of the air wing of Harriers and Sea Harriers on board '*Lusty*', whilst the majority of my support helicopters were based on board HMS *Ocean*, which was also in our armada. Other than preparing for and attending the JFC's morning and evening briefings and receiving updates from my three cells during their planning phase, there was little else for me to do until the plan began to come together. Each member of the JFC's team had been allocated an Omani shadow who we were supposed to be training as part of the exercise. My shadow was a RAFO group captain, whose name I no longer remember. He was a fighter controller by trade and, frankly, was totally disinterested in the task at hand. He spent all his time hanging over the back rail of the quarterdeck covered in a pall of cigarette smoke.

The exercise was interesting if not very arduous and I too occasionally found myself on the quarterdeck being introduced to naval ways by the admiral whilst we both took the warm sea air. He taught me how to calculate a ship's speed by using the 'speed by second bow wave' calculation and that whistling was forbidden on Her Majesty's ships as, historically, it had been used by mutineers to communicate with each other. I didn't have the heart to tell him that one of his ship's officers, a RAF Fighter Controller on an exchange tour on '*Lusty*' who went by the name of Flight Lieutenant Christian, was a direct descendant of one of the most famous mutineers of all time!

I spent hours captivated on the starboard rail as '*Lusty*' was replenished at sea from oilers and logistics ships. Dolphins and flying fish entertained me whenever I had the opportunity to visit the admiral's bridge and the occasional shark and whale could quite often be seen in the wake. There were

---

10. Joint Force Maritime Component Commander.

highlights too during my six weeks with the navy. Passing through the Suez Canal was a first, and probably a last, for me. Despite our Suez transit being undertaken in the pitch dark, at midnight, and with the ship in full lockdown with all its guns loaded, armed and manned as an anti-terrorist precaution, it was certainly one to tick off my bucket list. The canal is some 80nms long and it took until dawn to get through it. The subsequent transit of the Red Sea was quite fascinating. On either bank could be seen the detritus of wars various and an occasional active Soviet SAM system would test my recognition memory banks – were people still using SA-2 Guideline systems in 2001? Apparently the Egyptians were! When you look at the Red Sea on a map it looks somewhat insignificant. But from leaving the Canal Zone to reaching the Bab el Mandeb Strait – at its southern exit point – is just under 1200nms. Given the local demography on both shores of the Red Sea, *'Lusty'* remained on alert throughout the four-day voyage south. A port call at Salalah in Oman allowed a shopping trip in the souk to buy gifts for the family and a 'Jungly'[11] sortie into the searing heat of the Omani desert for a JFC's strategy meeting with his three component commanders was a major highlight.

Whilst my work as JFACC required my significant attention at critical points in the day, there were long periods when I was free to roam the ship and visit operational compartments to learn their role and how the ship's company executed their individual tasks. But it was a long six weeks and one wave top looks just like another after a while. Moreover, as the exercise progressed, it became very clear that the ship was indeed going to go to war once Saif Sareea was over. Plans were formulating to remove its fixed wing complement of Sea Harriers and Harrier GR9s and to then turn the ship into a helicopter platform to support HMS *Ocean*. War in Afghanistan was about to ensue. When the exercise finished all personnel that were surplus to requirement were quickly despatched ashore in a fleet of Junglies that deposited us at the former RAF base at Masirah. From there a RAF C-130 took us to RAFO Seeb and, following a night stop in tented accommodation, we flew home by RAF Tristar to Brize Norton.

Shortly after my return to Waddington the Commandant AWC, Stuart Peach, asked me if I might be interested in leading a small team to undertake research into an Air Warfare Training Strategy that had been called for by the

---

11. A Royal Navy Mark 4 Sea King helicopter used as a troop carrier, usually a Royal Marine Landing Force.

Air Force Board. The AFB's desire was to create a package of air power/air warfare doctrine training that could, eventually, be rolled out to every man and woman in the RAF. Its purpose, they hoped, was to better develop the strategic and tactical awareness of their personnel, thereby making the RAF as a whole more operationally aware and more career competitive with equivalent ranks in the other two Services. It was a subject that was very close to my heart. Reinforced by my visit to the Australian Defence Force Academy in Canberra, lack of formal air warfare training for all RAF personnel had been at the forefront of my mind for some considerable time. It was yet another project that I could get my teeth into. It meant greater autonomy in my working day. I had thrived in autonomous project work in the past and it would be, for me, a perfect conclusion to my RAF career. Selfishly, it also allowed me to get out of the Doctrine Office early and return to Cranwell, which meant that my plan to remain in Lincolnshire until my retirement could now be fulfilled. I leapt at the opportunity and promptly tidied my desk and moved ten miles south, back to Cranwell, and into the AWC's training school in Trenchard Hall. I was back in the very corridors where I had attended the Whitbread Enjoyment Course,[12] twice, earlier in my career.

My team consisted of me, as Head Air Warfare Training Project Team, and two squadron leaders. One was a navigator who had spent most of his flying in the AEW world and the other was a man from the Administrative (Training) Branch who was well versed in the management and production of Training Needs Analyses.[13] Our first task was to complete a TNA and to do so we needed to do a bunch of research at home and abroad. We spoke with RAF commanders in an attempt to discover their understanding of the level of doctrinal awareness of the RAF personnel who worked under them; we focused particularly on those holding staff jobs as SO2s.[14] We visited the other two Services and we ventured as far afield as the USAF's Air University at Maxwell AFB, in Alabama, to ascertain just how the largest air force in the free world went about its doctrine training. We gathered screeds and screeds of evidence and, with our TNA expert leading us, we put together a robust case that could eventually be put before a meeting of the AFB. We concentrated initially on the need to provide a cohesive training package

---

12. Weapons Employment Course.
13. Training Needs Analysis – the first stage in the training process; it involves a procedure to determine whether training will address the identified problem.
14. Staff Officer 2 – lieutenant commander, major, squadron leader.

for officers that would start at DIOT and, with through-life interventions, provide formal training courses at critical points in an officer's career, right up to and beyond ASC. Within the TNA additional on-base training opportunities were promoted that would ensure that every officer, on every station throughout the RAF, would have the opportunity to strengthen their understanding of air warfare and thus be truly able to call themselves a war fighter. We never lost sight of the fact that there was a definite need to provide similar training for airmen, but we knew that it was important to sort the officers out first and have them commit to the full training package that would then be developed for the fifty-four thousand personnel who formed the RAF in the first decade of the twenty-first century.

We were given two years to complete the task, but so hard did I drive my team and so well did we work together that we completed our TNA in three months. We were tenacious and, as has always been my wont, I scrutinised every word, line, paragraph and page to ensure that there was not one flaw in any of our spelling, grammar, defence writing, arguments or costs! Dare I say it, it was a masterpiece of coordinated thinking, coherent writing and cogent discussion. TNA experts within HQ PTC, who wished to have sight of our paper before it went forward to the AFB, were astounded at the depth of information, quality of our argument and speed with which our TNA had been undertaken. Such was their conviction that they used it as a model template for some years to come.

I supported the commandant at a briefing to the AFB 2-Star Steering Group in Whitehall where our TNA was accepted and our recommendations endorsed. Three million pounds was allocated to implement a package of training across the whole officer corps. With that significant hurdle crossed, the task now entered Phase 2 which demanded that by no later than 2005, a coherent cradle-to-grave air warfare package of training be developed for all officers, from pilot officer to air commodore, in the RAF; a replacement 'Single Component Phase' for all students attending the Advanced Command and Staff Course be established from 2006; a complete review of all extant AWT conducted by the RAF be carried out; and the commencement of a strategy to provide a comprehensive package of AWT for all ranks across the RAF be investigated. This was a much greater task than the one that had gone before and one that would take some time to complete.

I didn't have that time. I was already fifty-three and had, with annual and terminal leave and resettlement training, less than twelve months productive service left. Stuart Peach, however, had the answer. I grabbed at his offer of a three-year extension to my RAF career. Four more years would provide enough time to develop and implement much of what had been tasked. I had a track record of seeing projects through to the bitter end so was, once again, delighted to be able to do so with the AWT Strategy. And what is more retirement at fifty-eight, rather than fifty-five, from a life-long career in the RAF would allow me to sit back and relax afterwards, knowing that all my children would have completed their further education and would be settled into their careers – well, almost. Hannah was still in university when I retired, but the bulk of that expense for Jo and I was over by the time I actually left in 2007.

It was also decided that I would better accomplish all the tasks delegated if I was elevated to become the Boss of the AWC's training division at Cranwell. The previous incumbent was about to retire from the RAF and so a smooth path was cleared for me to take over command of AWC Cranwell. My remit was broad and a regular throughput of students had to be managed by my very capable staff. It included the provision, conduct and supervision of all aspects of Air Warfare, Battle Management, Weapons, Electronic Warfare, Targeting and Aerospace training for the RAF and those from the RN and British Army requiring these skills. I was also required to mount teams capable of delivering these subjects to national and foreign military units at both home and overseas. My weapons team, for example, had a regular commitment to lecture to the Bangladeshi Defence Services Command and Staff College students in Dhaka; unfortunately I never had the time to join them. My aerospace expert routinely lectured to the Joint Services Advanced Command and Staff Course at Shrivenham and was regularly required to brief very senior officers of all three Services on the growing and developing use of the space environment for warfare. Others were regularly on the road, either providing support to war-gaming activities and joint exercises or providing specialist lectures to other military establishments. In order to support my 'space man', who filled a digital post, I undertook his Space Study Period should he ever have had the need of an understudy to lecture to his students. That qualified me to travel with him twice to gain further 'space' knowledge at the United States Space Foundation's annual symposium in Colorado Springs! It was a busy department, but with a very professional and capable team, which made my task so much easier.

I was still, of course, fully engaged as Head of the AWTPT and closely involved, therefore, in the creation of the training packages being developed within the AWT Strategy. Manpower had to be established to run a two-week Basic Air Warfare Course within my department for DIOT students, who would undertake it in the third term of a revamped thirty-two week IOTC. Additional staff were also required to man a four-week Higher Air Warfare Course that was to be delivered both as a precursor for RAF SO2s and SO1s who were about to attend the year-long ACSC at Shrivenham and as a stand-alone course for SO1s not destined for ACSC.

On 1 January 2005 my sidekick in the AWTPT was promoted to wing commander and, eventually, began to take over responsibility for the longer term implementation of the strategy. This allowed me to concentrate on the more pressing issues of the imminent arrival of students on the BAWC and HAWC. We ran dummy courses with live students to test our means and methods and with a few tweaks, and some infrastructure alterations, we were ready to go when the first students on the new IOTC turned up in early 2006.

By October 2006 my replacement had arrived and I was able to start to think about life after the RAF. It had certainly been a fulfilling career. I had flown two unsurpassed aircraft in a rare period of general peace and calm in the history of the world's first air force. I had improved the operational capability of the RAF with the CWEM in 1985, a review of QWI training in 1993 and the procurement of new and potent weapons in 1997 and I had assisted the doctrinal education of its personnel with the AWT Strategy as my last act before retirement. Moreover, from 1997 to 2000 I had had an absolute ball introducing some two thousand new officers into the Royal Air Force. I had drunk rather too much beer and, as a result, I had probably got into too much trouble as a junior officer in too many officers' messes. I had flown with some incredibly capable pilots and had met and flown with some, on 237 OCU, that I'd rather forget about now. I had never got into an aircraft that didn't have an engine[15] and I had never had to get out of one whilst its engine was still going! Nor had I ever flown with a pilot who had been born after I had joined the RAF! Three philosophies that I had adopted early on in my career! I had met some fantastic characters along the way and had built an address book of friends whom I knew would, at any time, drop everything to stand by my side if I needed them. I had fathered two

_____

15. A glider.

magnificent children from my first marriage. I had recovered from a messy divorce and I had married the most wonderful woman in Jo and had brought up her two splendid daughters. I am distinctly proud of all of them. I have had the time of my life. From my early days in Glasgow, through a faltering scholastic career and a checkered history as a junior officer, right up until the day I left the RAF behind, I have loved every minute of it!

By the time I retired, my erstwhile Tornado pilot on 17 Squadron, Tim Anderson, had taken over as commandant of the AWC. He was the last man to ever write anything on my ACR. He summed me up as follows:

The investment made in extending Wg Cdr Herriot's service past his NRD[16] has been repaid fully. Herriot possesses a wealth of experience across a broad spectrum of roles and responsibilities bridging the operations, acquisition, training and doctrine domains. He has employed the knowledge and full range of skills that this experience generated during what has been a pivotal contribution to the development of a much more comprehensive AP/AW training capability resident at Cranwell. Through effective structural architecture, refined processes and efficient service provision, Herriot has ensured that available resources have been used to maximum effect by a workforce focused and motivated on clear outcomes.

Wg Cdr Herriot's forthcoming retirement at this rank undervalues his career contribution and ability. He has demonstrated clearly his suitability for the next rank and the positive promotion recommendation is entirely appropriate. Nevertheless, it is now clear that Herriot will see out the remainder of his service employed on duties associated with his current appointment within the AWC. In this, I have no doubt that he will continue to deliver in a consummately professional manner until the last.

Would I do it all again? Of course I bloody would, but this time I would make certain sure that I was never temporarily unsure of my position!

---

16. Notional Retirement Date.

Chapter Thirteen

Feet Up and On The Bench!

Since my retirement I have often been asked by civilian friends what I find to do with my time after thirty-eight years' service in the RAF. 'How', they would say, 'can anything compare with the active and exciting life that you had before?' Well, of course, it cannot. But stopping commuting to and from Cranwell on the A46 between Nottingham and Newark every day, which I did for the last eight years of my career, has helped greatly with my rehabilitation!

Rehabilitation! It sounds as though I have just completed a life sentence, which certainly it was not. The RAF call it resettlement and for my resettlement I was fortunate enough to negotiate attendance on a home DIY course for two weeks in West Wales and a week-long Italian cookery course in Umbria. I have to admit that I have had little call for my new-found bricklaying skills or my plumbing or plastering masterclass, but my Gorgonzola Soufflé and my Tiramisu are both to die for!

The course in Umbria was amazingly good fun. It was run by two retired wing commanders, husband and wife, who had bought Casa Panfili when they retired from the RAF. It was a large property that could sleep twelve and had a vast kitchen where the classes were held. I have always enjoyed cooking at home and I love Italy, so it had seemed natural to put the two together. The RAF acknowledged that a similar three-day course in London would cost them £1500 so were content to pay for the course in Italy, which cost less than half of the London course and lasted seven days. The rub, however, was that Resettlement Funds would not stretch to international air travel, but as long as I paid for the air tickets they were happy to send me. With a £16 return ticket with Ryanair from Stansted to Perugia in my pocket, it was a win/win situation for me.

Al and Betty Stewart had turned Casa Panfili from a rundown farmhouse into a thriving business. There was a 'granny flat' attached to the property that allowed them to decamp in the summer months when the main property was rented to sun and tranquillity seeking holidaymakers. They ran walking holidays, art class holidays and cooking courses. Al had trained as a sommelier and Betty as a chef as part of their own resettlement. The property also had its own vineyard and olive grove each with one hundred plants. The olives were pressed locally, but the wine preparation and bottling was all carried out on site. There were only three of us on the course in March 2007 and I was the only male. Betty had prepared a recipe book for the week and it was our task to prepare both lunch and dinner each day, which we would then consume with Panfili wine at lunchtime and the sommelier's choices with dinner. We were taken to the local markets to purchase fresh ingredients and out, for the occasional downtime, to such places as Assisi to view the relic of St Francis. We made some wonderfully gastronomic delights throughout the week and ate like kings every night, with mandatory free-flowing wine thrown in. Fully certificated at the end of the course, and with my very own Casa Panfili apron locked in my suitcase, I headed back to Stansted ready to experiment on my expectant friends and family.

As I approached retirement, one of my first acts was to apply to become a magistrate in Nottingham. My paternal grandfather had been a magistrate in Peebles and I had, over time, thought it might be an admirable way of giving something back to my adopted city and, at the same time, continue in my grandfather's footsteps. I had not been permitted to do so whilst serving, but as I approached retirement the opportunity now presented itself. The application process was lengthy. I suppose it had to be, because the responsibility of a magistrate is high and the close scrutiny of individuals is necessary, to ensure that people of good character and ability are appointed. Moreover, integrity and honesty are must have basic pillars of those who are tasked with dispensing local justice. If the application process was lengthy, the first interview was absolutely tortuous. Sat before a panel of three, two local magistrates and a co-opted social worker, I felt as if I was facing the Spanish Inquisition. It was not unlike the interrogation I had undergone having been captured in a snowy Bavaria at the RAF's Winter Survival School back in the early 70s. The only difference was that the 'nice guy' and the 'nasty guy' were in the room at the same time and I was never blindfolded! Thankfully, I managed to build a rapport with them both and seemed to be doing well until the chairwoman handed the floor over to the social worker. His first question knocked me sideways.

'Tell me, Mr Herriot, within the justice system, why do you think that men from Afro-Caribbean backgrounds make up over seventy per cent of the current prison population?'

Well, I quickly realised that my first and quickest thought was not the answer that would get me through the interview. So I deferred by asking him a question back about a contemporary news item that was topical at the time. The Cheshire Constabulary were, in 2006, being challenged about their apparent systemic racism. So I asked him if he included the police within the 'justice system'. He 'supposed he did', which allowed me to focus my answer on the police rather than the inmates themselves. I passed the interview and without too much delay found myself invited for a second, which was less arduous and focused more on case management and problem solving.

On 17 October 2006, I, along with twenty-seven other men and women, was sworn in as a Justice of the Peace in Nottingham's Crown Court. My wife and son accompanied me to witness the event and afterwards we headed for a celebratory lunch in town. There were, arranged on the Bench before the assembled magistrates in Number One Court: the Lord Lieutenant of Nottinghamshire, who represented Her Majesty the Queen; the Chief Constable of Nottinghamshire; the Chairman of the Nottingham Bench; and the senior presiding judge on the Midlands circuit. Each magistrate had to stand in turn and make two oaths. The first was the oath of allegiance to Her Majesty the Queen, which was not dissimilar to that that I had undertaken in January 1969 when I joined the RAF. The second was the judicial oath, which went as follows:

I do swear by Almighty God that I will well and truly serve our Sovereign Lady Queen Elizabeth the Second in the office of Justice of the Peace, and I will do right to all manner of people after the laws and usages of this realm, without fear or favour, affection or ill will.

Simple stuff, but exceedingly important. Without fear or favour, affection or ill will. In other words, no matter what affliction or appearance a defendant might have, my responsibility was to judge him or her fairly and that I did for twelve years before I resigned, on a point of principle, in 2018.

After I had made my oaths I sat quietly, contemplating my surroundings, whilst others made theirs. Whilst doing so, rather than him listen to the proceedings, I observed the judge reading what appeared to be trial papers. How rude, I thought. How wrong I was. When he stood to address us he explained that he had been reading through the list of our names and backgrounds to get a feel for where we had come from. He then set off into his speech and talked about the grave responsibility that we had now accepted and the task that was before us. He explained that we would now be properly referred to as 'Your Worship', but that we could anticipate many variations on that theme throughout our time in court. He let us know that he had been called many things throughout his time on the circuit. Everything from 'Your Majesty' through 'Your Lordship' down to 'mate'! But none, he said, could beat the day he was sitting in Birmingham when a delinquent defendant was brought before him and he asked him to provide his personal details to the court. His story went thus:

'Mr Smith, please give the court your full name, date of birth and where you currently reside.'

To which Mr Smith replied, 'What's it to you, you fat bastard!'

The punchline to this tale was, according to the judge, that Mr Smith went to prison and he went on the Atkins Diet. So you see it is not all doom and gloom in Her Majesty's Court Service. There is often time for a laugh, if you are sitting on the correct side of the Bench.

I thoroughly enjoyed my twelve years as a magistrate and worked both the Adult and the Youth Courts in Nottingham, rising to the position of a Bench Chairman in both environments. I learned an awful lot about society, which to a great degree I had been sheltered from previously because of my RAF service. I met many new friends on the Bench and, after all that time, began to recognise defendants who saw the justice system as just a speed bump in the path of their criminal careers. I even made the headlines in the local paper on a couple of occasions as the result of my position as a magistrate and, on one memorable occasion, because of my pronouncement in court on a particular individual who was a regular through the 'revolving door'.[1] This man had a string of low level convictions, predominantly to do with his begging for money to fuel his drug habit. However, on this occasion he had pleaded not guilty to a charge of fraud by false representation and was before me and my two colleagues to be tried. In short, he had been banned from being a Big Issue seller because he was interminably drunk and, consequently, abusive to his potential customers if they refused to hand over their hard earned cash. To overcome the ban, the evidence before the court was that he had bought a Big Issue from a mate at a reduced fee, attempted to sell it to passers-by and, when they offered him cash for it, he would tell them it was his last one,

_____

1. A judicial expression for those persistent criminals who regularly appear in court.

refuse to sell it to them, but take their cash anyway or abuse them if they refused to part with it. The evidence against him was compelling and it had all been captured on CCTV. Guilty as charged was a simple judgment as was the decision for sentence – twelve weeks custody, because of his repeat offending of a similar nature and for his failure to heed warnings that he had been given in the past. We had not bargained for his defence advocate's plea of mitigation, however. He pleaded with the court that the man had only just been allocated a place in a residential drug rehabilitation unit and, if incarcerated, would lose that place and a real opportunity to turn his life around. He was, his advocate stated, 'highly motivated to tackle a long-standing addiction'! Aren't they all when they are trapped like rabbits in a car's headlights? If we were not convinced we were, as a group of three, persuaded, so we suspended his custodial sentence for twelve months. But I chose my words very carefully when I addressed the individual in court. I told him in no uncertain terms, and was quoted in the *Nottingham Post*, 'If you commit any offences in the next twelve months, the next bench will throw the book at you.' Needless to say, he did. And happily, I was chairman of the sitting bench when he appeared yet again for trial! Having found him guilty, and I having explained the recent history to my fellow magistrates, he had done a runner from court by the time we returned our verdict and announced his custodial sentence. All we could do was issue a warrant, not backed for bail, and hope that the Nottinghamshire Constabulary picked him up from wherever he was lurking without too much delay.

As a magistrate I learned also that there are three types of felon in our society: bad; sad; and mad! The bad ones need locking up. The sad need some form of guidance. The mad need help, and not necessarily by locking them in prison.

I found the whole experience of being part of the justice system highly rewarding, but twelve years was enough and when the Bench voted in a 'Walter Mitty'[2] to be Chairman of the Bench I decided enough was enough. I had only a year left to do anyway because, good or bad, competent or incompetent, the justice system forces magistrates on to the scrap heap as soon as they hit seventy.

---

2. An expression used by military personnel to describe somebody who claims to have been in the military, but never was.

To keep myself out of my wife's way, I took a temporary job invigilating exams for a local college and joined the local golf club. I had been an occasional detachment golfer throughout my RAF career, but had never taken it up seriously. I have been at it now for twelve years and my deficient talent at sports that involve some form of implement and a ball has not helped me improve. However, I enjoy the walk, the company and the fresh air and, some days, I play quite well and can actually win the occasional match. Who cares, I am in my late sixties, and I am an old dog trying to learn new tricks whilst having fun.

Of course, my task as secretary of the BAA has not diminished. Indeed, if anything, it has increased, now that I am also editor of the association's biannual newsletter. Whilst I still very much enjoy keeping our nearly five hundred members updated, the saddest part of my task is that of recording and reporting on those who depart this life. Despite that fact, the association is vibrant, healthy and we regularly gather to share a beer or a formal dinner and recount tales of our past derring do.

I think one of the most important things in retirement is to stem the aging process. Walking my Labrador 'Bomber Harris', cycling with my wife and having grandchildren all help immensely in this regard. Writing stimulates the brain and keeps it from atrophying and so, in retirement, I have been more than involved in a number of written works, both in periodical and book form. Not least, of course, was the first part of this memoir,[3] but I have also had much fun contributing to 'Out Of The Blue', 'Out Of The Blue Too' and 'The Buccaneer Boys'. Also, at his request, I assisted Frederick Forsyth with technical details about the Buccaneer for his novel 'The Cobra'.[4] In my own right, in 2008, I published *The Buccaneer Songbook*.

Retirement has also given my wife and I an opportunity to travel that was more restricted whilst I was serving. We have cruised the fjords of Norway and, in 2011, took ourselves on a two and a half thousand mile road trip around Eastern Europe to see places that were off limits whilst I was serving. Berlin, Krakow, Prague, Dresden and Colditz were all covered in our trek around Europe. Berlin had changed much since I had first visited it in the early 70s by road with my first Buccaneer pilot, Iain Ross. The old border crossing at Helmstedt still had relics of its communist past and East Berlin,

---

3. *Adventures of a Cold War Fast-Jet Navigator: The Buccaneer Years* (Pen & Sword, 2017).

4. Although I have to admit he has used much poetic licence therein for which I bear no responsibility.

without 'the wall' was a most wonderful jewel. The former sparkle of West Berlin, the Kurfürstendamm, was much duller in 2011 and a shadow of its former neon-lit glory. We treated ourselves to a spot of luxury in Berlin, staying in the 5-Star 'Hotel Adlon Kempinski' on Unter den Linden, right by the Brandenburg Gate. We knew we were in the right place when we parked our rather tired Saab 9-5 Estate next to a vintage Rolls-Royce in the hotel's underground car park! It was luxury in the extreme, even to the extent that the hotel provided a 'bath butler' who would happily come to your room to run the bath for you. We declined the offer, as I did not think we would have afforded the tip. Breakfast in the hotel was wonderful – culinary delights abounded. Indeed, such was it that it had to be seen to be believed that, tourists would venture through the hotel at breakfast time, just so that they could see guests consuming the gastronomic delicacies. You may not know the Adlon in Berlin, but if I tell you it is where Michael Jackson dangled his child out of an upper storey window, you will know where we stayed.

Our purpose in going to Krakow was to visit Auschwitz. As a 13-year-old, I had been hosted by the Wallfisch family in Notting Hill over an Easter break from school. Peter Wallfisch was a concert pianist and a friend of my father's. His wife, Anita Lasker-Wallfisch, was a professional cellist, who had survived Auschwitz because she had been able to play the cello in the band that played as the Holocaust victims were marched to and from work every morning and evening. I wanted to see the place for myself and, having done so, I feel I have a better understanding of the misery that those poor people suffered under the Nazi regime. Every teenager in the Western World should go there – they then might understand what suffering was!

It was fascinating to travel in Eastern Europe, past places and airbases that had once been targets. Rural Poland was interesting, but its motorways were abominable with potholes every ten yards and filled in potholes every five! More importantly, there was no motorway between Krakow and the Czech border, so a planned six hour journey took nine hours to complete. We left Poland thinking it rather Third World and realising, perhaps, why so many of its residents now live and work in the United Kingdom. Prague was magnificent with its castle, Charles Bridge and astronomical clock. A short lunch stop in Dresden proved just how well the East Germans had recovered the city's gothic buildings, post the Second World War, back to their former glory. It also confirmed my view that Soviet built apartment blocks were as soulless in reality as they had appeared in photograph and film. Before a few days R&R in the Moselle, we spent two nights in Colditz so that we could visit its castle and view the place where many of my RAF forebears had been incarcerated, and had escaped from, in the 1940s.

Whilst our daughter Helen was serving in the Falkland Islands we managed to visit her for a long weekend. I had always wanted to visit the islands whilst I was serving, but, as a mud mover, was never able to do so. Thanks to the RAF's indulgence system and, upon application as parents of someone serving there, we had a very pleasant long weekend at RAF Mount Pleasant; there and back via RAF Ascension Island. Not everybody's idea of fun, but the thirty-eight hour round trip, on one of the RAF's scheduled twice-weekly Falklands Air Bridge[5] sorties, was no hardship for me. I just loved being back in the air again and all for the princely sum of £250 each.

East Falkland, with an area of 6,605 km², is the largest island in the archipelago. Other than its capital, Port Stanley, the islands are sparsely populated and it was easy to see how the 1982 Argentinian invasion was so successful, so quickly, with only a small garrison of Royal Marines to protect the islands. Not so in October 2014 when we visited. Mount Pleasant was a vast airfield sprawl with not only a flight of four RAF Typhoons, supported by a Voyager tanker, but also RAF Sea Kings to provide SAR and a couple of C-130s for in-theatre freight and passenger onward movement. British International Helicopters operated a flight of four civilian helicopters, from the airfield, that provided R&R travel to some of the remoter parts of the islands. In support of the British Army's resident infantry company, the RAF had deployed two Chinooks to Mount Pleasant. The British Army provided a Rapier detachment to provide point defence, whilst Mount Pleasant even had its own Royal Naval detachment at its dockyard at Mare Harbour. The resident Royal Navy vessel in the South Atlantic, based at Mare Harbour since 2007, is HMS *Clyde*, an offshore patrol vessel of the River Class. Just outside the gates of the base was the headquarters of the Commander British Forces South Atlantic Islands.

For me, it was a great opportunity to visit many of the battlefields such as Goose Green and San Carlos; names that strike remembrance for Britons since those dark spring days of 1982. Whilst in the Falklands, we were fortunate to be able to take a trip on a BIH Sea King to spend a day on

---

5. Operated by Air Tanker's passenger-role A330 Voyager.

Sea Lion Island.[6] It was fascinating, and thrilled my inner ornithologist, to walk amongst the resident flocks of penguins, Gentoo, Rockhopper and Magellan, but also to witness Orcas waiting offshore to catch a recently born, but unwary, Elephant Seal as it attempted its first swim in the sea. There were plenty more seabirds around and whilst I never saw an albatross, the widespread Upland Geese, the Falkland Steamer Ducks, Southern Giant Petrels, the beautifully red-breasted Long-tailed Meadow Lark and the occasional Southern Crested Caracara made up for the lack of a sighting of the world's largest flying bird.

In 2016, I returned to Australia, but not on business this time, but to visit my daughter Sarah, whose husband is Australian, and my two grandsons for a month. My visit coincided with my Canadian goddaughter's wedding in Edmonton, Alberta. Consequently, I flew the wrong way to Sydney and for the first time in my life flew across the Pacific. Almost twenty years on from my first trip to Australia, I completed my circumnavigation of the Globe.

So what of the two aircraft I flew operationally in my RAF career? The Buccaneer S2 and the Tornado GR1. Each aircraft had its own merits and its demerits. They came from different generations and, thus, are difficult to compare. An aircraft such as the Tornado, with its sophisticated avionics suite, will clearly be streets ahead in weapon delivery accuracy of an aircraft that was reliant on an analogue system, such as was the Buccaneer. Solid state systems will always have more capability than a system that relies on cogs and pulleys within its weapon system. Hard to believe, perhaps, but if you take the side wall off the Buccaneer's Control and Release Computer, which is the heart of its weapon aiming system, you will indeed find cogs and pulleys therein. Pretty damned accurate cogs and pulleys, but they are cogs and pulleys nonetheless. So in terms of weapon delivery the Tornado beat the Buccaneer hands down. Weapons load, however, is a different kettle of fish. With its internal bomb bay, the Buccaneer had quite a capability when it came to weapon carrying capacity. With four conventional stations and two nuclear hard-points in the bay, plus four weapon stations on the wings, each of which was capable of carrying a Twin Store Carrier, the Buccaneer could carry quite a punch. Of course the Tornado had multiple store stations on its wings and fuselage too, but both aircraft, especially those stationed in RAF Germany, routinely flew with wing tanks on the inboard pylons, thereby

---

6. Sea Lion Island is the southernmost inhabited island of the Falkland Islands.

denying two stations for weapon carriage. Additionally, the Buccaneer utilised one wing pylon to carry the Westinghouse AN/ALQ-101-10 ECM Pod and, towards the back end of its career in RAF colours, another to carry a Sidewinder missile. The same is true of the Tornado, however, which carried a Skyshadow ECM Pod on one outer pylon and a BOZ Chaff and Flare dispenser on the other. The latter had a Mauser cannon, for the 'get in close and smash it' ground attack requirement.

Cruise speeds were comparable as were high speed dash speeds when crossing the Forward Line of Own Troops and on the IP to Target run. The Buccaneer was not supersonic, but then nor was the Tornado with any external load. With its internal bomb bay the Buccaneer did not suffer the same drag penalty that the Tornado did and, consequently, it could go further. A quick comparison of both aircraft with a full war load, two wing tanks and appropriate defensive aids on the outer pylons gives the Buccaneer a Radius of Action advantage of greater than two hundred nautical miles over its successor on a Lo-Lo-Lo mission. On a Hi-Lo-Hi mission, with or without AAR, the Buccaneer's advantage was even greater.

So how to compare?

In my view, and notwithstanding the digital wizardry of the Tornado GR1, the Buccaneer was a much better platform for almost everything that it was required to do in both overland and over water roles in the RAF. It was a much more comfortable ride at low-level over land or sea and it could fly some 15,000 feet higher than a Tornado at high level. It was stable both as an AAR receiver and provider and whilst it could not match the Tornado for speed at low-level, when the latter was clean, it could actually carry more ordnance further and at a higher sustainable speed for longer thanks to its rotating bomb door. Indeed, as I wrote in the first volume of my memoir, a Buccaneer could actually fly around the world without having to air-to-air refuel. I planned just such a deployment in 1993 in response to the Laarbruch Station Commander's request, to see if it could be done, when the aircraft was being withdrawn from service in RAFG. Sadly, we were not cleared to execute our plan, which would have taken us away from Laarbruch for a month, because it would have been an embarrassing act that the Tornado could not have contemplated. But the accuracy of the Tornado's avionic system has to carry the day, even if some of the deeper targets that were within range of the Buccaneer could not have been reached by Tornado before the advent of Storm Shadow.

So what of my family? Our four children have now all flown the nest and have settled across the world with families of their own. I have watched, with admiration and pride, as each has blossomed into adulthood and secured not only gainful, but worthy, employment and success in their chosen career. Two qualified primary school teachers, one RAF officer and a training executive in hospitality is not a bad haul. The three girls have all chosen perfect husbands in Andrew, James and Gordon. The first an Australian, the second an Englishman and the third a Scot, which has ensured that I now have a diverse, in nationality terms, band of grandchildren who keep me eternally busy and well entertained. My son Christopher, the eternal bachelor, has settled in the French Alps with Caroline, his French partner. Sarah has moved to Sydney with Andrew and her family of two boys, Oscar and William. Helen, who is serving in the RAF in Lincolnshire, lives in the wilds of the county with James and her two young children, Beatrix and Montague, and Hannah and Gordon live in Leicestershire with their two young boys, Douglas and Stewart.

In the early years of my retirement, I maintained my link with the RAF College and, having held my fiftieth birthday celebration in College Hall, I very much enjoyed being able to return there in 2009 to celebrate my sixtieth birthday, surrounded by family and friends. That I thought would be my final formal connection with my alma mater. But later that year I was back to attend Helen's graduation parade when she was commissioned as an officer in the RAF. My connection with Cranwell did not stop there. In 2011, following a decision by the RAF to close the navigator branch I was lucky enough to gain a place at the Navigator Farewell Dinner in Daedalus Officers' Mess. What a momentous occasion. Some three hundred RAF navigators attended. Some young, some old, many serving and many retired, like me, attended to say farewell to a branch of the RAF that had provided them with a life that could never be repeated. The day of the airborne navigator in the RAF was over – or so the AFB thought. Aircraft coming into inventory would be guided by black boxes and those skills that I had been taught and had exercised throughout my flying career were no longer required.[7]

---

7. By 2011 RAF navigators had become Weapon System Officers, but with the forecast Out of Service Date for Tornado having been announced as 2018, plus the withdrawal of Nimrod and the C-130K, there was seen to be no future requirement for air navigators. In 2018, with the arrival of Rivet Joint and other like platforms that decision may have been somewhat premature!

In 2017, in recognition of my long association with aviation, I was accorded the honour of being certified as a Master Air Navigator by the Honourable Company of Air Pilots.[8] Prior to a sumptuous dinner in the magnificent surroundings of London's Guildhall, with Jo supporting me, I received my certificate from the livery company's Master. The certificate is signed by the Grand Master, His Royal Highness Prince Andrew.

So yes! Life after the air force has been different, but it has been just as much fun and has, quite routinely, been busier day-to-day than ever before. Of course, the happiest days of my retirement are those I spend with any one of my grandchildren to whom this book is dedicated. I hope that one day they will pick up both volumes and realise just what it was like to be a Cold War Fast-Jet Navigator.

---

8. Full title – Honourable Company of Air Pilots (including air navigators).

Appendix

Seventeen Squadron Songs

A s the result of events that unfolded during three major squadron detachments, each of the following songs was written, over a few beers in a bar, in Las Vegas, Sardinia or Goose Bay. Whilst the lyrics were committed to beer-stained paper at the time of writing the music is locked in my head. The Decimomannu and Goose Bay songs are both sung to recognisable tunes. Sadly, no music manuscript was ever written for the original Red Flag Song. These are the last squadron songs that I was ever involved in creating. I had learned 'my lyricist trade' on XV Squadron, at Laarbruch, on my first Buccaneer Tour. *The Buccaneer Songbook*[1] contains those songs, and more from the Fleet Air Arm and the South African Air Force.

The Red Flag Song

We're Seventeen Squadron, we're on detachment
And we're having lots of fun,
Drinking beer and playing hard
And bronzing in the sun
But we've got a lot of work to do
And I'm sure you'll all agree
Tha-at this is the life for you and me!

Chorus
This is the life! Travelling!
See the world!
It's sixteen forty-five and still no rain!
Travelling!
See the world!
This is the life!

---

1. *The Buccaneer Songbook* (Reading Room 2008) – available on Amazon.

AWACS sits above the range
Giving lots of clues
Bandits at belted time hack now
Just listen to the news
Dragnet you are awesome
As you sit up there on high
But with SAM 5s around the corner
You're gonna die!

Chorus
C'est la vie! En voyageant!
Voir le monde!
Il est seize heures quarante-cinq et pas de pluie!
En voyageant!
Voir le monde!
C'est la vie!

F-15s escort us in
Giving lots of cover
They sit above at a thousand feet
Like an overprotective mother
But they sure tie up the fighters
And allow the strikers through
Dear Queen, May we have some Eagles too!

Chorus (English)

106s, They're the boys
Flying in their Darts
Lawyers, bankers, farmers too
Giving it all their heart
Cos Montana's part-time flyers
Are a really shit-hot team
And as far as we're concerned
You are the cream.

Chorus (French)

Aggressors run the corridor
Doing one point four
Trying to catch Tornados
As they race the desert floor
But they very rarely kill us
As I'm sure you'll all agree
Cos they're constrained by Red Flag R O E!

Chorus (English)

SLUFs and BUFs and 16s too
Streaking across the sand
Weasels, Jammers, Chaff and Flares
Blanking every band
So the Commies better sharpen up
Before they do their thing
For this Red Flag has turned us into Kings!

Chorus (French)

All together now
We're the Red Flag boys we're in Las Vegas
And we're having lots of fun
Drinking beer and playing hard
And bronzing in the sun
But we've had a lot of work to do
And I'm sure you'll all agree
Tha-at this is the life for you and me!

Chorus (English)

The Decimomannu Song
(Tune: Heart and Soul)

Backing (6-8 persons) throughout:

Alcoholic, Alcoholic, Alcoholic, Alcoholic

Chorus:
Seventeen, we're on the piss again,
Frasca Range it's getting blitzed again
Sev'nteen in Deci – Mo – Man – Ooo.

Leader's brought, their own Tornados down
Hoping for, a really swinging town
How wrong can front line aircrew be?

Chorus

Some came down, by shiny Vee – Cee – Ten
We won't do, that awful stat again
Next time, we're going to bloody march!

Chorus

Q Wy Team, let off a lot of steam
Debrief time, they're always very mean
But the – ey don't practise what they preach.

Chorus

Jimbo James, he used the standby sight
And he gave, the R S O a fright
Bomb score, was off the plot at three!

Chorus

Gareth went, into the Pig and Tape
Got himself, into an awful state
Fell down, and split his head in two!

Chorus

'A' Team, went to Villa – sim – ius
A road block, soon put a stop to this
Twelve blats, for overloaded bus!

Chorus

Jimmy Gyp, prepared a super dish
Our Magoo,[2] was not impressed with this
Cos there, were beaks and eyeballs too.

Chorus

Went strafing, it's quite a cracking sport
Get too close, Q Wise'll have your throat
Poor Boss, you've blown the pass again.

Chorus
Seventeen, we're on the piss again,
Seventeen we're getting blitzed again
Seventeen in Deci – Mo – Man – Ooo.

Repeat last chorus Multo Forte!

---

2. Squadron Commander, Grant McLeod.

The Goose Bay Song

(Tune: Lily Marlene)

Seventeen in Goose Bay
What a happy mob
Never any women
Not even a blow job
We've been here for three weeks, far too long
We're so pissed off, we wrote this song,
So get me back to Brüggen
In time for Q–R–A!

Arrived out here by Shiny
What a bloody shag
The captain was a poofta
The hosties were in drag
We read stupid books and played at cards
We'd Gin & Tonics by the yard
But ended up in Goose Bay
Being briefed till we were bored.

Started flying Monday
What a happy day
Ten slots on the programme
And all for O–C–A
The Boss saw the schedule, got pissed off
Just change the plot he told the Auth
But Huck continued flying
Cos he's the Squadron Hog.

Delta's in the hangar
Without a bleeding donk
She has only been there
Since last we had a bonk
The engineers have got it wrong
They ought to sell her for a song
She'll still be there in autumn
When Seventeen return.

The Q Wy's been quite grumpy
Not a happy Joe
Not as good as Deci
Where he last ran the show
Jimbo went crazy, Herriot sad
They thought their man had gone quite mad
But he got pissed on Friday
And wasn't half as bad.

Magoo's a very hard man
Bared faces in a flash
He said the very first thing
Is grow a daft moustache
The boys said that he has thrown a fit
All we need now is gassie kit
Then we will have the answer
A three week Mineval.

Some go home on Friday
On Saturday the rest
We'll leave the aircraft ready
For those who're second best
We're hoping that they'll appreciate
The work you've done for it's been great
On their three weeks in Goose Bay
The Arsehole of the World.

Seventeen in Goose Bay
What a happy mob
Never any women
Not even a blow job
We've been here for three weeks, far too long
We're so pissed off, we wrote this song,
So get me back to Brüggen
In time for Q-R-A!

Glossary

AAA	Anti-Aircraft Artillery
A&AEE	Aircraft & Armament Experimental Establishment
AAAW	Advanced Air-Launched Anti-Armour Weapon
AAR	Air-to-Air Refuelling
ACDS OR(Air)	Assistant Chief of the Defence Staff Operational Requirements (Air)
ACL	Air Combat Leader
ACMI	Air Combat Manoeuvring Instrumentation
ACR	Annual Confidential Report
ACSC	Advanced Command and Staff Course
ACT	Air Combat Training
AD	Air Defence
ADC	Aide de Camp
AE	Aircraft Establishment
AEW	Airborne Early Warning
AFB	Air Force Base
AFB	Air Force Board
AFT	Advanced Flying Training
AGM	Air-to-Ground Missile
AIM	Air Intercept Missile
AIRNORTH	Allied Air Forces North
AIS	Airborne Instrumentation System
AMP	Air Member for Personnel
AMRAAM	Advanced Medium-Range Air-to-Air Missile
AMTC	Aeromedical Training Centre
AOC	Air Officer Commanding
AOTS	Aircrew Officer Training School
AOWG	Air Operations Working Group
APC	Armament Practice Camp
AR5	Aircrew Respirator 5
ASC	Advanced Staff Course

ASI	Air Speed Indicator
ASP	Aircraft Servicing Platform
AST	Advanced Staff Training
ATAF	Allied Tactical Air Force
ATC	Air Traffic Control
ATO	Air Tasking Order
AVM	Air Vice-Marshal
AWACS	Airborne Warning and Control System
AWC	Air Warfare Centre
AWT	Air Warfare Training
AWTPT	Air Warfare Training Project Team
BA	British Airways
BAA	Buccaneer Aircrew Association
BAe	British Aerospace
BAFO	Best and Final Offer
BAFTA	British Academy of Film and Television Arts
BARO	Barometric
BAWC	Basic Air Warfare Course
BBC	British Broadcasting Corporation
BFBS	British Forces Broadcasting Service
BIH	British International Helicopters
BP	Brooke-Popham
BRNC	Britannia Royal Naval College
BSC	Basic Staff Course
CAS	Close Air Support
CASOM	Conventionally Armed Stand Off Missile
CBFL(I)	Commander British Forces Lodestar (Italy)
CBU	Cluster Bomb Unit
CCF	Combined Cadet Force
CCTV	Close Circuit Television
CDS	Chief of the Defence Staff
CFB	Canadian Forces Base
CHOM	College Hall Officers' Mess
CO	Commanding Officer
CPGS	Cassette Preparation Ground Station
CR	Combat Ready
CRPMD	Combined Radar Projected Map Display

CSAR	Combat Search and Rescue
CSFC	Church of Scotland and Free Churches
CTP	Cocktail Party
CTTO	Central Tactics and Trials Organisation
CWEM	Conventional Weapons Employment Manual
CWO	College Warrant Officer
D Air Arm	Director of Air Armament
DACT	Dissimilar Air Combat Training
DAW	Department of Air Warfare
DDIOT	Director Department of Initial Officer Training
DDTO(RAF)	Deputy Director Training Operational (Royal Air Force)
DetCo	Detachment Commander
DG Arm	Director General (Armament)
DIOT	Department of Initial Officer Training
DIY	Do It Yourself
DoD	Department of Defence
DOR(Air)1	Director Operational Requirements (Air)1
DS	Directing Staff
EAC	Equipment Approvals Committee
ECG	Electrocardiogram
ECM	Electronic Counter-Measures
EW	Electronic Warfare
F1369	Officer's Confidential Report
FAA	Fleet Air Arm
FIR	Flight Information Region
FJ	Fast-Jet
FLC	Field Leadership Camp
Flt	Flight
Flt Lt	Flight Lieutenant
FOB	Forward Operating Base
G&T	Gin and Tonic
GCA	Ground Control Approach
GMR	Ground Mapping Radar
Gp Capt	Group Captain
GPS	Global Positioning System
HAS	Hardened Aircraft Shelter
HAWC	Higher Air Warfare Course

HEL	Hunting Engineering Limited
Hi-Lo-Hi	High Level sortie with a Low Level phase
HMG	Her Majesty's Government
HMSO	Her Majesty's Stationery Office
HQ	Headquarters
HQ PTC	Headquarters Personnel & Training Command
HQSTC	Headquarters Strike Command
HT	High Tension
IDS	Interdictor/Strike
ILT	Intermediate Leadership Training
IMC	Instrument Meteorological Conditions
IOTC	Initial Officer Training Course
IP	Initial Point
ISD	In Service Date
ISS	Individual Staff Studies
ItAF	Italian Air Force
JDAM	Joint Direct Attack Munition
JFACC	Joint Force Air Component Commander
JFACHQ	Joint Force Air Component Headquarters
JFC	Joint Force Commander
JFMCC	Joint Force Maritime Component Commander
JMEM	Joint Munitions Effectiveness Manual
JSOW	Joint Stand Off Weapon
LCR	Limited Combat Ready
LGB	Laser Guided Bomb
LOA	Local Overseas Allowance
Lo-Lo-Lo	Low Level Mission
MAEB	Mean Area of Effectiveness (Blast)
MAEF	Mean Area of Effectiveness (Fragment)
MARTEL	Missile Anti-Radar Television
MASH	Medical and Special Holding Flight
MB	Main Building
MBDA	Matra British Aerospace (Dynamics)
MNF	Multi-National Force
MO	Medical Officer
MOD	Ministry of Defence
MOD(PE)	Ministry of Defence (Procurement Executive)

MT	Motor Transport
NAAFI	Navy, Army and Air Force Institutes
NAS	Naval Air Station
NATO	North Atlantic Treaty Organisation
Nav	Navigator/Navigation
NBC	Nuclear, Biological and Chemical
NFU	Non-Formed Unit
nm	Nautical Mile
NMCP	Nav Mode Control Panel
NOTAM	Notice to Airmen
O_2	Oxygen
OASC	Officer and Aircrew Selection Centre
OC	Officer Commanding/Officer Cadet
OCA	Offensive Counter Air
OCU	Operational Conversion Unit
OHMS	On Her Majesty's Service
OHP	Overhead Projector
OLF	Operational Low Flying
OMQ	Officer's Married Quarter
Ops	Operations
OR	Operational Requirement(s)
OR(Air)	Operational Requirements(Air)
OR51(Air)	Operational Requirements 51(Air)
ORB	Operational Research Branch
OTR	Over Target Requirement
OTS	Officer Training School
PA	Personal Assistant
PBF	Pilot Briefing Facility
P_k	Kill Probability
PMA	Personnel Management Agency (formerly Personnel Management Centre)
PMC	President of the Mess Committee
PMS	Personnel Management Squadron
POC	Point of Contact
POW	Prisoner of War
PSO	Personal Staff Officer
PTC	Personnel and Training Command

PTI	Physical Training Instructor
PTO$_k$	Prevent Take Off Kill
QFI	Qualified Flying Instructor
QRA	Quick Reaction Alert
qs	Qualified Basic Staff Course
QWI	Qualified Weapons Instructor
R&R	Rest and Recuperation
RAAF	Royal Australian Air Force
Rad Alt	Radar/Radio Altimeter
RAF	Royal Air Force
RAFASUPU	Royal Air Force Armament Support Unit
RAFG	Royal Air Force Germany
RAFO	Royal Air Force of Oman
RARDE	Royal Armament Research and Development Establishment
RCDI	Rate of Climb and Descent Indicator
RDAF	Royal Danish Air Force
RIC	Reconnaissance and Intelligence Centre
RMA	Royal Military Academy
RN	Royal Navy
RHWR	Radar Homing and Warning Receiver
SAAF	South African Air Force
SACEUR	Supreme Allied Commander Europe
SACLANT	Supreme Allied Commander Atlantic
SAM	Surface to Air Missile
SAP	Simulated Attack Profile
SAR	Search and Rescue
SAS	Special Air Service
SASO	Senior Air Staff Officer
SCALP	Système de Croisière Autonome à Longue Portée
SD	Service Dress
SHAPE	Supreme Headquarters Allied Powers Europe
SHQ	Station Headquarters
SMC	Station Medical Centre
SNEB	Societé Nouvelle des Etablissements Brandt
SO	Student Officer
SOP	Standard Operating Procedure
Sqn Cdr	Squadron Commander

SR(A)	Staff Requirement(Air)
ST(A)	Staff Target(Air)
STAN(F)	STANEVAL (Flying)
STAN(W)	STANEVAL (Weapons)
STANEVAL	Standards and Evaluation
STCAAME	Strike Command Air-to-Air Missile Establishment
STRIPRO	Strike Progression
T&S	Travel and Subsistence
TA	Training Area
TACAN	Tactical Air Navigation System
TACEVAL	Tactical Evaluation
TAP	Terminal Approach Procedure
TF	Terrain Following
TF2a(RAF)	Training Flying 2a (Royal Air Force)
TFR	Terrain Following Radar
TNA	Training Needs Analysis
TO2(RAF)	Training Operational 2 (Royal Air Force)
TO2a(RAF)	Training Operational 2a (Royal Air Force)
TOCU	Tornado Operational Conversion Unit
TSU	Tornado Standardisation Unit
TTSG	Tri-national Tornado Steering Group
TTTE	Tri-national Tornado Training Establishment
TV Tab	Television Tabulation
TWCU	Tornado Weapons Conversion Unit
TWU	Tactical Weapons Unit
UDI	Unilateral Declaration of Independence
UE	Unit Establishment
UK	United Kingdom
UKADR	United Kingdom Air Defence Region
ULL	Ultra Low Level
UN	United Nations
UOR	Urgent Operational Requirement
USAF	United States Air Force
USMC	United States Marine Corps
USN	United States Navy
VAS	Visiting Aircraft Squadron
VAT	Value Added Tax

VHF	Very High Frequency
VMC	Visual Meteorology Conditions
WAMS	Weapon Aiming Mode Selector
WEC	Weapons Employment Course
WEP	Weapon Effort Planning
Wg Cdr	Wing Commander
Wg Cdr Cdts	Wing Commander Cadets
Wg Cdr Trg	Wing Commander Training
WP	Warsaw Pact
YAM	Yorkshire Air Museum

Index

Note: Where ranks are stated it is the last known rank of an officer/OR.

244   The Tornado Years

Lovell, Wg Cdr Graham, Plates
McClymont, Sqn Ldr Gordon, Plates
McFadyen, AM Sir Ian, 137
McLeod, Wg Cdr Grant, 42, 46, 227,
    Plates
McNicoll, AM Iain, ix, 45, Plates
McRobbie, Air Cdre Gordon, 39, 93–4
Middleton, Gp Capt Dick, ix, 188, 190,
    192–4, 196, 201
Miller, AM Sir Leslie "Dusty" Miller,
    137
Molloy, Gp Capt Martin, 104–105
Moore, Sqn Ldr (Rev) Gerry, 151
Nichol, Flt Lt John, 107
Osborn, AM Phil 'Osby', 139, Plates
O'Shea, Flt Lt John, ii, Plates
Parkinson, Air Cdre Steve, 63, 71
Peach, ACM Sir Stuart, 205, 208
Peters, AVM Bob, 113, 128
Peters, Sqn Ldr John, 107
Pitchfork, Air Cdre Graham, 155
Prissick, Air Cdre Mal, Plates
Prytherch, Flt Lt Nick, 166, Plates
Reekie, Sqn Ldr Gordon, 65
Rimmer, AVM Bill, 190, 194, 197,
    Plates
Risdale, Sqn Ldr Nigel, 92
Roberts, Flt Lt 'Paddy', Plates
Ross, Wg Cdr Iain, 24–6, 46, 83, 216
Seaward, Wg Cdr Graham, Plates
Squelch, Wg Cdr Jim, 60, Plates
Stevenson, Air Cdre Ashley, 168
Stewart, Wg Cdr Al, 211
Stewart, Wg Cdr Betty, 211
Thomas, Flt Lt Richard, 33
Trace, Sqn Ldr Brian, Plates
Trenchard, MRAF Lord, 169
Tyack, Air Cdre Bill, 137, 152–3
Waddington, Sqn Ldr Frank, 39
Waldwyn, Sqn Ldr Cliff, ix
Walker, Sqn Ldr Ivor, 78
West, Wg Cdr Paul 'Stringy', Plates
Whybro, Sqn Ldr Mick, 18
Williams, Sqn Ldr David, Plates
Witts, Air Cdre Jerry, 107, 127
Woodroffe, Wg Cdr Rick, 81
Wright, Sqn Ldr Mike, 186
Wright, Flt Lt Phil, 43–4
Wright, AM Sir Robert, 79–80
Young, Sqn Ldr Simon "Shifty", 83

RAF Squadrons/Units:
  2 Air Navigation School/2 ANS, 3, 190
  9 Squadron, 74–5, 79
  12 Squadron, 7-8, 37, 160, 198
  14 Squadron, 41, 78
  XV Squadron, 5–6, 24–6, 39, 46, 92–3,
    107, 127, 223
  16 Squadron, 9–10, 23, 39, 54–5, 60, 65,
    87
  17 Squadron, x, 41–2, 45–6,64, 68–71,
    73, 75, 79, 108, 135, 137, 188, 210
  20 Squadron, 92
  31 Squadron, 74, 78, 102, 107, 127, 134
  208 Squadron, 25, 79
  237 Operational Conversion Unit, 4, 7–8,
    24–5, 39, 89, 106, 209
  Aeromedical Training Centre/AMTC,
    28–9
  Aircrew Officer Training School/AOTS,
    3, 31
  Air Refuelling School, 99
  Air Warfare Centre/AWC, x, 198,
    200–202, 205, 208, 210
  Air Warfare Training Project Team/
    AWTPT, 206, 209
  Central Tactics and Trials Organisation/
    CTTO, 72, 127, 130, 136
  Department of Air Warfare/DAW, 16, 26
  Department of Initial Officer Training/
    DIOT, 17–18, 160, 170–6, 178–80,
    183–4, 188, 191–5, 197, 200, 207
  Individual Studies School/ISS, 8–9, 13,
    23, 97, 112
  Medical and Special Holding Flight,
    192–3
  Mobile Meteorology Unit, 161
  Officer and Aircrew Selection Centre/
    OASC, 2, 172, 186–7, 195–6
  Operational Research Branch/ORB, 14,
    26
  Royal Air Force Armament Support
    Unit/RAFASUPU, 72, 156
  Royal Air Force College Cranwell, 3,
    16–17, 31, 151, 160, 169–70, 179–80,
    189, 194, 196, 199, 221
  Royal Air Force Germany/RAFG, 44, 48,
    87, 92, 102, 220
  RAF Hospital Wegberg, 91
  RAF School of Fighter Control, 116
  RAF Staff College, 97, 112–13, 122, 127–8